SHAKESPEARE AND HIS BETTERS

TOP (*left*), Francis Bacon, Baron Verulam, 1561–1626; (*right*), Sir Walter Raleigh, 1552(?)–1618. CENTRE, William Shakespeare, 1564–1616, the 'Chandos' portrait. BOTTOM (*left*), Edward de Vere, 17th Earl of Oxford, 1540–1604; (*right*), William Stanley, 6th Earl of Derby, 1561–1642.

SHAKESPEARE
AND HIS BETTERS,

A HISTORY AND A CRITICISM OF THE ATTEMPTS

WHICH HAVE BEEN MADE TO PROVE THAT

SHAKESPEARE'S WORKS WERE

WRITTEN BY OTHERS

by

R. C. CHURCHILL

WITH COLLABORATION IN

BIBLIOGRAPHY AND RESEARCH BY

MAURICE HUSSEY

FOREWORD BY

IVOR BROWN

INDIANA UNIVERSITY PRESS
BLOOMINGTON

TO MY WIFE

First published in the U.S.A. 1959
Manufactured in Great Britain
Library of Congress Catalogue Card Number 59-5124

CONTENTS

PORTRAITS IN THE FRONTISPIECE

The portraits in the frontispiece are reproduced by kind permission of the following:

National Portrait Gallery

WILLIAM SHAKESPEARE: detail from the "Chandos" portrait, traditionally said to be painted by Richard Burbage (see Note 4 on page 69)

FRANCIS BACON: detail from the portrait after Paul Van Somer

SIR WALTER RALEIGH: detail from a panel by an unknown artist

Bodleian Library, Sutherland Collection

WILLIAM STANLEY, 6th Earl of Derby: detail from a replica by Silvester Harding of the family portrait at Knowsley

Mansell Collection:

EDWARD DE VERE, 17th Earl of Oxford: detail from an original painting

---

NOTES

Notes designated by an asterisk are given at the foot of the page.
Numbered notes are given at the end of the chapter.

ACKNOWLEDGMENTS

It is pleasant to be able to begin a book on such a controversial subject by expressing thanks to people whose views differ considerably from my own. Mr. Edward D. Johnson, the present President of the Francis Bacon Society, is one to whom I should like to acknowledge a particular debt: not only has he sent me many of his own books and pamphlets, he has furnished me with some insight into the Baconian mind by means of a correspondence lasting many months. It is to him that I owe the occasion of my first counter-arguments against certain Baconian positions, arguments that I have developed in the Critical part of this book.

Another Baconian, Mr. J. S. L. Millar, W.S., kindly sent me a pamphlet of his own, and I must acknowledge a similar kindness on the part of Mr. William Kent, F.S.A., one of the Vice-Presidents of the Shakespeare Fellowship, a body primarily but not exclusively concerned with advocating the claims of the Earl of Oxford. The Fellowship has an excellent library, which I was very glad to make use of. I should like to express here my grateful thanks to the Hon. Librarian, Miss Ruth M. D. Wainewright, for her kind attention and courtesy.

On his visit to England during 1956, Mr. Calvin Hoffman, advocate of the claims of Christopher Marlowe, kindly favoured me with an answer to one or two questions of fact. For the gift or loan of books, I must thank Mr. William Margrie, whose views are similar to mine; Mr. John Atkins; my former colleague, Mr. R. E. Kellett; and my collaborator in research, Mr. Maurice Hussey.

In the History part of this book, I should, quite frankly, have been lost without Mr. Hussey's co-operation. Many of the foreign works on the question, and some of the minor theories, were unknown to me until I had the results of his research. He himself would like to thank, on our joint behalf, the Librarian of the Shakespeare Memorial Library, Birmingham, for the loan of invaluable books and a microfilm; and the University Library, Cambridge, for the kindness of their staff upon innumerable matters. A personal note of thanks (Mr. Hussey adds) is also due to Mr. Morris Shapira of Downing College, Cambridge, and to Mr. W. G. Moore of St. John's College, Oxford. Needless to say, Mr. Hussey is not responsible for any mistakes I may have made in the writing of this book.

R. C. C.

May 1957

FOREWORD

BY IVOR BROWN

The disbelief in William Shakespeare's authorship of what were, and still are, acted and printed as William Shakespeare's plays is a very old one, as Mr. Churchill reminds the reader in his ample and fair-minded study of the many heterodox opinions. The subject has always interested me, not only because everything that we can discover about the work and personality of Shakespeare is, for me, exciting, but because the emotions aroused have been strangely intense.

Those who wish to depose the man of Stratford from his plinth of world-renown have often turned on him in fury. Shagsper the actor, as his name is frequently spelled by those who regard him as thief, usurper and pretender, has been railed at as a barbarous oaf, 'a sordid money-lender . . . drunken, ignorant, and absolutely unlettered, who never in his life wrote so much as his own name and in all probability was totally unable to read one single line of print'. Thus Sir Edwin Durning-Lawrence, in *Bacon is Shake-speare*. There have been others to dismiss as a mere 'clod without a spark' the Stratford Shagsper. I have always found it difficult to understand how a man supposedly unable to read could yet manage to study a part and take a share in company management and theatrical finance, as well as performing on the stage. All anti-Stratfordians are not, however, so extreme in their contempt for 'Avonian Willy', nor do they make such sweeping assertions of his illiteracy.

On the other hand, the heretics, those who put their case with reasonable moderation, have been subjected at times to unnecessary ridicule and to misrepresentation of their argument. Their company has included many distinguished brains and cool minds. One of Sir Max Beerbohm's cartoons shows Shakespeare surreptitiously receiving a script from Bacon. Among the more illustrious doubters was Henry James, whose presence in their ranks was the more important since he was himself a creative artist, and so understood the significance of style which most of his fellow-sceptics do not. It is one great merit of Mr. Churchill's book that he is both equitable and urbane: he gives the various pleaders a good run for their theories, explaining their ideas after immense and careful reading. He cannot, of course, state all their arguments in a single volume: but he has given the gist without prejudice.

He does, after his exposition of these views, decide against them. But he does not use mockery and insult as additions to his logical method. Those readers who wish to know what has been said against the Shakespearean authorship will find the bulk of it justly summarized: should they wish to study the case further, there is added a bibliography of such size that the extent of the anti-Stratfordian campaigns is fully and fairly made evident.

The underlying motives of these campaigns and the bursts of temper which I have mentioned have their own fascination. As Mr. Churchill justly says, when supreme honours are at stake, like turns to like. The milord would have the greatest of English writers a milord: the lawyer would have him a lawyer: the sailor would have him a notable voyager. I have not met with a retort from the glove-makers and shop-keepers that, to satisfy their professional pride, the author must have been a haberdasher or a tradesman, and that the son of John Shakespeare, glover of Stratford, was the man for them. But the feeling that 'this man is ours' has obviously been at work and it is at least a pleasant occurrence among the British, so often charged with neglect of their literature, that so much toil, as well as passion, should have been spent upon the identity of a poet.

Another motive, which none can deride, is the chivalrous determination to right a supposed wrong. If Another Hand was what I have called in my book on 'Shakespeare' the Hand of Glory, then it is indeed a gross injustice that the world should for centuries have been attaching that hand to the wrong body. The anti-Stratfordians see themselves as a rescue-party, with justice their end. Such a claim inevitably heightens the emotions and leads to a view of the orthodox as shielders of a scandalous mistake. It is true that the Other Hand or Group of Hands, if there were such a company of genius, made it easy, by their method of secrecy, for the world to go wrong. Never mind, say the defenders, at long last the Truth will be revealed and justice done. That feeling, even if it reaches the level of conspiracy-mania and dramatizes the orthodox as evil-minded plotters, is not to be despised. The thinking may be wrong, but the emotion is generous.

To dismiss as cranks and crack-pots those who hold a minority opinion is easy and the dismissal may often be well-earned. Preposterous nonsense has been talked by some, as the following chapters will show. But not by all. I have known some of the disputants on the anti-Stratfordian side and have always respected the sanity of these, as well as their integrity and their zeal for truth. So it is only fair that they should get the mannerly treatment of their various creeds, which Mr. Churchill has properly given them.

What is, I think, untenable is the assertion made by neutrals in this war that the name of the poet really does not matter. There are those who say that, since we have the poems and plays, the author's identity is of no importance. That is an astonishing attitude. The man who wrote the greatest poetry in the English language and the plays which many think the finest in the history of the world's theatre deserves more than a shoulder-shrugging indifference about his name. Furthermore, a detective story has its own excitement and, if there is indeed a Shakespeare Mystery, one must be singularly lacking in curiosity to remain thus aloof and unconcerned in its presence. The allure of a detective story has been added to the other motives which have provoked so much (and sometimes embittered) controversy and have evoked such a tremendous output of anti-Stratfordian books and articles. A fair amount of this output I have read: like Mr. Churchill, I do not oppose without consideration.

In agreeing with his reply to the heretics, I may add one or two reflections of my own. If the allegations that Another Hand, preferably that of a savant or a nobleman, passed on the plays to a lowly agent since it was deemed improper for the uncommonly eminent to write for the common stages, it is indeed remarkable that the chosen agent should have been a player whom so many anti-Stratfordians describe as ignorant, if not illiterate. Since they argue that the knowledge of courtly procedure and of the grandee's way of life could not have been acquired by the small-town lad turned vagabond player, then the use of the supposed yokel as the agent would be ridiculous. The Other Hand's only hope of keeping his secret was to plant the plays on somebody as well informed and as learned as himself, though not of the highest social rank, say, perhaps, a clever youngster at the Inns of Court.

If Shakespeare the actor was known to be the ignoramus suggested by many of the heretics, the play-goers would have ridiculed the idea of his authorship. In any case, to keep a secret of this kind in so small a society as that of Elizabethan London would surely have been impossible: to escape from this by asserting that the secret was widely known but respected does not help. It is most unlikely that so good a story would not have leaked out amid the talk of the town and it is equally obvious that the name of Shakespeare as a writer was familiar to his fellow-poets and to the young men at the Universities, who doted on his poems. 'O sweet Mr. Shakespeare. I'le have his picture in my study at the courte. . . . I'le worshipp sweet Mr. Shakespeare and to honoure him will lay his *Venus and Adonis* under my pillow.' Thus a character in a University comedy of 1599.

Those (and they seem to be an increasing number) who believe in a Group of Eminents as the source of the plays have to persuade us that a masterpiece can be written by a committee. This is beyond my powers of belief. It is widely known that collaboration was common among the Elizabethan dramatists and Shakespeare, as a beginner, probably had had to start that way: the plays belonged to the company and there was little sense of private property in writing. *Titus Andronicus* is considered to be largely Peele's. Perhaps. But if such lines as 'Come and take choice of all my library, And so beguile thy sorrow' were not Shakespeare's I should be much surprised.

Shakespeare was ready to help other men out, for the company's sake, long after he was established and successful. In that case, he showed his modesty and friendliness. Did his team, the King's Men, have in hand poorish plays about 'Timon of Athens' and 'Pericles' and did they need a piece quickly? Then even the author of the great tragedies would turn aside to pour his genius into them. In a pessimistic mood, Timon appealed to him and the raging misanthropy of the play's latter half has produced poetry as essentially Shakespearean as any in the Folio. Similarly the second half of *Pericles* is signed by Shakespeare again and again. Was it Wilkins from whom he took over? That name is inessential. Certainly Shakespeare collaborated there and also, I am sure, in the apocryphal play, *Two Noble Kinsmen*, where a few passages seem to leap right out of the text as though signed by the master-hand.

Incidentally, I have noticed in this piece the use of a strange adjective for tired or jaded, which is otherwise unknown except once in Shakespeare and also as a Cotswold and Gloucestershire dialect word. That is wappened or wappered, whose negative form is unwappered. The former occurs in the Shakespearean part of *Timon of Athens* (Act IV, Scene 3) where we hear of the wappered widow who may be lured by gold to a second marriage. The latter appears in *Two Noble Kinsmen* (Act V, Scene 4)

> We come towards the gods,
> Young and unwappered, not halting under crimes.

Now if that dialect word were associated with St. Albans, what joy for the Baconians, with Lancashire what joy for the Derbyites, and with Hackney what joy for the Oxfordians! But it came from Shakespeare's 'Cotsall', those hills above the valley where Stratford lies and which Shakespeare knew.

That Shakespeare did sometimes, both early and late in his career, collaborate does not turn him into a Group. Nor is there any evidence that the great plays were not his own. (There may have been later insertions in *Macbeth* whose text raises several problems.) His style is unmistakeable: the Hand of Glory is continually there. There are the tricks of rhythm and alliteration which he loved and used to perfection. Only one man could possess such felicity of words and music.

Therefore, for the Groupists to say that one hand (Southampton's) contributed *Macbeth*, because its owner had been to Scotland, and that another hand (Raleigh's) wrote *The Tempest*, because Sir Walter had sailed to the Indies, is nonsensical to anyone who is at all sensitive to style. The believers in a single Other Hand, whether it were Bacon's, Oxford's, or Derby's, or belonged to any other of the numerous names suggested, are not on such sticky ground as are the Groupists. But they have to face the fact that no other products of their candidates show anything approaching the same traits of poetic style or genius in the use of it.

But I must not any longer anticipate Mr. Churchill's outline of the pleas put forward by the anti-Stratfordian claimants, and his reply to them. The literature on and around Shakespeare's life and work is of such gigantic size that it is very hard to discover ground that has not been covered already. Mr. Churchill has found it. By assembling all the theories of authorship and the attributions to one or more Other Hands he has provided the general reader with a most serviceable survey of what has been surmised down the centuries—in scores of books and periodicals, many of which are now difficult to obtain. It cannot be complained that he has treated in a careless or discourteous way the views with which he, like the great majority, disagrees. He has been in no mood to sneer at a lonely opinion because of its solitude. With his counter-arguments I agree as cordially as I admire the labour which he, with an associate, has undertaken. It was a most severe task, as his bibliography shows, and it has been carried out not only with scholarship but with an equanimity too often missing in this too often passionate debate.

INTRODUCTION

O, be some other name!
What's in a name! that which we call a rose
By any other name would smell as sweet.
SHAKESPEARE: *Romeo and Juliet.*

I

'His thesis is the perennially fascinating one—one that has become almost a national pastime—that our greatest poet was not the person we suppose him to have been.'

Thus the distinguished historian, Sir Arthur Bryant, introducing a book by Claud W. Sykes which claims that Roger Manners fifth Earl of Rutland, wrote the plays and poems commonly attributed to the actor William Shakespeare of Stratford-on-Avon (*Alias William Shakespeare?*, 1947). Sir Arthur does not himself agree with the Rutland theory: 'Nothing in Mr. Sykes's narrative . . . makes me think that the William Shakespeare commemorated in Stratford church did not write his own plays.' But he admits the fascination of the thesis, and most readers, whatever their opinion, will agree with him.

The 'pastime', however, is much more than a national one: it can truly be called international. The particular theory with which the book of Mr. Sykes was concerned, the theory which gives the works of Shakespeare to the Earl of Rutland, was first put forward by German writers, then taken up by Belgian, American, and Argentinian, and has more recently been made the subject of a book written by a Russian. The Baconian theory has included in its ranks writers from England, Ireland, the United States, Canada, South Africa, Australia, France, Holland, Germany, Austria, Serbia, Hungary, Poland, and Italy. The chief propagandists for the Earl of Derby have been Frenchmen; for Florio German and Italian; for Sir Walter Raleigh American and Australian; for the Earl of Oxford British and American; while the advocates for various Group and Dual Theories have come from England, Scotland, the United States, Germany, and France. There are, in fact, few countries which have not produced at least one writer on the subject, as there are few members of the Elizabethan aristocracy

15

who have not been credited with at least a share in the works of Shakespeare.

Attempts to deal with the question as a whole have been remarkably rare. The present book is the only one, I believe, which tries to cover the entire field, past and present, though an orthodox scholar, M. Georges Connes, formerly Professor of English Literature at the University of Dijon, in *Le Mystère Shakespearien*, published in Paris in 1926, and a Group Theorist, the late Professor Slater, in *Seven Shakespeares*, published in London in 1931, have dealt with the main theories advanced in the late nineteenth and early twentieth centuries. I myself divide the question into two parts: first I give the history of the subject, from the seventeenth century to the time of writing; secondly, I subject the theories to a literary and cultural analysis, from which—it may be agreed—very little remains.

It may be asked: what qualifications do I possess for tackling such a complicated subject? In the first place, I am a literary critic, and it is remarkable how few literary critics there have been among the thousands of writers, often eminent in other fields, who have taken unorthodox views upon the authorship of Shakespeare's works. Some disclaim literary criticism in somewhat lofty an accent, as if a writer on astronomy should disclaim any specialized knowledge of the stars. 'It was not a problem, he felt, for a literary critic, which he did not pretend to be, but for a detective; in Dr. Gilbert Slater's pungent phrase, "for the man from Scotland Yard".'* Looney himself said that 'It is the kind of enquiry with which lawyers and juries are faced every day' ('*Shakespeare*' *Identified*, p. 72). I hope to make clear in the course of this book that it is not in the least this kind of enquiry and that the prerequisite for any enquirer is a training in literary criticism and a knowledge of literary and cultural history.

The next essential is a thorough acquaintance with the subject. How thorough is my own acquaintance? It must be confessed at once that if any writer paused, like another Lord Acton, until he had read every book, pamphlet, and article on the subject, he would never put pen to paper at all. A French critic, Firmin Roz,

---

* William McFee, Introduction to new American edition of J. Thomas Looney's '*Shakespeare*' *Identified in Edward de Vere, the Seventeenth Earl of Oxford* (1949). p. xvii. Compare Slater, *Seven Shakespeares*, p. vii: 'Literature and literary history are not exactly my *métier*.'

writing in the *Revue des Deux Mondes* in 1916, estimated the Baconian books and pamphlets published in all countries up to that date to be somewhere in the region of 500 to 600. Forty years more have produced at least as fecund a crop, and this is only one theory —admittedly the most fertile—among the many that have been advanced. M. Connes told his students at Dijon that Célestin Demblon, one of the Belgian advocates of the Rutlandian theory, had read some 5,000 works on the Shakespeare authorship question. 'Let us respectfully salute his memory,' the Professor smoothly added (*The Shakespeare Mystery*, p. 202). I cannot claim to have read 5,000 myself, nor was there any need for me to do so. Those who have read ten Baconian books have read a hundred, for the repetition of arguments, often in the same words, is so great that one can make the assumption with perfect justice. Much the same is true of the Oxfordian books and pamphlets, which are only less numerous than the Baconian. If you have read ten or twenty of them, then you have virtually explored the complete case. I myself have read about fifty Baconian books and pamphlets, and have read parts of twenty to thirty others, besides articles: I should be much surprised if by so doing I have not examined at least 90 per cent. of their case. I have similarly read about twenty Oxfordian books and pamphlets, besides parts of a dozen others and several articles: I shall be much surprised if by so doing I have left unexamined more than a few unimportant details. The books on the Group and Dual theories, and on the theories supporting Raleigh, Derby, Rutland, Florio, and others, have not been nearly so numerous, and I can claim to have read (or read *in*) at least a third of the total output. That, after all, is the important point: to have covered the field in reasonable selection, past and present, not to have read a thousand different pamphlets all making the same unoriginal points in the same unoriginal words.

II

I can claim, then, two out of what I conceive to be the three most essential qualifications for the task I have set myself. The third essential I can only hope I shall not be found lacking in: that is, of keeping a civil tongue in my head. Too many books on the question have been disfigured by abuse of their opponents. It is impossible to say who are the chief culprits, because all sides have

B

been equally guilty: the 'pastime' has too often become a war of words. M. Connes gives some distressing examples of abuse by Baconians against orthodox scholars and by these 'Stratfordians' against Baconian and other theorists (*Shakespeare Mystery*, Ch. IV. Compare John Appleby, *The Stuffed Swan*, Ch. 11). The most famous critics have not been entirely guiltless. For instance, the great Danish critic, Georg Brandes, who wrote his book on Shakespeare partly as a counterblast to Baconian ideas, wrote of the 'ignorant and arrogant attack' of the 'wretched group of dilettanti' who have 'been bold enough, in England and America, to deny William Shakespeare the right to his own life-work, to give to another the honour due to his genius, and to bespatter him and his invulnerable name with an insane abuse which has re-echoed through every land' (*William Shakespeare*, Vol. II, p. 413).

Abuse has led to counter-abuse, and I take that as a warning. I prefer to remember that J. M. Robertson, one of the chief opponents of the Baconian position, and Sir George Greenwood, one of the chief opponents of the orthodox position, were personal friends and remained friends after the untold knocks they inflicted upon each other in their various books and articles. I shall inflict some knocks myself upon the unorthodox cases in the second part of this book, but in the first part I intend to give the history of the various cases almost entirely free of comment, so that the reader can know in brief what the different positions actually stand for. I think myself that they all stand upon extremely rickety foundations, that the title of the actor Shakespeare to the plays he is commonly credited with is perfectly sound, without a single serious question to be imputed against it; but those beliefs will not be obtruded into the History section of the book, which is the history of unorthodoxy without orthodox comment.

In my reading for this book, I have been struck by two false assumptions commonly advanced, one by orthodox Shakespeareans, the other by unorthodox theorists. I should like to remove both assumptions straight away, so that we can proceed with more care.

The first false assumption is by the orthodox, in whose camp I belong. It takes different forms with different writers, but the gist is that the unorthodox are entirely or mostly composed of cranks. Now it is perfectly true that unorthodox theorists are more likely to be cranks than to be literary critics, but this is the utmost that we can say. It is simply not the case that we can dismiss the unorthodox as composed almost entirely of 'incorrigible cranks whose different piety assigns all the work called Shakespeare's to numerous members of the peerage' (*Concise Cambridge History of English Literature*, p. 256). Among the unorthodox, either wholly or in part, have appeared such distinguished figures as Lord Palmerston, John Bright, John Greenleaf Whittier, Prince Bismarck, Mark Twain, Henry James, George Moore, and Sigmund Freud.* These are hardly 'incorrigible cranks', nor yet 'a troop of less than half-educated people', as Brandes described them.

So much for the false assumption made by the orthodox. The second common false assumption is made by the unorthodox, and is to the effect that their case has never been answered. Now it is perfectly true that against some thousands of unorthodox works there have been only a few score of refutations; but, as I have pointed out, the unorthodox books repeat each other to such an extent that their number can be reduced, to all intents and purposes, to about ten for each theory. Recent unorthodox works repeat arguments that were demolished years ago by Mrs. Stopes, Andrew Lang, Sir Walter Greg, Canon Beeching, J. M. Robertson, Charles Crawford, Richard Grant White, Judge Willis, William Devecmon, Dr. Nicholson, or some other critic. Their authors may not agree that their case has been refuted, but it is futile to pretend that no answer has taken place at all.

III

I have only one more point which I should like to raise before we proceed to our History section. And that concerns the spelling of the name 'Shakespeare'. As is well known, the name was spelt in Elizabethan and Jacobean times in many different ways, including Shakespeare, Shake-speare (with a hyphen), Shakespear, Shakspeare, Shak-speare (with a hyphen), Shakespere, Shakesper, Shaksper, Shagspere, Shaxpere, Shaxpur, Shexpere, Shayksper, Shaxber, Shaxberd, Shaxper, Shakspur, Shackspeare, Shackspere, Shakspeer, Sheakspear, Shaksperr, Shaykspeyr, Shakspeyr, and Shaksporre. (Not content with all these alternative spellings, French

---

* The claim often made by Baconians (even by M. Connes in his *résumé* of their case) that Dickens, Hawthorne, Emerson, and Gervinus were Baconians cannot be substantiated. See below, pp. 33, 38, 68, 206.

critics in the eighteenth century were so independent as to call him Shakpear, Shakespehar, Shakespeart, or Shakees Pear.)

This extremely varied spelling has led most unorthodox writers to assume that there must have been *two* men: one, the actor, whom they mostly call 'Shaksper' or 'Shakspere', the other the real author (Bacon, Derby, Rutland, etc.) whom they call 'Shakespeare' or 'Shake-speare' (with the hyphen). Some Oxfordians even find *three* men: one, the man from Stratford, 'Shaksper' or 'Shakspere'; the second, the boy actor 'Shakespeare', Oxford's illegitimate son; and the third the author of the plays, 'Shakespeare' (with the hyphen), which is assumed to be a pseudonym for Oxford or for a group of writers led by Oxford. (See, for example, Graf Vitzthum, *Shakespeare und Shakspere*, p. 5 sq., and Louis P. Bénézet, *Shakspere, Shakespeare and de Vere*, p. 25.)

All these ingenious theories rest upon the false assumption that it was unusual for an Elizabethan name to be spelt in a number of different ways. It was not only *not* unusual, it was the common rule. The Elizabethans were not very free in some respects; they had, for instance, no religious freedom. But they had infinite freedom of spelling, and all Elizabethans availed themselves of this liberty with—to a modern eye—very curious results. In a recent article, Dr. Hotson had occasion to list the contemporary spellings of the famous Elizabethan admiral usually known to us, through Tennyson's poem, as Sir Richard Grenville of the *Revenge*. According to Dr. Hotson, the man we call Grenville was known to his contemporaries as Grenefield, Grenfeld, Greenefeild, Greenefeelde, Grenefild, Greenfield, Greenfeild, Greynfild, or Grenefeld (Leslie Hotson, 'Falstaff's Death and Greenfield's'. *Times Literary Supplement*, 6 April 1956).

The name of Sir Walter Raleigh was written by his contemporaries either Raleigh, Raliegh, Ralegh, Raghley, Rawley, Rawly, Rawlie, Rawleigh, Raulighe, Raughlie, or Rayly. The name of Thomas Dekker was written either Dekker, Decker, Deckar, Deckers, Dicker, Dickers, Dyckers, or (interestingly enough) Dickens. Admiral Holland, in his book *Shakespeare through Oxford Glasses* (p. 32), points out that the name Cecil was often spelt Cysell; also, of course, Cecill, Cecyll, Ciecill, Cyssell, Secyll, and Syssell. The name of Francis Bacon, Durning-Lawrence admitted in his *Shakespeare Myth* (p. 23), was 'spelled in many different ways, as students of various books will find to be the fact'.

The name of Christopher Marlowe was written either Marlowe, Marlow, Mar-low (with a hyphen), Marloe, Marley, Marly, Marlen, Marlin, or Morley. Greenwood, in *Baconian Essays* (p. 91), claimed that 'the name "Shakespeare" is, in truth, a quite different name from that of "Shakspere" or "Shaksper" or "Shaxpur".' Only in the sense that Grenville is a different name from Greenfield, Dekker from Dickens, or Marlowe from Morley.

If you lived in Elizabethan or Jacobean times, you could even change your mind in the middle of a sentence, as Izaak Walton (or the printer) did in his *Life of Donne* when he referred to 'M. Samuel Brooke . . . and his brother M. Christopher Brook'. In this case, of course, there could be another explanation: the two brothers might have decided to spell their name in different ways— a procedure equally acceptable at the time.

The deposition against Marlowe by Richard Cholmeley contains the following paragraph (italics mine): 'That hee saieth & verely beleueth that one *Marlowe* is able to shewe more sounde reasons for Atheisme then any devine in Englande is able to geue to prove devinitie & that *Marloe* tolde him . . .' In the *Anatomy of Melancholy* Burton notes in the margin the authors to whom he makes reference in the text: against a reference to *Venus and Adonis* he notes 'Shakspere', against one to *Much Ado About Nothing* he notes 'Shakespeare's'. The Stationers' Registers under date 10 August 1579 (italics mine) refer to 'Richard *Feilde*, sonne of Henry *Fielde*'. The title-page of *Love's Labour's Lost* (1598) spells the name of the publisher 'Cutbert Burby'; the title-page of *Palladis Tamia* (same year) spells him 'Cuthbert Burbie'.

The hyphenated form of proper names, as in 'Shake-speare', was less common, but by no means unheard of. Mr. Calvin Hoffman, American advocate of the theory that Shakespeare's works were written by Marlowe, gives the following examples: Munday written Mun-day; Holinshed, Holin-shed; Burleigh, Bur-leigh; Cranmer, Cran-mer; Marlowe, Mar-low; and Walsingham, Wal-sing-ham (*The Man who was Shakespeare*, pp. 139–40). So there does not seem to be any reason why unorthodox theorists should assume that 'Shake-speare' (with the hyphen) was necessarily a pseudonym.

The false assumption comes, of course, from considering Shakespeare in isolation. Once we realize that the multiple spelling of the dramatist's name was in accordance with the usage of the time, the apparent mystery vanishes. Not that all the unorthodox have fallen into the trap. Just as a good many orthodox writers— such as Mrs. Stopes, J. R. Green, Bernard Shaw—have preferred the spelling 'Shakspere', 'Shakespere', or 'Shakespear' to the common form, so some of the unorthodox, like the late Prof. Lefranc, do not make the false assumption of their colleagues. Lefranc, with true French logic, invariably calls the actor from Stratford by the name given to him in some of the London references at the time and in the First Folio.

From the evidence of his surviving signatures, such as they are, Shakespeare seems to have spelt his name 'Shaksper' or 'Shakspere'. Raleigh spelt his name, though not invariably, 'Ralegh'; but this does not mean that the other spellings of the name on record refer to other people: they all refer to Raleigh. The actor was spelt 'Shakespeare' in the Court Treasurer's Accounts of 15 March, 1594, which recorded payment to 'William Kempe, William Shakespeare and Richard Burbage servauntes to the Lord Chamberleyne . . . for twoe severall Comedies or Enterludes shewed by them before her majestie in Christmas tyme laste paste.' Another Court record, of 1604, gives the name of the author of *Measure for Measure* as 'Shaxberd'. In 1609 Thomas Thorpe published the *Sonnets* with the title-page reading: 'SHAKE-SPEARES SONNETS'. The entry in the Stationers' Register reads: 'a Booke called Shakespeares sonnettes'. Edward Alleyn, the actor, bought a copy and jotted down the price in a list of purchases on the back of a letter dated 19 June, 1609: he spelled it 'Shakspers Sonnets 5d.' This proves that 'Shaksper', 'Shakespeare' and 'Shake-speare' (with the hyphen) were merely variant spellings of the same person's name.

Throughout this book, then, I refer to Shakespeare as Shakespeare. Some of the less logical among the unorthodox will ask me: Do you mean the actor or the dramatist? To which the reply is: I mean the actor-dramatist. For it is most illogical to speak, as Slater does, of a 'Stratfordian theory': this is a misuse of language. That William Shakespeare of Stratford wrote the plays and poems commonly attributed to him is not a *theory* at the present time, it is a *fact* at the present time—and will continue to be a fact until it is definitely proved wrong. What are correctly termed theories are the arguments which are the subject of this book: the arguments 'proving' that Shakespeare's works were written by Bacon, Raleigh, Rutland, or by some other aristocrat (as he usually is) or by a combination of such aristocrats. These are the theories, and they will remain theories until one of them is accepted as a definite proof. When that day dawns—it may be tomorrow or (more likely) it may *always* be tomorrow—the Baconian theory or one of its rivals will become the *fact*; and then, and not till then, can we speak logically of a Stratfordian *theory*. The orthodox will then be heretics, and some of the heretics orthodox, but I am writing this book today, not tomorrow, and accordingly cannot admit that the fact of the actor Shakespeare's authorship—as stated in the First Folio and in all subsequent editions—is a mere theory like the Baconian.

The argument, of course, works in protection of Bacon as much as it does in protection of Shakespeare. If some writer in the future should deny Bacon's authorship of *New Atlantis*, giving that celebrated work to King James I or John Donne, that theory will remain a theory until it is definitely proved. Until it is proved, nobody can have the right to call Bacon's authorship of *New Atlantis* a Baconian or St. Albans theory.

I have no particular bias in favour of the spelling 'Shakespeare'. It is the commonest form today, and therefore I use it, as I use the spellings 'Raleigh' and 'Marlowe'. This procedure holds good throughout this book except where I quote Elizabethan literature in contemporary spelling or cite unorthodox theorists who make a distinction between the actor 'Shakspere' and the dramatist 'Shakespeare'. Such a distinction, I believe, cannot be substantiated.

PART ONE

HISTORY

I am 'sort of' haunted by the conviction that the divine William is the biggest and most successful fraud ever practised on a patient world. The more I turn him round and round the more he so affects me. But that is all—I am not pretending to treat the question or carry it any further. It bristles with difficulties and I can only express my general sense by saying I find it *almost* as impossible to conceive that Bacon wrote the plays as to conceive that the man from Stratford, as we know the man from Stratford, did.

HENRY JAMES: Letter to Violet Hunt,
26 August 1903

The name 'William Shakespeare' is most probably a pseudonym behind which there lies concealed a great unknown.

SIGMUND FREUD: *Outline of Psychoanalysis* (1940)

CHAPTER I

THE ORIGINS
1601–1857

Thou wretched, rash, intruding fool, farewell!
I took thee for thy better.
SHAKESPEARE: *Hamlet.*

Some are born great, some achieve greatness, and
some have greatness thrust upon 'em.
SHAKESPEARE: *Twelfth Night.*

I

The common view about the origin of the Shakespeare authorship question assigns it to the nineteenth century. George Sampson, for instance, tells us that nobody ever doubted Shakespeare's authorship 'till America in the nineteenth century began to throw up a succession of cranks representing the extremes of ignorant credulity and morbid ingenuity' (*Concise Cambridge History of English Literature*, p. 256). Compare B.J.A., 'The Humbug of Bacon', *New York Herald*, 5 October 1874: 'The idea of robbing the world of Shakespeare for such a stiff, legal-headed old jack-ass as Bacon, is a modern invention of fools'. Even Marchette Chute, the author of what is probably the best recent biography of Shakespeare, inclines to the popular view when she takes the question as springing entirely from nineteenth-century reaction to some Restoration legends:

'. . . Many people felt almost relieved when Delia Bacon took the final logical step in 1857 and suggested that the plays of Shakespeare were written by someone else entirely. Delia chose Sir Francis Bacon for the honour.* Later candidates to be suggested have been the Earl of Oxford, Sir Edward Dyer, the fifth Earl of Rutland, the sixth Earl of Derby and even the Countess of Pembroke, who worked as part of a syndicate and supplied womanly touches here and there. This respect for the literary value of noble birth is impressive in its unanimity but a little hard to explain logically, since the most learned of Elizabethan dramatists was a

---

* Not entirely, of course. See below, pp. 37–8.

27

bricklayer, and the most poetic, next to Shakespeare, was the son of a cobbler.' (*Shakespeare of London*, p. 314, *note*.)

There is an impressive unanimity also in the crediting of the origins of the question to the nineteenth century. But this is as wrong as is the respect for the literary value of noble birth. Whether the origins go back to the seventeenth century or merely to the eighteenth is, admittedly, a matter of opinion. It depends whether we give any credit at all to evidence that lies outside the reach of literary criticism. If we do give such credit, then the origins of the question go back at least to 1624; if we decide not to give credit to anything outside strictly literary opinion, then the origins go back to 1759 or perhaps to 1738. The reasons for my own date of 1601 will become clear in the second part of this book.

The non-literary evidence referred to concerns some pictorial title-pages of the seventeenth century, described by W. H. Mallock—before the days of Hollywood—as 'talking pictures'. ('New Facts Relating to the Bacon–Shakespeare Question', *Pall Mall Magazine*, January 1903, p. 80.) There is no doubt that title-pages containing symbolic, not merely decorative, drawings were familiar to scholars of the sixteenth and seventeenth centuries and that Bacon was interested in the rules that had been worked out for representing ideas by pictorial symbols. In the preface to his *Recueil d'Emblèmes Divers*, published in Paris in 1638, the French writer Baudoin refers to the assistance given to scholars on this subject by the late Lord Chancellor of England: 'I venture to say that there is very little in philosophy which cannot be represented by means of symbols or emblems. Here, O reader, I have attempted to deal with the principles of the matter, aided by the explanations given by the learned Chancellor Bacon.' [1] Thus far we can tread with comparative safety. It is amusing to see how Mallock, himself not a Baconian, guards himself against the assumption later developed by his friend Sir Edwin Durning-Lawrence:

'The utmost in the way of theory, on which I should personally venture, is this: That the facts indicate, not that Bacon was the real Shakespeare, but that he had certain connections, of one sort or another, with the literature and the *literati* of his time, which he never publicly acknowledged, and which have thus far never been recognized. . . . Should subsequent study of the matter show that this position is not warranted I shall abandon it without regret' (*loc. cit.*, p. 77).

Whether Mallock ever made any further study is not known to me; what is certain is that Durning-Lawrence did, embodying his findings in a book *Bacon is Shake-speare* (1910) and a pamphlet *The Shakespeare Myth* (1912). Later Baconians have mostly accepted his beliefs on this particular matter of the pictorial title-pages; later non-Baconians have either been as cautious as Mallock or have dismissed the whole thing as nonsense.

It is not in the procedure which I intend to follow in this historical part of my book to dismiss any theory as nonsensical, however great the temptation; what matters is when and where the theory has been held. The problem in regard to these pictorial title-pages is one of interpretation; lacking other evidence, we can only say that some people have interpreted them in a certain way, others have denied that this interpretation is valid.

The chief title-pages in question are those to the following books: *Cryptomenytices et Cryptographiae*, a book published at Lüneburg in 1624 under the auspices of the Duke of Brunswick, the author being 'Gustavus Selenus', possibly a pseudonym for the Duke himself; the third edition of Florio's translation of Montaigne, published in London in 1632; Bacon's *Sermones Fideles, Ethici, Politici, Oeconomici*, published in Holland in 1641; Bacon's *Historia Regni Henrici Septimi*, published in Holland, 1642; and Book IX of Bacon's *De Augmentis Scientiarum*, published in Holland in 1645, 1662, and 1694. All these are reproduced in Mallock's articles in the *Pall Mall Magazine* and in the book and pamphlet by Durning-Lawrence.

The contention is that the figures depicted on these title-pages symbolize the actor Shakespeare stealing the crown of fame from the philosopher Bacon—or other symbols to a similar effect. Durning-Lawrence was convinced that these represent the first indications of the dramatist's real identity; he also believed that the book by 'Gustavus Selenus' (1624) 'was issued as the key to the Shakespeare Folio of 1623' (*Bacon is Shake-speare*, pp. 107–8). Mallock believed that the title-pages mean only that Bacon was connected in some way with the publication, not the authorship, of

Shakespeare's plays. The interested reader is referred to the
seventeenth-century works mentioned or to their title-pages reproduced in Mallock and Durning-Lawrence.[2]

II

The first literary, as distinct from pictorial, evidence belongs to
the eighteenth century, in the shape of a farce in two acts entitled
High Life below Stairs, written by the Rev. James Townley and
acted in London in 1759. In this play a character named Mrs. Kitty
asks the question: 'Who wrote Shakespeare?' And the Duke re-
plies gravely: 'Ben Jonson'. 'Oh, no!' cries Lady Bab: 'Shakespeare was written by one Mr. Finis, for I saw his name at the end
of the book.'

The joke is not a very profound one, even if the whole dialogue
was invented, as we must suspect, for the express purpose of making it. The passage cannot, however, be taken as accidental; there
is no reason to think that Townley could have written 'Who wrote
Milton?' instead. There must have been, in the mid-eighteenth
century, a certain amount of discussion as to the authenticity of the
traditional authorship of Shakespeare, and the substitution of Ben
Jonson is significant. All through the seventeenth century,
Shakespeare's 'Nature' was constantly being contrasted with Jonson's 'Art'. By the mid-eighteenth century, if this passage of
Townley's is any guide, readers were no longer quite so sure that
Shakespeare's plays were the work of a relatively unlearned author.
There were plenty of critics who still supported the old view, but
now there had apparently grown up a minority to whom the idea
of Shakespeare and Jonson being the same person was not one to
be automatically dismissed.

Ten years after Townley's comedy, there was published in London an anonymous book entitled *The Life and Adventures of Common Sense: An Historical Allegory*. Its author is generally considered to have been the physician Herbert Lawrence, friend of the
actor Garrick; it was so far popular that it attained a second
edition in London, and was afterwards translated into French and
published at Avignon and at Yverdon, Switzerland, in 1777. This
book relates the various adventures of Common Sense, son of Wisdom and Truth, from the time of Cicero to the reign of George I.
Chapter IX of Book II sees the symbolic hero landing at Dover in

1588, whence he proceeds to London and writes plays which are passed off as his own by the actor Shakespeare. How seriously this is meant, or even precisely *what* is meant, depends primarily on the individual reader. Baconians have taken it to mean that the symbolic hero represents Francis Bacon; other anti-Shakespeareans have denied the identification. (See, for example, Roderick Eagle, *Shakespeare: New Views for Old*, pp. 8–9; William Kent, *Edward de Vere, the Real Shakespeare*, p. 10.) It is possible that nothing of the sort was intended at all, that the author was merely paying a humorous compliment to Shakespeare as the 'thief' of Wisdom and Truth. The chief propagandist for the Earl of Derby, however, the late Prof. Lefranc, cites in this connection Louis Riccoboni's curious remark about 'Shakpear' in his *Réflexions historiques et critiques sur les différents Théâtres de l'Europe* (1738): '*Ayant consumé son patrimoine, il entreprit le métier de voleur.*' Perhaps this idea of Shakespeare as a professional thief stems rather from Restoration legends about his career as a poacher than from any suggestion that he might have stolen the plays from the Earl of Derby.

Sixteen years later, in 1785, James Corton Cowell, a gentleman of Ipswich, was in Stratford-on-Avon in search of material for a lecture on Shakespeare he had promised to deliver to the Ipswich Philosophical Society. He fell in with a certain Rev. James Wilmot, D.D., formerly scholar of Trinity College, Oxford, and at that time rector of Barton-on-the-Heath, a village a few miles to the north of Stratford. Wilmot had long been struck by the similarity of thought between Shakespeare and Bacon, and had come to the conclusion that they must have been the same person. He confided his views to Cowell, who accepted them. Thus the first Baconian known to us by name is the Rev. James Wilmot, and the first Baconian who expressed his views in writing that has survived was James Corton Cowell.[3] For the first Baconian who expressed his views in print, we have to wait till 1856.

Or, alternatively, till the very next year after the meeting between Wilmot and Cowell. For in 1786 there appeared in London a similar anonymous publication to that of 1769. Whether the author was the same, we do not know, but it seems very likely. Mr. Eagle, however, has 'a strong suspicion' that the author may have been Wilmot, afterwards credited by his daughter, who wrote his Life, with the authorship of the mysterious *Letters of Junius*.

The new anonymous allegory had the title of *The Learned Pig*, and the author tells us that this symbolic animal has appeared on earth in many reincarnations since the time of Romulus, the founder of Rome. One of these reincarnations was in the time of Queen Elizabeth, when the Pig met Shakespeare, who got all the credit for the plays the learned animal had written. 'He has been fathered', says the Pig, 'with many spurious dramatic pieces: *Hamlet, Othello, As You Like It, The Tempest*, and *A Midsummer Night's Dream*, for five; of all which I confess myself to be the author.' If we take this work seriously, and in the sense in which Baconians take it, then its writer was the first Baconian to express his views in print.

The eighteenth century, then, while still being cryptical, is much less so than the seventeenth in its opinions on this question. It gives us two definite Baconians in Wilmot and Cowell, and a possible third in the author of *The Learned Pig*, who may have been Wilmot himself. The view of the author of *The Life and Adventures of Common Sense* is more difficult to place. The reader must take his choice of three opinions: (1) that he was paying a compliment to Shakespeare as a genius 'thieving' Wisdom and Truth; (2) that he was indicating that Shakespeare stole the honours due to the real author; or (3) that he was indicating that this real author was Bacon.

Cowell's opinions were the reflection of Wilmot's, and I believe that modern Baconians are right when they hail the Rector of Barton as the virtual founder of their theory. It remains to enquire what led him to think that Shakespeare and Bacon were the same person. He was not a literary critic, and in fact his opinion was not founded on the literary qualities of Shakespeare and Bacon at all, but in what he conceived to be their parallel 'philosophies'—for example, in the views expressed by the character Coriolanus in the play of that name and the views expressed by Francis Bacon in his own person. Wilmot was also struck by the intimate knowledge which Shakespeare seemed to reveal of the Court of Navarre in *Love's Labour's Lost*. For this reason, among others of a similar nature, he was forced to the conclusion that the author of the plays must have been a much-travelled philosopher, not an actor-dramatist who probably did not leave his native country in his life. As all his points were developed by later Baconians, the title of 'first Baconian' is justly held by him.

III

Now occurs a silence of more than thirty years—or more than fifty years if we regard Cowell's manuscript of 1805 as expressing the views held by Wilmot and the author of *The Learned Pig* in the 1780's. It is true that the great poet and critic Samuel Taylor Coleridge is often called a Baconian by Baconians, but the only evidence they produce is a passage in which he dissents from the opinion of 'our daily criticism' about the nature of Shakespeare's genius. So far as I am aware, Coleridge expressed no views at all on the subject of the authorship.

On similar 'evidence', Dickens and the great German critic Gervinus have been claimed as Baconians. In the former case, the evidence rests upon a single sentence, extracted I believe from one of Dickens's letters: 'The Life of Shakespeare is a fine mystery and I tremble every day lest something should turn up.' This hardly qualifies as Baconianism or even indicates that Dickens believed Shakespeare's plays were written by someone else. In the latter case, Baconians have been misled by the passage in which Gervinus compares the work of Shakespeare with the work of Bacon (*Shakespeare Commentaries*, revised translation, 1875, p. 884 sq.). Nowhere does the critic suggest that the two writers were the same. Indeed, on p. 26 of the same work he writes as follows: 'The commentators of the last century, on account of a few historical, geographical and chronological errors, looked down upon the ignorant poet with an air of superiority. Now, however, whole volumes are written to prove his knowledge of true and fabulous natural history, to evidence his familiarity with the Bible, to establish his agreement with Aristotle, and to make him one and the same person as the philosopher Bacon!' The exclamation mark shows what Gervinus thought of the last-named opinion. The passage comes, by the way, from a chapter entitled 'Shakespeare at Stratford'.

There may have been, however, some discussion on the question by some of Coleridge's contemporaries. The evidence is slight, but must be mentioned. It consists of a passage in Chapter VI of Disraeli's novel *Venetia* (1837), in which the character Lord Carducis expresses doubts about Shakespeare's authorship. This character is supposed to have been based on the poet Byron, so there is indication that Byron himself had said something of the

c

sort. Whether Disraeli agreed is not known to me, but I should think it very likely.

Eleven years later, in 1848,[4] Joseph C. Hart, American Consul at Santa Cruz, published a book entitled *The Romance of Yachting*. One would not immediately connect a book of this title with discussion of the Shakespeare authorship, but Hart had ideas of his own about the matter and duly expressed them here. He believed that Shakespeare merely owned the plays as property of the theatre and that they were written by poorly paid collaborators. Bringing Riccoboni up to date, Hart wrote that Shakespeare

'grew up in ignorance and viciousness and became a common poacher. And the latter title, in literary matters, he carried to his grave. . . . It is a fraud upon the world to thrust his surreptitious fame upon us. . . . The enquiry will be, Who were the able literary men who wrote the dramas imputed to him?'

Much the same position was taken up by Robert Jamieson, in an article he contributed anonymously to *Chambers's Edinburgh Journal*, 7 August 1852. 'Who Wrote Shakespeare?' was his title, and he began by quoting Townley's farce *High Life below Stairs*, still a popular piece upon the stage. He did not agree with the Duke in that play, that Shakespeare was written by Ben Jonson, but rather with Hart, that the so-called dramatist was really nothing more than the manager of a theatre. He believed that Shakespeare 'kept a poet'—not a number of different poets, as Hart had thought—and that when the poet died about 1610–12 plays ceased to appear and Shakespeare, the manager, retired rich.

Four years later, in 1856, we reach the first full-scale work on the subject: *Bacon and Shakespeare: An Inquiry touching Players, Playhouses and Play-Writers in the Days of Elizabeth*, by William Henry Smith—the book which is said to have convinced Lord Palmerston. Smith was the first to put forward the suggestion that Shakespeare was illiterate. In general, he agreed with Hart and Jamieson:

'Prior to the year 1611, a number of plays . . . were produced of which William Shakespeare was reputed to be the author, and which undoubtedly were, in some way, the property of the company of actors of which he was an active member. Not one single manuscript has ever been found to identify him as the author of these productions.'

We reach, too, the first controversy. For Smith's book was answered by a pamphlet entitled *William Shakespeare Not an Impostor: by an English Critic*, published in 1857. The author was George H. Townsend. The battle is now joined, and will continue for a hundred years. Our search for the origins can be considered over. . . .

But it may be asked: what of Delia Bacon? That she is often *believed* to have been the first Baconian is a fact, but it is not a fact that she was actually so. Wilmot, Cowell, and Smith preceded her,[5] and she is not even to be regarded as a Baconian at all, if we define the name as applying to somebody who believes that Francis Bacon wrote all the works generally attributed to Shakespeare. Delia Bacon was not a Baconian in this sense, not a Baconian *tout court*. She was the chief foundress of the Group Theory—originally hinted at by Hart—and that too has continued for a hundred years.

NOTES

1. See also, for the use of ciphers and secret writing during these centuries, Baptista Porta, *De Furtivis Literarum Notis* (Naples, 1568); Blaise de Vigenère, *Traité des chiffres, ou Secrètes manières d'escrire* (Paris, 1586); John Wilkins, Bishop of Chester, *Mercury, or The Secret and Swift Messenger* (London, 1641); and Thomas Tenison, Archbishop of Canterbury, *Baconiana* (London, 1679). The last-named contains a guide to the cipher actually used by Bacon—said by Mrs. Stopes to have been stolen from Vigenère. 'The very cipher which Bacon claims, which suggested to Mr. Donnelly his years of patient labour, was cribbed from Vigenère's volume, and taken possession of *without acknowledgment*' (*The Bacon-Shakspere Question Answered*, p. 220).

2. There is a similar pictorial title-page in an edition of Spenser's poems published in London in 1611. Some Baconians believe that this means that Bacon wrote Spenser's poems, others that he edited them. Mallock thought that 'The design, if it refers to him, can mean only that he was connected with their production in some unspecified way.' The same design was apparently used on the title-pages of Bedingfield's translation of Machiavelli's *Florentine History* and the sixth edition (1623) of Sidney's *Arcadia*. See A. W. Pollard, *The History of the Title-page*.

3. See Allardyce Nicoll, 'The First Baconian', *Times Literary Supplement*, 25 February 1932; and Lord Sydenham's pamphlet, undated, of the same title. Cowell's lecture exists in a manuscript dated 7 February 1805, now in the possession of the Library of the University of London; it was part of a bequest of books and manuscripts by Sir Edwin Durning-Lawrence.

4. 'The year of my birth,' adds Lord Sydenham. Other Baconians see significance in the fact that Wilmot was born exactly a hundred years after the death

of Bacon. Durning-Lawrence counted all the letters in the verses 'To the Reader' in the First Folio and found that they amounted to 287, 'a masonic number often repeated throughout the Folio. My book *Bacon is Shake-speare* was published in 1910 (i.e., 287 years after 1623), and tells for the first time the true meaning of these lines' (*The Shakespeare Myth*, p. 7).

  5. There was some controversy at one time as to whether Smith had copied from Delia Bacon. But he was able to prove that his book was in the press before hers or her previous article was published and that he had held his Baconian views for years. His book caused discussion both in England and in France.

CHAPTER II

A CENTURY OF GROUP THEORIES
1856-1956

Sir Walter . . . William Stanley;
Oxford, redoubted Pembroke . . .
And many moe of noble fame and worth.
SHAKESPEARE: *King Richard the Third.*

I

The Group Theory, with which can be considered the various
Dual Theories which have been advanced,[1] has always proved the
most popular of all the arguments which hold that Shakespeare
either did not write his own plays at all or that he wrote only certain
parts of them. Its history covers now a complete century, with the
publication in 1956 of A. J. Evans's *Shakespeare's Magic Circle.*

Its genesis is in Delia Bacon's *The Philosophy of Shakespeare's
Plays Unfolded*, which was published in London in 1857, a small
part of it having appeared the previous year in an article in
Putnam's Magazine, New York. Delia Bacon was unfortunate in
her life and has been doubly unfortunate in her reputation. It has
already been mentioned that she has been credited with the founding of the Baconian Theory, whereas what she really founded (on
perhaps the original impulse of Hart) was the Group Theory;
more serious, she has been dismissed as 'more than half-crazed' [2]
because she was unfortunate enough to end her days in a lunatic
asylum. Now this period of insanity no more affects her Group
Theory than the insanity of Collins affects the *Ode to Evening* or
than the fact that George Townsend committed suicide affects
the value of his answer to Smith. Theories, whether we agree with
them or not, must be considered strictly on their merits, without
regard to the personalities of their creators.

It is safe to say that a woman whose ideas and conversation were
found stimulating by so great a novelist as Hawthorne was not of
unsound mind. I would certainly call her an eccentric, but no
more so than Ignatius Donnelly or Mrs. Pott or than that other
American enthusiast, Orville Owen, who searched the bed of the

River Wye in the hope of discovering Bacon's Shakespeare manuscripts.

Hawthorne, however, wrote the Preface to Delia Bacon's book purely out of friendship. He was not himself a Group Theorist—still less a Baconian, as he has often been called. I have read his Preface with great care, and nowhere in it does he express his agreement with his friend's theory. He obviously thinks it a theory worth consideration, but that is all. He is concerned above all to stress his friend's complete sincerity:

'The volume now before the reader . . . is the product of a most faithful and conscientious labour, and a truly heroic devotion of intellect and heart. No man or woman has ever thought or written more sincerely. . . .

'It is for the public to say whether my countrywoman has proved her theory. In the worst event, if she has failed, her failure will be more honorable than most people's triumphs; since it must fling upon the old tombstone, at Stratford-on-Avon, the noblest tributary wreath that has ever lain there' (Preface, pp. xii, xv).

I have called Delia Bacon's theory a Group Theory. So it was, indeed, but a case could be made out for calling it a Dual Theory. The 'philosophy' in her title evidently agrees with the former opinion (unknown to her) of the Rector of Barton-on-the-Heath. But she did not share Wilmot's opinion that, because of the apparent resemblance between the philosophy of Bacon and the 'philosophy' of the plays, therefore the Viscount St. Albans must have written the entire works. Instead she put forward what is, on the face of it, a much more plausible theory, though she offered no evidence in support. She postulated a group authorship, with a supreme friendship as the original impulse—a friendship between the Poet, Sir Walter Raleigh, and the Philosopher, Francis Bacon. The chief writer of the plays, she believed, was Raleigh, 'that great Political and Military Chief, and not less illustrious Man of Letters', aided by the philosophy of Bacon and to a certain extent by the assistance of such men as Edmund Spenser, Sir Philip Sidney, Thomas Sackville, Henry Lord Paget, Edward Earl of Oxford, and some others. These latter poets and gentlemen make only a brief appearance in her book: most of her 700 pages is given over to the friendship between Raleigh, the master poet of the plays, and Bacon, the master philosopher. She asks on p. 518:

'When shall the friendship of such "a twain" gladden our earth again, and build its "eternal summer" in our common things? When shall a "marriage of true minds" so even be celebrated on the lips and in the lives of men again?'

Raleigh-Bacon: a Dual Authorship. But also a Group Authorship, for Delia Bacon believed that these two men formed and led a secret association 'for the culture and instruction of the masses' —secret, because it was directed against the governments of Elizabeth and James I:

'It was an enterprise which originated in the Court of Queen Elizabeth, in that little company of wits, and poets, and philosophers, which was the first-fruit of the new development of the national genius, that followed the revival of the learning of antiquity in this island. . . .

'Ciphers were employed in the writings of this school . . . through the works they could not own' (pp. 519, 572-3).

In her Introduction, a comparatively modest affair of a hundred pages, she gives us a few preliminary details of this group of poets and philosophers. I will content myself with three quotations from this Introduction, which is more quotable than the main text:

'Driven from one field, they showed themselves in another. Driven from the open field, they fought in secret . . . Elizabethan England rejected the Elizabethan Man. She would have none of his meddling with her affairs. She sent him to the Tower, and to the block, if ever she caught him . . . She took the seals of office, she took the sword, from his hands and put a pen in it. She would have of him a Man of Letters, and a Man of Letters he became. A Man of Runes' (p. xlix).

'The brave, bold genius of Raleigh flashed new life into that little nucleus of the Elizabethan development. The new "Round Table" . . . with its new weapons and devices . . . was not yet "full" till he came in. The Round Table grew rounder with this knight's presence . . . The Round Table grew spheral, as he sat talking by it; the Round Table dissolved, as he brought forth his lore, and unrolled his maps upon it . . . "THE GLOBE"—the Globe, with its TWO hemispheres, became henceforth their device' (pp. lv-lvi).

'It is not too much to say that the works of Raleigh and Bacon and others . . . are written throughout in the language of this school. "Our glorious Willy" . . . was born in it, and knew no other speech . . . It was there, where the young wits and scholars, fresh from their continental tours . . . the Mercutios, the Benedicts, the Birons, the Longuevilles, came together fresh from the Court of Navarre, and smelling of the lore of their foreign "Academe" . . . it was *there*, in those *réunions*, that our Poet caught those gracious airs of his . . . those aristocratic notions that haunt him everywhere. It was there that he picked up his various knowledge of men and manners, his acquaintance with foreign life, his bits of travelled wit, that flash through all' (pp. lxxi–ii).

It is often considered that the idea of a secret cipher, inserted in Shakespeare's plays to reveal the true identity of the author, was first put forward by Mrs. Windle and Ignatius Donnelly in the late nineteenth century. But the notion appears to have been first thought of by Delia Bacon in 1857. In the Introduction from which we have quoted occurs the following passage (she is imagining Raleigh in the Tower):

'It is not a chapter in the *History of the World* which he is composing at present, though that work is there at this moment on the table, and forms the ostensible state-prison work of this convict. This is the man who made one so long ago in those brilliant "Round Table" reunions, in which the idea of converting the new *belles lettres* of that new time to such grave and politic uses was first suggested; he is the genius of that company, that even in such frolic mad-cap games as *Love's Labour's Lost*, and *The Taming of the Shrew*, and *Midsummer Night's Dream*, could contrive to insert . . . the cipher in which the secret of the authorship of these works was infolded' (p. lxxxi).

If much of later unorthodox theorizing goes back to Wilmot and Smith, much also goes back to Delia Bacon. Her book is difficult to read, but her main position has been made clear, I hope, by my quotations. An association, and a secret one, wrote the plays commonly attributed to Shakespeare; the chief poet was Raleigh, the chief philosopher was Bacon. 'To evade political restrictions, and to meet the popular mind on its own ground, was the double purpose of the disguise' (p. 32). The plays, she believes (p. 332), were part of 'that great question which was so soon to become the out-spoken question of the nation and the age . . . in swarms of English pamphlets, in harangues from English pulpits, in English parliaments and on English battlefields'.

II

We need not wonder that the Group Theory has since proved so popular. It lends itself to infinite variety of conjecture, and a great number of Elizabethans, mostly aristocrats, have been pressed into its service. Here I can only deal with some of the chief Group and Dual Theories; a full history would take a complete volume.

The first to follow Delia Bacon were her fellow-Americans, William D. O'Connor and Appleton Morgan. In two books published in Boston, *Harrington: A Story of True Love* (1860) and—more important—*Hamlet's Note-Book* (1886), O'Connor developed his own Group Theory, laying the stress upon Raleigh's part in the authorship rather than upon Bacon's. Not that he was at all anti-Baconian; indeed, in *Mr. Donnelly's Reviewers*, he ably defended the cryptographic theories of Ignatius Donnelly against the hostile treatment they had received in the American press. But Raleigh's claim engaged most of his attention, both for the plays of Shakespeare and the poems. He believed, for example, that the mysterious dedication of the *Sonnets*—to 'Mr. W. H.'—refers to 'Walter RaleigH', and that the publisher's initials, 'T.T.' (Thomas Thorpe), really refer to the noted mathematician, 'Thomas HarioT', one of Raleigh's literary circle, the so-called 'School of Night', which was suspected of atheism.

Appleton Morgan was more of a scholar; in his *Study of the Warwickshire Dialect* he discovered traces of the dialect of Shakespeare's native county in all the plays, especially in *Hamlet* (34 instances), *Henry the Fifth* (34), *The Winter's Tale* (23), the Second Part of *King Henry the Sixth* (21), *Troilus and Cressida* (20), and *Othello* and *Love's Labour's Lost* (17 each).

Compare the view of an orthodox scholar, Miss E. M. Wright, in her study *Rustic Speech and Folk-Lore* (Oxford, 1913): 'The Shakespeare-Bacon theory, if not too dead and gone to be worth further combat, could easily be completely overthrown by anyone who chose to array against it the convincing mass of evidence

which proves Shakespeare's intimate acquaintance with the Warwickshire dialect. Numbers of the words and phrases which
Shakespeare used, and which we have since lost, still exist in his
native county, and in the other counties bordering on Warwickshire' (p. 54). Morgan himself entered into a debate on this subject with a Baconian, Isaac Hull Platt, in the American journal *New
Shakespeareana*, April–July 1903.

But Morgan did not believe that Shakespeare wrote the plays:
'Our gratitude is due to William Shakespeare as editor, though
not as author, of the plays . . . His own real plays are apparently
lost.'

The quotation comes from *The Shakespeare Myth: William
Shakespeare and Circumstantial Evidence*, which Morgan published
at Cincinnati in 1881. He followed this by a further volume:
Shakespeare in Fact and in Criticism (New York, 1888). In these
books he put forward the belief that there are three anti-Shakespearean theories: (1) the Delia Bacon or Junta Theory; (2) the
Baconian or Unitary Theory; and (3) the New Theory. This New
Theory was, of course, the Morgan theory of Shakespeare's
editorship; he believed 'that various noblemen wrote these plays,
and that they used Shakespeare's name as a *nom de plume*'. He disagreed with Delia Bacon about Raleigh's predominance and with
the Baconians about their unitary claim for Francis Bacon.
'Experts have proved that the styles of Bacon and Shakespeare are
as far apart as the poles. . . . The New Theory is that all the
learned parts are by a learned hand, but that Shakespeare put in all
the clown business.' The contribution of Bacon was limited to the
legal and philosophical knowledge which he supplied to the group
of noble authors.

This part of Morgan's theory was repeated, though in a very
different form, by a more orthodox scholar, Edward James
Castle, in his book *Shakespeare, Jonson, Bacon and Greene: A
Study*, published in London in 1897. Castle was a qualified
lawyer—formerly Recorder of Carlisle—but he did not agree with
the Baconians that the author of the plays must have been a professional legal man (see below, p. 65 sq.). Instead, he divided the
plays into two classes, which he designated 'legal' and 'non-legal'.
In the latter, more numerous, he found so many 'laughable mistakes' as to convince him that the author 'personally had not the
education of a lawyer'. In the former plays, he found evidence to

prove that Shakespeare must have had some assistance from a professional legal man, probably Bacon. In Castle, the Group Theory becomes a Dual Theory, with Bacon acting merely as legal adviser to the actor-dramatist from Stratford. (For the wide diversity of opinion among legal authorities, on the question of the authorship, see below, p. 159 sq.)

Morgan's first book on the New Theory was translated into German (*Der Shakespeare-Mythus*, Leipzig, 1885) by Karl Müller-Mylius, himself the author of a work on the Shakespeare–Bacon controversy, *Der Shakespeare-und-Bacon Streit*, published in the same city—the home of German Shakespeare studies—the year before. The influence of Morgan is perhaps seen in two curious theories propounded by another German writer, Eugen Reichel. In his first book, *Shakespeare-Litteratur* (Stuttgart, 1887), he put forward the theory that a great writer named William Shakespeare died about 1586, that Bacon got possession of the manuscripts of his plays, edited them and 'fathered' them on the actor Shakspere from Stratford. In 1902, in the journal *Die Gegenwart*, he put forward another theory in an article entitled 'Das Porträt des Herrn W.H.' He kept to the idea of Bacon's editorship, but now suggested that the plays were the combined work of a father and a son, as he believed was indicated in the *Sonnets*. The father was Walter Devereux, who in 1572 had been created Earl of Essex; the son was the ill-starred second Earl, Robert Devereux, who in 1601 was executed for his rebellion against the Queen's government. The connection between German and American theories still persists, for in 1905 an American, Latham Davis, was to put forward the theory that this second Earl of Essex was the author of all Shakespeare's works.

But we have not yet completely finished with the nineteenth century. Other Group and Dual Theories belong to the century of Delia Bacon, and we must briefly glance at the chief ones in turn. In 1887 an anonymous writer with the initials J.G.B. produced a very original theory under the unoriginal title *Who wrote Shakespeare's Plays?* His answer to the question was none other than Cardinal Wolsey—who died, of course, many years before the plays were acted. Wolsey's manuscripts, J. G. B. believed, came into the possession of Bacon, who edited them for the stage and himself wrote the concluding historical play, *Henry the Eighth*, in which Wolsey is the chief character.

The next year, 1888, saw the publication of General J. Watts de Peyster's *Was THE Shakespeare after all a Myth?* De Peyster answered his question in the affirmative, being convinced that the plays wcrc written in collaboration by a number of aristocratic Elizabethans, including Raleigh and Bacon. The actor Shakespeare's authorship the General dismissed with contempt:

'It almost seems ridiculous to talk about the writings of any man, when not a line of his has come down to us, and not a word, except his own signature. Is it a matter of possibility or probability that if Shaksper wrote so well in every sense of the word and such a vast amount, that no manuscript of his, good, bad or indifferent, has been preserved, when the writings of so many men of far lesser note, conceding any greatness to Shaksper, should not only exist but abound?'

The de Peyster family were friends and neighbours in New York of the James family, so perhaps it is to the General's book and conversation that we can trace the origin of Henry James's attitude to the Shakespeare question.

In *Our English Homer* (1892) T. W. White described the plays as the result of collaboration between Greene, Peele, Daniel, Marlowe, Shakespeare, Nashe, and Lodge, Bacon again acting as editor. In *The Gentle Shakspere* (1896) J. P. Yeatman described them as written by Shakespeare with the assistance of Bartholomew Griffin, Henry Ferrers, the Earl of Derby, the Earl of Southampton, and the Earl of Pembroke. While in *It was Marlowe: a Story of the Secret of Three Centuries*, a novel published in Chicago in 1895, Wilbur Gleason Zeigler described them as the work of Christopher Marlowe, assisted among others by Raleigh and the Earl of Rutland. . . . The popularity of the Group Theory, I make no apology for repeating, lies in the fact that it lends itself to infinite variety of conjecture.

III

And as much in the twentieth century as in the nineteenth. The first twentieth-century Group Theorist whom we must consider is John H. Stotsenburg, who published at Louisville, Kentucky, in 1904 a book entitled *An Impartial Study of the Shakespeare Title*.

Although dedicated to Mrs. Pott, with reference to her 'exposure' of 'the Shaksper fraud',* this book presents one of the more scholarly of the unorthodox theories, useful as a source for previous unorthodox opinions. Judge Stotsenburg believed that the plays were 'originally composed by collaborators' and then 'corrected, revised, and added to' by others (p. vii). 'No one but a scholar or coterie of scholars could have written the Shakespeare poems and plays' (p. 15). He develops this case on a later page:

'When I assert that William Shaksper, even if a very learned man, [the Judge believes him to have been illiterate] could not have written the plays, I mean by that assertion that no one man, however gifted . . . could by any possibility have written the plays. I assert the same as to the scholarly Bacon, rare Ben Jonson, or any other writer of the period . . . I support my assertion by two infallible propositions . . . first . . . that no one man . . . could use as many words as are found in the plays, and the second . . . that an examination of the plays . . . shows that three men at the very least participated in the preparation and composition' (pp. 174–5).

Stotsenburg believed that this theory of collaboration removes all the difficulties facing any assertion of single authorship, whether by Shakespeare, by Bacon, or by another:

'. . . all the difficulties vanish. The use of so many words is naturally explained. The difference in style and methods of expression are properly accounted for, and there is room enough in the glorious company of the poets to account for all the knowledge —legal, medical, scientific, theological, special or general—that has hitherto bothered the brains of the admirers of the Shakespeare plays in their attempts to palm them upon the public as the offspring of one man' (pp. 178–9).

The main authors of the plays, he believed, were Drayton and Dekker, assisted at different times by Bacon, Munday, Webster,

---

* Mrs. Henry Pott was, of course, one of the most eminent of American Baconians, whom we shall be considering in her proper place in the next chapter. But she can be regarded also as a Dual Theorist, because of her conviction that Anthony Bacon as well as Francis was 'a considerable author, poet, and playwright'. She asks: 'What share did Anthony Bacon take in his brother's works? . . . Did he, perhaps, frame the plots of many of the plays which Francis polished and finished?' (*Francis Bacon and his Secret Society*, pp. 47, 367).

Chettle, Wentworth Smythe, Heywood, Porter, Middleton, Fletcher, Wilson, and possibly Jonson. For example, *Julius Caesar* was written by Drayton, Middleton, Webster, and Munday (p. 415 sq.) and *All's Well That Ends Well* by Heywood and Chettle (p. 514); *Troilus and Cressida* was originally written by Dekker and Chettle, 'added to and philosophically dressed by Francis Bacon' (p. 379); Drayton was the principal author of *Richard the Second*, added to by Wilson, Dekker, and Chettle (pp. 408, 413); while *Measure for Measure* was written by Heywood and Chettle, later 'dressed and beautified' by Bacon 'with his views upon life, death, justice and mercy' (pp. 386–7, 393).

Venus and Adonis and *The Rape of Lucrece* Stotsenburg believed to have been written by Bacon, because of their legal allusions. The *Sonnets* he gave to Sir Philip Sidney (Ch. XXII) for a number of reasons. Sidney's name among his intimates was 'Will' or 'Willy', as indicated in Sonnets 135–6; his close friend was Sir Edward Dyer, obviously indicated by the pun in Sonnet 20: 'A man in hue all hues in his controlling'; and he 'bore the canopy' (Sonnet 125) as a gentleman-in-waiting on the Queen in the summer of 1578. Stotsenburg had previously credited Sidney with the authorship of the *Sonnets* in an article in *Baconiana* in October 1892, in the course of which he refuted the counter-claim put forward on behalf of Sir Anthony Shirley.

We have mentioned that the name of the Earl of Rutland was first put forward by Zeigler in Chicago in 1895. Once again we see the close connection between American theories and German, for in 1906 Peter Alvor—pen-name of Burkhard Herrmann—published a book in Munich entitled *Das neue Shakespeare-Evangelium* in which he put forward the suggestion that the plays and poems were the result of collaboration between two earls: Henry Wriothesley, third Earl of Southampton, and Roger Manners, fifth Earl of Rutland. The connection of Southampton with Shakespeare is well known, though when Mrs. Stopes wrote his biography, in the hope of discovering more about their relationship, she was forced to confess that her researches had found out little new. But it is, at any rate, a fact that it was to Southampton that Shakespeare dedicated *Venus and Adonis* and *Lucrece*. Whether it is a fact or a mere legend that Southampton gave him a present of a thousand pounds is not known; the sum seems to me enormous.

Alvor gave to Southampton the posthumous present of having been the author of *King John, Richard the Second, Henry the Sixth, Titus Andronicus, Romeo and Juliet, Richard the Third, Henry the Fourth, Henry the Fifth, Othello, Julius Caesar, Macbeth, Antony and Cleopatra, King Lear, Cymbeline, Henry the Eighth,* and *Coriolanus.* Rutland, he believed, wrote all the other plays, as well as *Venus and Adonis, Lucrece,* and the *Sonnets.* (*Das Neue Shakespeare-Evangelium,* 2nd ed., p. 118.) The models for the various characters were as follows: Romeo was the author Southampton, Juliet being Elizabeth Vernon; in *Much Ado About Nothing,* Claudio was Southampton, Hero Elizabeth Vernon, Benedict the author Rutland, Beatrice Elizabeth Sidney, Countess Rutland, and Don Pedro Essex; in *Henry the Fourth,* Percy was Essex, Prince Hal the author Southampton, Falstaff Shaksper, '*der Stratforder Schauspieler*', and Bardolph Ben Jonson; in *The Merchant of Venice,* Bassanio was Bacon; in *Julius Caesar,* Brutus was the author Southampton, Portia the Countess of Southampton, and Cassius Essex; while Coriolanus was Raleigh, Aufidius Essex, and Menenius the author Southampton (pp. 94–5).

Alvor appears not to have rested on the laurels of this attractive theory. I have not read his later books, but I am told that in *Die Lösung der Shakespeare-Frage* (Leipzig, 1909) he advocated the authorship of Anthony Bacon, presumably assisted by his brother Francis, and in *Neue Shakespeare Biographie* (Würzburg, 1930) he suggested that the works of Shakespeare were written by Lord Mountjoy, second husband of Sidney's 'Stella' (Penelope Devereux), who became the Earl of Devonshire. Whether this last theory was for a single candidate, or perhaps for Devonshire as collaborator in a group, is not known to me for certain at the time of writing.

Anthony Bacon as author of the *Sonnets* was suggested by W. H. Denning in an article, 'Who wrote the Shakespeare Sonnets?', in the *English Review,* June 1925, and in a pamphlet, *Dressing Old Words New* (1933). He was judging partly by the reference to 'lameness' in Sonnet 89, a remark which he took literally and applied to the crippled brother of Francis. This reference has also been taken literally by writers who have advocated the claims of Raleigh and Oxford. In his pamphlet Mr. Denning draws comparisons between the *Sonnets* and Anthony's letters to his mother.

IV

The most startling attribution, to an Elizabethan or Jacobean eye, would have been that put forward in Chicago in 1916 by Harold Johnson: *Did the Jesuits write 'Shakespeare'?* Johnson suggests that certain members of the Society of Jesus, living in forced seclusion, wrote the plays using as a pseudonym a name suggested by that of Nicolas Breakspear, Pope Adrian IV (1154–9), the only Englishman to attain the Papacy. The names are certainly alike, and the background of the two men was not dissimilar ('of humble stock' say the reference books of Pope Adrian); but there the resemblance ends. There is no real evidence to show that Shakespeare was a Catholic; he has been *called* a Catholic, of course, but on the other hand he has been called a Puritan.[3]

We have said nothing so far in this chapter of that rather lonely figure among the unorthodox, Sir George Greenwood. He is often supposed to have been an 'orthodox Baconian', but he pointed out several times that he was not. He can be included among the Group Theorists by reason of many remarks he made: for instance, in *Baconian Essays*: 'That the work of many pens appears in the Folio of 1623 is surely indisputable' (Introduction, p. 10). He accepted the Baconian claim to the extent of thinking that Bacon probably wrote *Love's Labour's Lost*, but he was distinguished among unorthodox writers by his refusal to commit himself to any one theory. He wrote many books on the authorship question, and we shall meet him again in later chapters.

He was a personal friend, as has been mentioned, of J. M. Robertson, author of *The Baconian Heresy: A Confutation*. Can Robertson himself be included among the Group Theorists? He can in so far as he was a leader of the pre-war scholars who sought to 'disintegrate' the text of Shakespeare: that is, to examine the accepted canon in the hope of removing all non-Shakespearean parts. Robertson was a most intelligent man, but in the opinion of most scholars today he took his disintegration much too far. He rejected entirely *Titus* and *Henry the Sixth*, considered there were 'weighty reasons for regarding *Richard the Second* and *Richard the Third* as plays really composed by Marlowe and only touched at points by Shakespeare' (*Introduction to the Study of the Shakespeare Canon*, p. 474), believed that Marlowe was the principal author of *The Comedy of Errors* and *Henry the Fifth* and that he also contributed to *Romeo* and *Julius Caesar*, including Antony's oration to the crowd; and thought that about fifty of the *Sonnets* were spurious.

Another otherwise orthodox writer, H. T. S. Forrest, in *The Five Authors of Shakespeare's Sonnets* (1923), believed that they were the result of a competition instigated by the Earl of Southampton. The five authors competing for the prize—perhaps of that legendary thousand pounds—Forrest believed to have been Shakespeare, Barnabe Barnes, William Warner or Walker, John Donne, and Samuel Daniel. He also thought *Venus and Adonis* the work of two men. Among other authors of the *Sonnets*, Thomas Watson has been advocated. The evidence in his case rests primarily upon certain initial letters of lines in Sonnet 76.

Wilhelm Marschall, in *Aus Shakespeares Briefwechsel* (Heidelberg, 1926), believed that the *Sonnets* were private letters addressed to each other by two poets known as 'R' and 'W'. In *Die neun Dichter des 'Hamlet'* (1929) he put forward the theory, based upon what he conceived to be the different styles in the play, that *Hamlet* was the result of collaboration between nine authors: Shakespeare, Burbage, Dekker, Munday, Chettle, Jonson, Nashe, the Earl of Rutland, and an unknown writer who was mainly responsible for Hamlet's soliloquies. Another German theory belongs to the nineteen-twenties: that of C. G. Muskat, who in *Die Lösung der Shakespeare-Frage* (Leipzig, 1925) maintained that the works were written by the Earl of Oxford, the Earl and Countess of Rutland, and Francis Bacon.

A similar theory was advocated by Gilbert Slater in *Seven Shakespeares* (1931), a book that has already been mentioned. This is partly a review of evidence put forward on behalf of various single candidates, partly an able exposition of a Group Theory with the Earl of Oxford as presiding genius. Slater believed that no theory postulating a single authorship can be shown to be probable: 'The true alternative to the traditional doctrine is, I consider, that the Shakespeare Plays came from a group of writers, closely connected with one another and with the Elizabethan Court' (*Seven Shakespeares*, pp. ix–x. Contrast Titherley, *Shakespeare's Identity: William Stanley*: 'There is no escape from single authorship').

D

Slater believed there to be

'striking evidence for at least the part authorship of *Richard the Second* and *Richard the Third* by Bacon, of *Love's Labour's Lost* by Derby, and of *Hamlet* by Oxford. This is an awkward situation for the extremists of all three schools, but all the evidence supports the theory that the three men were in the Shakespeare group. Since Derby was Oxford's son-in-law, and Oxford Burleigh's, and Bacon a nephew of Lady Burleigh's, all three men were closely connected' (Pp. x–xi. Contrast Sykes: 'It is, in fact, Shakespeare's *Richard the Second* that puts Bacon's claim absolutely out of court').

Slater suggested that the Countess of Pembroke was a member of the group. He based the theory mainly on Ben Jonson's famous lines in the First Folio about the 'Sweet Swan of Avon', pointing out truly that 'the map of England shows, not one only, but six rivers Avon'. Mary Herbert, to whom her brother Sir Philip Sidney dedicated his *Arcadia* ('it was currently believed that she had a share in its composition'), lived at Wilton on the banks of the Wylye, which is a tributary of the Wiltshire Avon. She was the most eminent patroness of literature at the time, and Slater goes on to enquire : 'Does the title "Sweet Swan" better fit the money-lending maltster of Stratford or the "peerless Ladie bright" of Wilton? Which of the two would Jonson most naturally think of as "My Beloved"?' As additional proof, Slater points out that *Julius Caesar*, *Antony and Cleopatra* and *Coriolanus* show 'feminine intuition'. He considers, too, that *As You Like It* is 'distinctly feminine' and that Rosalind, 'whether intentionally or not', is a self-portrait of the authoress. In *King Lear* she wrote all the feminine parts, and Slater believes 'that to her it is due that we are made to see that there was something to be said for Goneril, and that Lear was a most undesirable visitor in the house, sure to upset any hostess's nerves' (pp. 77, 208, 216–30).

Sir Edmund Chambers, in his *William Shakespeare: A Study of Facts and Problems* (Vol. II, p. 329), quotes William Cory's diary, referring to the diarist's visit to Wilton House in 1865: 'The house (Lady Herbert said) is full of interest. . . . We have a letter, never printed, from Lady Pembroke to her son, telling him to bring James the First from Salisbury to see *As You Like It*: "we have the man Shakespeare with us".' This letter has since been lost, but Slater agrees with Col. Ward that the reference is not to

Shakespeare of Stratford but to the Earl of Oxford, 'the *Man* Shakespeare', as the guest of Lady Pembroke, 'the *Woman* Shakespeare' (pp. 78, 229–30). 'This conclusion [that a woman may have been Shakespeare or partly so] is not new,' adds Slater. 'Among the hypothetical Shakespeares the name of Queen Elizabeth has been suggested.'

Slater's 'Seven Shakespeares', then, formed a group, with Oxford in the leading position and Bacon and Derby as his chief lieutenants; the Countess of Pembroke wrote the more feminine parts; Marlowe was a member of the group in its early days; Rutland helped with *Hamlet*; and Raleigh 'collaborated to a considerable extent in the writing of *The Tempest*'. A similar Group Theory, with Oxford as the Master Mind, is envisaged in Gilbert Standen's *Shakespeare Authorship* (1930) and in Col. Montagu Douglas's *Lord Oxford and the Shakespeare Group* (1952).

Those who are not widely acquainted with unorthodox literature may be surprised to find Slater referring to Shakespeare as a 'money-lending maltster'. This, though, is quite the usual thing and must not disturb the reader. If Shakespeare is not referred to as 'the illiterate actor', then he is most likely to be named 'the drunken money-lender' or 'the maltster' or both at once.

Examples could fill a dozen pages. A few of the more notable I give here. 'The drunken, illiterate clown of Stratford-on-Avon', 'a miser', 'a lying rascal', 'the sordid money-lender of Stratford', 'the mean, drunken, ignorant and absolutely unlettered rustic of Stratford', 'a drunken Warwickshire rustic', 'the miser Shakespeare, the lying rascal' (all by Durning-Lawrence); 'the Stratford butcher boy', 'this unlettered rustic of Stratford, who cared neither for honesty nor morality', 'the huckster Shagsper of Stratford' (all by Walter Ellis: *The Shakespeare Myth*).

This is not meant to be the same as calling the author of *Lear* a money-lending actor or an illiterate maltster, for the unorthodox consider themselves to have proved that the plays were written by someone else entirely. So there is no occasion for the orthodox to be upset by these remarks, though to call Shakespeare a money-lender or a maltster, with the implication that he was professionally engaged in either business, is about as accurate—as I hope to make clear in a later chapter—as to call the Earl of Oxford a professional assassin because he once killed, presumably by accident, a serving-man of Lord Burghley's.

Shakespeare is given a new title in a book by Alden Brooks published in New York in 1937: *Will Shakspere: Factotum and Agent*. In this the author believes he has made it 'apparent that Shakspere cannot have been the genius the world knows as William Shakespeare, poet of all ages'. Not that Mr. Brooks denies the Stratford man's authorship altogether: 'Although Shakspere contributed nothing more to the text of the plays than passages of comic matter, I believe he was a supervisor and critic of their general composition.' More positively:

'Will Shakspere did not write the plays of the Shakespearean canon. Who then did write them? Marlowe? Greene? Lyly? Nashe? Peele? Lodge? Kyd? All these at different moments contributed their share . . . they and still other dramatists but all remained subsidiary to one who oversaw and revised, sometimes entirely, what they had written—the genius of the Shakespearean thought and verse . . . The Poet, gentleman of birth, courtier of the Elizabethan world, poet and philosopher by temperament . . . was the genius of the Shakespearean plays. Will Shakspere, man of the theatre, braggart of natural wit, play-broker, was the go-between, agent, willing figurehead' (pp. 159, 168–9, 176, 186).

The name of this courtly genius is not given in Mr. Brooks's first book. His identity is revealed in his second: *Will Shakespere and the Dyer's Hand* (New York, 1943). He is Sir Edward Dyer, friend of Sidney and known as a courtly poet and patron of letters. The famous lines in Sonnet 111 refer to him:

> Thence comes it that my name receives a brand,
> And almost thence my nature is subdu'd
> To what it works in, like the dyer's hand.

The *Sonnets* Mr. Brooks believes to have been written by Nashe, Barnes, Daniel, the Earl of Southampton, and others, and *Lucrece* to have been a poem ordered by Southampton to satirize Raleigh, the Earl supervising it and possibly having a share in its composition.

V

We are now reaching the end of our Century of Group and Dual Theories, but there are still a few interesting books to be recorded. A Dual Theory of curious origin was put forward by two Scotsmen in books published in Glasgow: *The Story of Anne Whateley and William Shaxper as revealed by 'the Sonnets to Mr. W. H.' and other Elizabethan Poetry* (1939) by William Ross; and *Shakespeare's Other Anne* (1950) by W. J. Fraser Hutcheson. The books are mostly in agreement with each other, so can be considered together.

Now who was Anne Whateley? It is by no means certain that she ever existed. Marchette Chute believes the name to have been simply a clerical error for 'Anne Hathaway' or 'Hathwey', adding that 'Mistakes of this kind were not unusual, since the year after Shakespeare's marriage the name of a bridegroom was written in the bond as "Robert Bradeley" and on the bishop's register as "Robert Darby" ' (*Shakespeare of London*, p. 46 and *note*). But Mr. Ross and his friend Mr. Hutcheson agree that a girl of this name actually existed, that she was probably the daughter or the natural daughter of the famous merchant explorer, Capt. Anthony Jenkinson. They believe that she loved Shakespeare passionately, that her love was returned, that the two were going to be married (Mr. Hutcheson's version) but that Shakespeare having in an idle moment seduced Anne Hathaway he was forced by the Hathaway family to marry her instead.

Mr. Ross's version is slightly different in regard to the romance: he believes that Anne Whateley was a nun and that the marriage was one 'of true minds'—'the fruits of that "marriage" are the great tragedies, comedies and poems known in every tongue as "the Works of William Shakespeare" ' (Ross, pp. 11, 15 sq., 16–17, 123; Hutcheson, pp. 11, 125, etc.). Mr. Hutcheson even gives a portrait of this probably non-existent lady: he believes her to have been the subject of the portrait of an unknown girl in the Devonshire Collection at Chatsworth House. The theory of these two Scotsmen is almost as attractive as the girl portrayed, but the amount of real evidence for it may strike the reader as somewhat meagre. Seldom can a small clerical error have produced so great a conjecture.

For it is not simply the accepted authorship of Shakespeare that will have to be modified if this theory gains general acceptance; almost the entire literature of Elizabethan England is affected. Mr. Ross believes that Anne Whateley wrote the plays 'attributed to Marlowe' and that 'the invention of stage blank verse' must be put to her credit (pp. 207–8); Mr. Hutcheson thinks she wrote or edited much of Spenser and some of Gascoigne, Lyly, Munday, Nashe, Drayton, Daniel, both Harveys, Sidney, and Marston, and that all the anonymous poems of the Elizabethan era signed 'Ignoto' were her work (pp. 25 sq., 68 sq.).

The *Sonnets*, Mr. Ross believes, were written by this young maiden to Will Shaxpere. 'The youth to whom they were addressed, and whose beauty and worth are immortalised by them, was William Shaxpere of Stratford.' Mr. Hutcheson agrees that the *Sonnets* tell the three-cornered story of Shakespeare–Whateley–Hathaway, and that *The Phoenix and the Turtle* refers to her, Shakespeare being the turtle. After her death (about 1600) Shaxpere, 'himself a poet of distinction', wrote a poem to her memory entitled 'The Twenty-First and Last Book of the Ocean, to Cynthia'—'hitherto attributed', adds Mr. Ross, 'to Sir Walter Raleigh.'

We have seen how previous unorthodox theories have sought to strengthen their case by casting all manner of abuse upon 'the illiterate maltster of Stratford'. Mr. Ross has likewise a villain—or rather a villainess. Her name is Anne Hathaway: 'In Shaxpere's wife', he tells us, 'the dark forces of the earth were potent. She was lustful, cruel, selfish' and obviously deserved only the second-best bed.

But there are compensations for Anne Hathaway. Just as 'the drunken money-lender' of Durning-Lawrence's invention becomes in Mr. Ross's story the beautiful youth to whom Anne Whateley's sonnets were addressed, so the 'lustful, cruel, selfish' Mrs. Shakespeare has been credited with the writing of Shakespeare's works. The evidence is contained in an article entitled 'The Plays of Mrs. Shakespeare', by J. P. de Fonseka, in *G.K's Weekly*, 3 March 1938. If this is not a burlesque—and it is naturally difficult to see the difference sometimes between burlesque theories and theories which are held seriously—then I presume it is a Dual Theory like that featuring Anne Whateley. The case presented I take to be that Mrs. Shakespeare wrote the plays at Stratford and her husband edited them for the stage.

Another theory which may or may not have been meant seriously appeared in the *Academy* in the late 'nineties. This gave the works to Patrick O'Toole of Ennis. The evidence was cryptographic, based on Hamlet's 'St. Patrick' oath, and was put forward by George Newcomen in an article entitled 'A New Shakespeare

Cryptogram: Was the Author of Shakespeare's Plays an Irishman?' (*Academy*, 25 December 1897). The case was answered by H. L. Allen in 'Was Shakespeare an Irishman?' in the 26 February 1898 number. Allen was so far facetious as to quote another line from *Hamlet*: 'Now might I do it Pat.'

I mentioned in my Introduction that there was a recent book on the Rutlandian theory written by a Russian. This is *Shakespeare Unmasked*, by Pierre S. Porohovshikov, M.A. of Moscow University, and now Professor of History at Oglethorpe University, U.S.A. The book was published in New York in 1940, but did not attain a London edition till 1955. It will concern us more fully in our chapter on Rutland, but must be mentioned briefly here because Professor Porohovshikov, while giving most of the works to Roger Manners, believes that 'it is open to the wise, though hidden from the vulgar' that the author of *Love's Labour's Lost*, and also *Venus and Adonis* and *Lucrece*, was Francis Bacon (pp. 99–100). I am happy to count myself, in this respect, among the irredeemably vulgar. I do not believe that either Rutland or Bacon, or any other aristocrat, had anything to do, or could possibly have had anything to do, with the writing of Shakespeare's works. I shall be devoting the first chapter of the second part of this book to a consideration of the aristocratic assumption which lies behind most of these Group Theories and behind almost all the theories which have attributed the works to a single candidate.

It was part of the background of the original Group Theory advanced by Delia Bacon. Now a whole century has gone by, and we find in the latest book on the subject, A. J. Evans's *Shakespeare's Magic Circle* (1956), a similar argument being maintained, the place of presiding genius being given to William Stanley, sixth Earl of Derby. Mr. Evans postulates two poets, Derby and Oxford, who wrote the plays in collaboration, afterwards passing them round to their aristocratic friends, including Bacon and Rutland, who added their own knowledge, ideas and phrases to them. For instance, Rutland, on his return to England from Denmark, passed on to the authors of *Hamlet* the knowledge gained by his embassy. *Venus and Adonis* and *Lucrece*, Mr. Evans believes, were written by Derby alone, though Oxford may have collaborated in the *Sonnets*. . . . The wheel of a century has come full 'circle', and the seed sown by Delia Bacon has borne strange fruit.

NOTES

1. The first Dual Theory was perhaps that advanced, none too seriously, by the anonymous author of *An Essay against too much Reading*, published in London in 1728. The author, who may have been Capt. Goulding, said that he would give the public 'a short account of Mr. Shakespeare's proceeding, and that I had from one of his intimate acquaintance [which may be doubted]. His being perfect in some things was owing to his not being a scholar, which obliged him to have one of those chuckle-pated historians for his particular associate, that could scarce speak a word but upon that subject . . . Shakespeare . . . was no scholar . . . no historian . . . Although his plays were historical . . . the history part was given him . . . by one of those chuckles that could give him nothing else.'

2. *Chambers's Biographical Dictionary.* Compare William McFee: 'Sometimes the [Baconian] revelation took the form of religious ecstasy. Delia Bacon, an American girl [she was 42 when she first visited England] of good family but no relation to the author of *Novum Organum*, obtained permission from the Vicar of Stratford to spend the night in the sacred edifice where the playwright's bones were buried. The result of her hallucinations was the notion that the plays were written by Lord Bacon and several other Elizabethans. The curious will find a fascinating picture of this excellent but unbalanced lady in Nathaniel Hawthorne's essay in *Our Old Home*, which he calls "Recollections of a Gifted Woman" ' (Introduction to Looney, pp. xv–xvi).

3. By the Rev. T. Carter, *Shakespeare: Puritan and Recusant* (1897). The statement that he 'died a Papist' was first made by the Rev. Richard Davies in 1685. 'That this was the local tradition in the latter part of the seventeenth century does not admit of rational question' (Halliwell-Phillipps, *Outline of the Life of Shakespeare*, Vol. I, p. 264). See also John Henry de Groot, *The Shakespeares and 'the Old Faith'* (New York, 1946) and articles in the *Month* by Fr. Herbert Thurston (May 1882 and November 1911) and J. H. Pollen (October–November 1917).

CHAPTER III

THE BACONIAN CASE CONTINUED
1866–1957

Soule of the Age!
The applause! delight! the wonder of our Stage!
My Bacon, rise!
BEN JONSON: *To the Memory of my Beloved, the Author*
(revised by Smithson, *Baconian Essays*, p. 118).

I

It has been remarked in our chapter on the Origins that the case
for attributing Shakespeare to Francis Bacon, Lord Verulam,
Viscount St. Albans, is the oldest of the unorthodox theories,
though whether it goes back to the seventeenth or to the eighteenth
century must remain a matter of individual opinion. In one sense,
of course, it must go back to Bacon himself, for most Baconians
firmly believe that in 1623 he edited the First Folio, putting into
the text certain cryptic allusions to be deciphered in the late nineteenth century by Mrs. Windle, Ignatius Donnelly, Mrs. Gallup,
and Mrs. Henry Pott. In this sense, the first Baconian was Bacon.[1]
It is even believed by at least one advocate of a rival theory that
Bacon deliberately fooled posterity by means of these ciphers into
thinking him the author of the works, thereby robbing the real
author—the Earl of Rutland—of his rightful glory.[2]

Our present chapter concerns the continuation of the Baconian
case from the mid-Victorian age. It was continued both in time
and in extent, it having gradually dawned on Baconians that Bacon
was not simply the author of Shakespeare but of most of Elizabethan literature. Mr. Edward D. Johnson, the present President
of the Francis Bacon Society,* considers that Bacon wrote, besides
his own undisputed works, the whole of Shakespeare, most of the
works of Lyly, Peele, Greene, Marlowe, Spenser, Nashe, Kyd, and
Burton, and also Cervantes' *Don Quixote* (*The Shaksper Illusion*,
pp. 91–104, 170 sq.). In believing so, Mr. Johnson is echoing the
beliefs, or some of them, of many Baconians of past generations.

* As this book goes to press, I learn that Mr. Johnson has been succeeded as
President by Commander Martin Pares, R.N.

Graf Vitzthum gave Bacon the works of Marlowe, Greene, and
Ben Jonson as well as Shakespeare's (*Shakespeare und Shakspere*,
pp. 7, 150); Parker Woodward gave him Spenser's *Fairie Queene*,
Lyly's *Euphues*, Burton's *Anatomy of Melancholy*, Puttenham's
Arte of English Poesie, and all the works of Shakespeare, Greene,
Peele, Kyd, and Marlowe; Durning-Lawrence gave him Mon-
taigne, Ben Jonson, Francis Meres's *Palladis Tamia*, and the
editorship of the Authorized Version of the Bible, believing him
to have so remodelled the phrasing of the translation that 'the
Bible and Shakespeare embody the language of the great master'
(*Shakespeare Myth*, p. 29); Donnelly found in the verses on
Shakespeare's tombstone the ciphered message FRANCIS BACON
WROTE THE GREENE, MARLOWE AND SHAKESPEARE PLAYES and also
gave him Jonson and 'a great Spanish work', presumably *Don
Quixote* (*The Cipher in the Plays and on the Tombstone*, pp. 83, 87);
Mrs. Pott gave him Montaigne, Marlowe, and the minor Elizabethan
dramatists, and the Douai translation of the Bible, which he pro-
duced with the assistance of his old friend Sir Tobie Mathew, who
had become a priest in the Jesuit College there (*op. cit.*, pp. 33, 42
sq., 109–10, 221–2); Mrs. Windle gave him Montaigne; Dr. R. M.
Theobald gave him Marlowe; Mrs. Gallup gave him part of
Spenser; Granville Cuningham (*Bacon's Secret Disclosed in Contemporary Books*) believed that 'the masques [*sic*] under which he
wrote were Spenser, Greene, Marlowe and Shakespeare'; while
J. E. Roe (*The Mortal Moon: Bacon and his Masks*) credited him
with the authorship, among other works, of Bunyan's *Holy War*
and *Pilgrim's Progress*, Milton's *Paradise Lost*, Defoe's *Robinson
Crusoe*, Hobbes's *Leviathan*, Swift's *Tale of a Tub* and *Gulliver*,
and Carlyle's *Sartor Resartus*.

Bacon having died in 1626, it might be considered odd that he
managed to write works which belong to the late seventeenth,
eighteenth and nineteenth centuries. But some Baconians reject
the commonly accepted date of Bacon's death as rigorously as they
reject the commonly accepted authorship of Shakespeare's plays.
Durning-Lawrence refers to 'the 1632 edition of Shakespeare's
plays when Bacon was (supposed to be) dead', and both Parker
Woodward and the Dutch Baconian, H. A. W. Speckman, maintained that he died in Stuttgart in 1647. Other Baconians think
that he is still alive,[3] living in retirement in some English country
house, having never ceased to pour forth literary masterpieces

under various pseudonyms from the seventeenth century onwards. Whether he now draws his old age pension, under the National Insurance Scheme, is one of the points on which I have not been able to get any precise information.

Dr. Titherley, in *Shakespeare's Identity: William Stanley*, p. 150, writes as follows: 'In 1623 Bacon, then Viscount St. Alban, had fallen from greatness, had failed to secure even the minor post of Provost of Eton and had retreated to his three-storey chambers at Gray's Inn *where he still was in October 1924*' (*sic*; my italics). This would have given Bacon the opportunity to write Eliot's *Waste Land* and Joyce's *Ulysses*, but I fear that '1924' is a misprint for '1624'.

Greenwood held that there are 'Baconians and Baconians', that not much notice should be taken of those who believe that the master is still living, that he was the son of Queen Elizabeth, that he wrote secret messages in ciphers and cryptograms, that he wrote all the literature of his time, or that he hid his Shakespeare manuscripts in the mud of the River Wye (*Baconian Essays*, pp 24–5). I agree that there does not seem much point in arguing with those who believe Bacon wrote the *Pilgrim's Progress*, but I cannot agree that either ciphers or extraordinary ascriptions are marginal to the Baconian case. The present President of the Francis Bacon Society, Mr. Johnson, has written a great deal on ciphers; he has also ascribed to Bacon, as we have mentioned, the authorship of *Don Quixote*. I personally consider this to be an even more extraordinary ascription than that which gives to Bacon the *Pilgrim's Progress*. After all, both he and Bunyan were Englishmen, though not contemporaries, whereas the ascription to Bacon of the work regarded as typically Spanish is like saying that Dr. Johnson wrote *Candide* and Voltaire *Rasselas*.

We can go no higher than the President of the Francis Bacon Society, if we attempt to summarize the Baconian case. So I cannot dismiss the ciphering theories as irrelevant. The most I can do is to deal with them in very brief form, taking for granted that those readers who are interested will explore further for themselves. The list of Baconian books in my Bibliography should be enough to satisfy the hunger of even the most ardent seeker after knowledge.

II

In our Origins chapter we left the Baconian theory just a century ago, in the year 1856, when William Henry Smith produced his book *Bacon and Shakespeare*. Smith was an Englishman, and his book was published in London, but what is so remarkable about the later history of Baconianism is the way its doctrines have spread all over the world. The pioneer study in the United States was Judge Nathaniel Holmes's *The Authorship of Shakespeare* (New York, 1866), a book owing something to Delia Bacon's Group Theory. It was followed in America by, among others, Mrs. Windle's *On the Discovery of the Cipher of Francis Bacon* (San Francisco, 1881), Mrs. Pott's edition of Bacon's *Promus* and her *Francis Bacon and his Secret Society* (New York, 1883, 1891), Ignatius Donnelly's *The Great Cryptogram* and *The Cipher in the Plays and on the Tombstone* (New York, 1888, 1899), J. E. Roe's *The Mortal Moon* (New York, 1891), Orville Owen's *Francis Bacon's Cipher Story* (Detroit, 1893–5), Isaac Hull Platt's *Are the Shakespeare Plays Signed by Francis Bacon?* (Philadelphia, 1897) and Mrs. Gallup's *The Biliteral Cypher of Francis Bacon* (Detroit, 1899).

Australia entered the controversy as early as 1878, when Dr. William Thompson published in Melbourne the first of seven pamphlets, *The Political Purpose of the Renascence Drama*. Canada produced the first Baconian to look for a cipher on Shakespeare's tombstone: Hugh Black, who preceded Donnelly on this point in an article in the *North American Review* entitled 'Bacon's Claim and Shakespeare's "Aye".' An orthodox reply to Judge Holmes, *Bacon versus Shakespeare: A Plea for the Defendant* by Thomas King, was published in Montreal in 1875. India seems also to have had Baconian adherents, judging by a defence of Shakespeare by Mukhopadhyaya Harendrakumara, *The Authorship of the Shakespearean Plays: An Answer to the Baconians*, published in Calcutta in 1915. South Africa appears not to have entered the fray till 1927, with the publication in Cape Town of *Who Wrote Shakespeare?* by E. Crewe.

We have mentioned, in our chapter on the Origins, that Smith's theory was known in Paris in 1857. The controversy was re-opened in France in 1885 with essays by M. Cochin in the *Revue des Deux Mondes* and by Alexandre Büchner in the *Revue Britan-*

nique and with a book by Louis de Raynal, *Une controverse littèraire: Shakespeare et Bacon* (Paris, 1888). Henrik Schuck appears to have been the pioneer in Sweden, with a *résumé* of the Baconian case, 'Den nya Teorien om Författerskapet till Shakesperes arbeten', in *Ny Svensk Tidskrift* (Stockholm, 1883). The same year, the Serbian writer, V. Ilijć, published in Sobodija his book *Šekspir ili Bekon*, to be followed by another of the same title by his fellow-countryman, B. Popović, published in Glasnik in 1907. Dr. Karl Müller-Mylius, the translator of Appleton Morgan, published in Leipzig in 1884 the critical study we have mentioned: *Der Shakespeare-und-Bacon-Streit*. He was followed in Germany by, among others, Carl Friedrich, Graf Vitzthum von Eckstädt, whose book *Shakespeare und Shakspere* (Stuttgart, 1888) has been quoted; and by Edwin Bormann, whose score or so of Baconian works, some of which have been translated into English, include *Das Shakespeare Geheimniss* and *Neue Shakespeare-Enthüllungen* (Leipzig, 1894–5). Denmark appears to have had her Baconians, judging by the defence of Shakespeare contained in the famous book by Georg Brandes—quoted in our Introduction—and in Niels Bögholm's *Bacon og Shakespeare* (Copenhagen, 1906).

The Baconian question, for or against, penetrated to Poland with Adolf Strzelecki's *Szekspir i Bakon* (Krakow, 1898); to Austria with Jakob Schipper's *Zur Kritik des Shakespeare-Bacon-Frage*, Alfred von Weber-Ebenhoff's *Bacon-Shakespeare-Cervantes*, and Albert Eichler's *Anti-Baconianus: Shakespeare-Bacon?*, published in Vienna in 1889, 1917, and 1919 respectively; to Italy with Giuseppe Chiarini's *Studii Shakespeariani* (Leghorn, 1897) and O. Masnovo's *Come Shakespeare potè leggere Euripide?: piccolo contributo alla questione baconiana* (Parma, 1909); to Hungary with *Shakespeare or Bacon* by A. B. Yolland (Budapest, 1906) and *A Shakespeare-drámák-szerzöségi kérdése* by F. Hoos (Ersekujvar, 1914); and to Holland with D. Croll's *De Bacon-Shakespeare mythe* (Rotterdam, 1914) and H. A. W. Speckman's book we have mentioned, *Francis Bacon is Shakespeare* (Arnhem, 1916).

Whether Russia produced any native Baconians is not known to me, but literary circles in St. Petersburg knew about the controversy from *résumés* that appeared in books and articles from 1887 to 1898. (The German Baconian, Graf Vitzthum, was Ambassador to the Tsarist Court.) French-speaking inhabitants of Egypt, too, were not entirely unacquainted with the question:

an article by V. Nourisson, 'Shakspere et Shakespeare', was published in the *Nouvelle Revue*, Alexandria, in November 1903.

In England itself the most important step was the formation in
1885 of the Bacon Society, now called the Francis Bacon Society.
From 1886 it published its own *Journal*, which received from
1891 the prefix of *Baconiana*. A German quarterly of the same
nature, *Deutsche Baconiana*, appears to have lasted only from 1930
to 1932. The Bacon Society of America was founded in 1922.

Baconian arguments can most easily be divided into those
which can only be understood by the initiated and those which can
be understood by ordinary people like ourselves. Mrs. Windle of
San Francisco was the first to follow Delia in announcing the discovery that Francis Bacon had put a secret cipher into the plays
of Shakespeare, proving that he had indeed written them, as Smith
and Holmes had maintained. Mrs. Windle believed herself to be
'the favoured human agent, to recover him to the world', though
she did not claim, as Mrs. Gallup was to do, that Bacon had put a
cipher message explaining that one day his secret would be revealed by a lady living in the farthest west.

Mrs. Windle's pamphlets were modest in size, but her successor Ignatius Donnelly spread his *Great Cryptogram* theory over
a thousand pages and Orville Owen took five volumes to tell
Francis Bacon's Cipher Story. One of the secret messages Donnelly picked out of the Folio was the following: 'Seas ill [Cecil]
said that More low [Marlowe] or Shak'st spurre [Shakespeare]
never writ a word of them'. In his later book, *The Cipher in the
Plays*, he tells us how Bacon managed to insert such messages:

'Clearly, before Francis Bacon put pen to paper to write these
plays, he had mapped out the cipher story; and had his pages
blocked off in little squares, each square numbered according to
its place from the top or the bottom of the page. He next adjusted
the length of his columns, and their subdivisions, to enable him
to use significant words like "written", "playes", "shakst", "spur",
etc., over and over again. And, when all this was in place, he proceeded to write out the plays; using his miraculous ingenuity to
bring the right words in the proper positions' (pp. 191–2).

This ingenuity enabled Bacon, with some assistance from
Ignatius Donnelly, to insert messages like 'Shak'st-spurre is the

first-born sonne of a poor, sickly, woe-begone creature, much given to drink' and 'The man hath not knowledge wit nor wisdom or imagination enough to have ever writ these well-known shows'.

Mrs. Gallup and Mrs. Henry Pott believed that two founts were used in the printing of the Folio and that a hidden message could be deciphered out of them which gave the story of Bacon's life. They duly deciphered it, beginning with the discovery that Bacon and Essex were the unacknowledged sons of a secret marriage between Queen Elizabeth and Leicester. This theory has found widespread support among later Baconians, for example in Ludwig Mathy's *Der Wahre William Shakespeare: Prinz Francis Tudor* (Frankfurt-on-Main, 1929), A. B. Cornwall's *Francis, the First Uncrowned King of England* (Birmingham, 1936), C. Y. C. Dawbarn's *Uncrowned: The Story of Queen Elizabeth and Bacon* (London, 1913), and Alfred Mudie's *The Self-Named William Shakespeare* (London, 1925).

Naturally enough, the general theory of the cipher has found even wider support. You can scarcely open a Baconian book without finding arguments like this of Mr. Roderick Eagle in *Shakespeare: New Views for Old*. Mr. Eagle first tells us that 'It was quite a common practice in Elizabethan ciphers to refer to a particular person by a number'. Thus the name 'Bacon' is 33: that is, $B(2) + A(1) + C(3) + O(14) + N(13) = 33$. 'Bacon–Shakespeare' together equals 136, by the Elizabethan alphabet of twenty-four letters. 'Now', continues Mr. Eagle, 'turning to Sonnet 136. . . .'

It was arguments like this that convinced the Rutlandian, Prof. Porohovshikov, that Bacon must have had a hand in the works. Mr. Percy Allen, one of the most fertile supporters of the Earl of Oxford, was convinced by similar reasoning on the part of Bertram G. Theobald in *Shake-speare's Sonnets Unmasked* (pp. 29–40). 'By the use of three simple ciphers,' Mr. Allen explains, 'Bacon has written his signature into the title-page of the Sonnets. . . . For these surprising, not to say astonishing results, we owe warm thanks to the ingenious discoverer' (*The Case for Edward de Vere*, p. 148). The Oxfordians, however, can use these results for their own purposes. It was pointed out to Mr. Allen by Col. Ward that line 7 in the Dedication, if interpreted by the same cipher as Mr. Theobald had used for lines 2, 3, and 5, spells the name of the Earl of Oxford! 'I regard Col. Ward's discovery,' concludes Mr.

Allen, 'as a genuine, and extremely important, vindication' of the Oxfordian claim.

It will be seen, therefore, that ciphers, cryptograms, and the like, are not only central to the Baconian case, but are even accepted in part by those concerned to press the claims of rival candidates. And those so concerned, while sometimes scoffing at the more extreme cryptographic efforts of the Baconians, are not above being strongly influenced by them.

Much of modern Baconian reasoning on this matter goes back to the book and pamphlet by Sir Edwin Durning-Lawrence which we mentioned in our Origins chapter 4. Under the startling subheading 'Bacon signed the Shakespeare Plays', Durning-Lawrence takes the following quotation from *The Merry Wives of Windsor*, which is in the First Folio, Comedy Section, p. 53 (the quotation being in the original spelling and punctuation). The context will be remembered; the Welsh schoolmaster Evans is instructing the boy William, with Dame Quickly looking on:

> EVA. I pray you have your remembrance (childe) Accusativo, hing, hang, hog.
> QU. Hang-hog, is latten for Bacon, I warrant you.

This may seem to the uninformed a simple pun, but Durning-Lawrence relates this mention of 'Bacon' in the Comedy Section, p. 53, to 'the Gammon of Bacon' mentioned in *King Henry the Fourth*, Part One, which is in the History Section, p. 53. He does not think this entirely convincing proof that Bacon wrote Shakespeare: 'we must remember', he tells us, 'that a Baconian revelation, in order to be complete, satisfactory, and certain, requires to be repeated three times.' And the argument continues:

'The uninitiated inquirer will not be able to perceive upon the third page 53 [p. 53 in the Tragedy Section] any trace of Bacon, or hog or pig, or anything suggesting such things. The initiated will know that the great "Master-Mason" will supply two visible pillars, but that the third pillar will be the invisible pillar, the Shibboleth; therefore, the informed will not expect to find the third key upon the visible page 53, but upon THE INVISIBLE PAGE 53. Most of my readers will not fail to perceive that the invisible page 53 must be the page that is 53, when we count not from the beginning, but from the end of the volume. The last page in the Folio is 399.

This is falsely numbered 993, not by accident or by a misprint, but (as the great cryptographic book, by Gustavus Selenus, the man in the Moon, published in 1624, will tell those who are able to read it), because 993 forms the word "Baconus", a signature of Bacon. . . . Deducting 53 from 399 we obtain the number 346, which is THE PAGE 53 FROM THE END. . . . Now here we perceive that "Pompey", "in", and "got", by the manner in which the type is arranged in the column, come directly under each other, and their initial letters being P.I.G., we quite easily read "pig", which is what we were looking for' (*The Shakespeare Myth*, p. 20).

Such arguments, able to be understood by the initiated only, form at least half of the volume of the Baconian case. The appeal here is frankly esoteric, and it is significant that a Baconian once wrote a book entitled *Shakespeare: Creator of Freemasonry*.

A pamphlet by the same author, Alfred Dodd, *Who Was Shakespeare?* (1947) contains the following passage:

'This is the man, FRANCIS BACON . . . the man whom I KNOW to be the MIGHTY SHAKESPEARE, the Inspirer of the English Renaissance, assisted by "his Compeers by night", the Secret Rosicrosse Literary Society, the Builder of Solomon's Temple of Ethical Symbolism, the real Creator of Solomon's House of Science which led to the establishment of the Royal Society. . . . His first task on taking up his legal residence at Gray's Inn was to found a secret Literary Society (afterwards called the Rosicrosse) for the Universal Advancement of Learning. . . . Thus there arose in Gray's Inn an earnest band of Brothers—of Shake-speares—of whom Francis was the Head Shake-speare. From this society there arose the Rosicrucian College and the Masonic Lodge' (pp. 6, 16).

For further esoteric information, see Mrs. Pott's *Francis Bacon and his Secret Society* and W. F. C. Wigston's *Bacon and the Rosicrucians*.

The other arguments that have been brought forward are more easily understood by ordinary people like ourselves. Some of them we have met before: for instance, the argument that Shakespeare's works show intimate knowledge of aristocratic life, at home and abroad. 'A lawyer, a scholar, and a courtier': these are the three persons the Baconians find in the plays, and as Bacon was one of the

E

most learned lawyers of the age, it is naturally the legal allusions in Shakespeare the Baconians make most of. A whole series of eminent British and American lawyers, from the eighteenth century onwards, are quoted in evidence. Some of these were quite orthodox in regard to the authorship question, even anti-Baconian; some were Baconians themselves or sympathetic to their case. The chief books are *Shakespeare a Lawyer* by W. L. Rushton (Liverpool, 1858); *Shakespeare's Legal Acquirements Considered* by Lord Campbell (London, 1859); *The Law in Shakespeare* by Senator Cushman Davis (St. Paul, Minnesota, 1884); *A Judicial Summing-Up on the Bacon-Shakespeare Controversy* by Lord Penzance (London, 1902); *The Shakespeare Mystery* by Judge Webb (New York, 1902); and *Shakespeare's Law* by Sir George Greenwood (London, 1920). Some of their comments can be briefly quoted. Shakespeare 'had a deep technical knowledge of the law' (Campbell); 'He seems almost to have thought in legal phrases. . . . His knowledge of law protruded itself on all occasions, appropriate or inappropriate' (Penzance); 'It is certain that the author was a lawyer' (Webb); 'Shakespeare uses this legal terminology with a persistency and an accuracy . . . which cannot be paralleled in the writings of any layman of the time' (Greenwood). And Mr. Crump, Q.C., once editor of the *Law Times*, declared that the plays were written by the greatest lawyer the world has ever seen or ever would see. In the appropriate chapter of the second part of this book I shall be examining in more detail this legal argument of the Baconians.

There is also the argument, first advanced by Wilmot and repeated by Smith and Holmes, concerning the thoughts and style of the two writers. This has been partly developed by means of comparisons between the opinions expressed by Bacon and those expressed by certain of Shakespeare's characters, partly by means of comparisons between the actual phrasing of the two men in their accepted works. Donnelly gave long lists of similar phrases, lists which were quoted by Lord Penzance in his *Judicial Summing-Up*. The first two of Donnelly's parallels can be quoted again here:

> Shakespeare (*Hamlet*): It is very cold.
> It is a nipping and an *eager* air.
> Bacon (*Natural History*): Whereby the cold becomes
> more *eager*.

Shakespeare (*Macbeth*): Light *thickens*, and the crow
  Makes wing to the rooky wood.
Bacon (*Nat. Hist.*): For the over-moisture of the brain
  doth *thicken* the spirits visual.

The late Dr. W. S. Melsome, former President of the Bacon Society, compiled a whole book of such parallelisms called *The Bacon–Shakespeare Anatomy* (1945), a book which I reviewed for the *Nineteenth Century and After*. This is a representative passage:

'We now come to the seventh reminder of Bacon [in a speech by Angelo in *Measure for Measure*]:

> "New-conceived,
> And so in progress to be hatch'd and born."

"Born" applies to animals and "hatch'd" to birds; and between the conception and the hatching of the egg some time must elapse; and this is what interested Bacon, who says: "For birds there is double enquiry: the distance between the treading or coupling and the laying of the egg; and again between the egg laid, and the DISCLOSING or HATCHING". . . . While Hamlet's "melancholy sits on brood"; his uncle said . . .

> "I do doubt the HATCH and the DISCLOSE
> Will be some danger." '

III

The Baconian case can now be summarized as follows. First, the belief that Bacon signed the First Folio by various ciphers and cryptograms—a belief that, if accepted, would render superfluous all other evidences that have been put forward. Secondly, the belief that the philosophy expressed by Bacon, and his very turns of phrase, can be matched in Shakespeare. Thirdly, the belief that Shakespeare's works show that he must have been a courtier, a scholar and—most significantly—a *lawyer*. These three beliefs, and the various minor conjectures that have sprung from them, constitute the positive side of the Baconian case.

There is also a negative side, partly the work of Baconians, partly of non-Baconians. This attempts to show that, no matter who wrote the works commonly attributed to Shakespeare,

Shakespeare himself could not have done so. The most fertile exponent of this belief was Greenwood, who did not himself accept the Baconian case entirely; other writers who sought to denigrate Shakespeare included Mark Twain, who was not a Baconian when he wrote his book *Is Shakespeare Dead?* (1909) but is said to have 'died a Baconian' the year after. Twain's title did not refer to the alleged immortality of Francis Bacon, but to what he supposed to be the lack of evidence concerning the life of Shakespeare. The great humorist made these two main points: (1) Shakespeare was of no account in Stratford in his lifetime and was utterly forgotten afterwards; and (2) the plays are saturated with a technical knowledge of law which the actor could not possibly have acquired.

Twain was particularly concerned with Shakespeare's will, which he described as 'eminently and conspicuously a business man's will, not a poet's'. He went on: 'The will mentioned *not a play, not a poem, not an unfinished literary work, not a scrap of manuscript of any kind*. Many poets have died poor, but this is the only one in history who has died *this* poor' (p. 30 sq.). Since then, all Baconians have devoted a section of their writings to a discussion of Shakespeare's will, it being particularly remarked that he mentioned no books (e.g. Johnson, *The Shaksper Illusion*, p. 14; Smithson, *Baconian Essays*, p. 150; Eagle, *Shakespeare: New Views for Old*, p. 78; Ellis, *The Shakespeare Myth*, p. 3. Also an Oxfordian, William Kent, *Edward de Vere*, p. 7).

The main object of Greenwood was to show that the plays of Shakespeare and the life of Shakespeare were incompatible. Greenwood it was who developed the sermon, or rather many sermons, from the text of Emerson, so often quoted by Baconians. Emerson was not a Baconian himself, though often claimed by Baconians to be one; in fact, he was perfectly orthodox and would have been dismayed to see the methods by which Baconians and Oxfordians have twisted his words for their own purposes (see below, p. 206). The text in question is a passage from *Representative Men* (1849):

'The Egyptian verdict of the Shakespeare Societies comes to mind, that he was a jovial actor and manager. I cannot marry this fact to his verse. Other admirable men have led lives in some sort of keeping with their thought; but this man, in wide contrast.'

The development of this remark of Emerson's, taken out of its context, constitutes the negative side of the Baconian case. Both this and the positive side will be discussed further in the second part of this book.

NOTES

1. Donnelly believed that the Bacon–Shakespeare *controversy* goes back to Bacon's lifetime. He found in the Folio the cipher message: 'I am constrained to deny the uncounted rumours, surmises, jealousies and reports that I have written these plays' (*The Cipher in the Plays and on the Tombstone*, p. 174 sq.).

2. Porohovshikov, *Shakespeare Unmasked*, pp. 255–8. The Professor adds: 'Bacon's ciphered messages offer not the slightest hint of joint authorship. He claimed all . . . as his own. The inevitable conclusion is that he betrayed a dead friend as he had before betrayed, face to face, a man [Essex] who had not been his friend only, but his patron and benefactor.'

3. According to Connes, *Shakespeare Mystery*, p. 17. Compare Thomas Sheppard, *Bacon is Alive!* (Hull, 1911).

4. It was Durning-Lawrence, too, who originated the theory that the Droeshout engraving prefixed to the First Folio is not a proper portrait but a mask. Baconians have since often contrasted this admittedly crude engraving with one of the portraits painted of Bacon. But the truth is that one cannot compare an engraving with a painting but only with another engraving. There are only two portraits of Shakespeare which are generally accepted as authentic: the Droeshout engraving and the bust on the Stratford monument. Thus in my Frontispiece, if I had reproduced either of these, I should have had to reproduce also engravings or busts of Bacon, Raleigh, Derby, and Oxford—which were not available. The only compromise solution was to reproduce paintings of them all, including the 'Chandos' portrait, which, while not so authentic as the engraving or the bust, is the nearest we have to a geniune contemporary portrait of Shakespeare. There is an authentic engraving of Lady Pembroke, but the usual portrait of her reproduced in modern books is not regarded as authentic.

CHAPTER IV

RALEIGH: ESSEX: CECIL
1877–1916

Welcome, Sir Walter . . .
Some of us love you well.
SHAKESPEARE: *The First Part of*
King Henry the Fourth.

I

To Delia Bacon and O'Connor, Sir Walter Raleigh was the chief of a number of mainly aristocratic poets who wrote the works commonly attributed to Shakespeare. Other Group Theorists, including de Peyster, Zeigler, and Slater, see Raleigh as part-author, particularly of *The Tempest*. The theory that he was the sole author has been held by few, but on the other hand it could claim in its forty years' existence to have appeared in three widely scattered countries—a theory suitably widespread for one of the most celebrated explorers of the Elizabethan age.

The theory was first put forward in Australia, a country to which even the intrepid Raleigh never penetrated. The pioneer was G. S. Caldwell in a book entitled *Is Sir Walter Ralegh the Author of Shakespeare's Plays?*, published at Melbourne in 1877. Quite independently, it seems, the case was then advocated in the United States, no doubt partly influenced by the Group Theories of Delia Bacon and O'Connor. The American advocate was Henry Pemberton, Jr., first in an article in the journal *New Shakespeareana*, published at Westfield, New Jersey, in May 1909, then in a book *Shakspere and Sir Walter Ralegh*, edited from his unfinished manuscript and published in Philadelphia and London in 1914. Two years later, there appeared in *The Times Literary Supplement*, London, a letter on Sir Walter Raleigh and Shakespeare by Robert Palk—and with that letter the theory seems to have come to a stop, so far as publication is concerned. In the following summary I rely almost entirely on the American book of 1914.

Pemberton agreed with the Baconians that the author of Shakespeare's works must have been a courtier. On the other hand, as

Pemberton saw it, the man from Stratford was not only *not* a courtier but was 'continually found in close and intimate association with the common actors of the day. . . . No reliable evidence can be produced showing that he ever was present in circles higher than these.' He was, moreover, 'a notorious money-lender', and Pemberton further discovered from Dr. Wallace's famous article on Shakespeare and the Mountjoy family (*Harper's Magazine*, April 1910) that he had been a lodger for years with this Huguenot wig-maker and hairdresser, and his wife and daughter, 'common folk, most ordinary people' who lived at the corner of Muggle Street in the ward of Cripplegate: he 'knew the family well, and was on terms of intimacy with them'. Pemberton concludes that the money-lending associate of actors and wig-makers could not possibly have written the plays and poems he is supposed to have written (pp. 4 sq., 16 sq., 24 sq., 36 sq.).

So far, then, Pemberton follows the Baconians, with minor additions of his own, but he does not favour their candidate. A courtier, yes; but not Bacon. For Pemberton, believing—like most unorthodox theorists—that Shakespeare's works are disguised autobiography, had failed to find any evidence that this autobiography paralleled the life-story of Francis Bacon. Take the reference to lameness in Sonnets 37 and 89: it could not possibly apply to Bacon, any more than to Shakespeare, for neither was in battle in his life; but everyone knows that Raleigh suffered 'a grievous wound' at Cadiz in 1596. Why, again, should either Shakespeare or Bacon be asked to write sonnets urging William Herbert, the young Earl of Pembroke, to marry? (p. 79 sq.) Raleigh, on the other hand, was an intimate friend and a 'former flame' of the widowed Countess, so who more likely to be asked the favour and to write?

> Thou art thy mother's glass and she in thee
> Calls back the lovely April of her prime.

Robert Palk, in the letter to *The Times Literary Supplement* mentioned, put forward the belief that Sonnet 146 contains references to Raleigh's dark curly hair and magnificent dress, and that Sonnet 125 is Raleigh's comment upon the false charge of his complicity in the Gunpowder Plot.

II

Pemberton's case rests primarily on the *Sonnets*, *Twelfth Night*, *Hamlet*, *The Tempest*, and various references to maritime life and exploration scattered throughout the plays. In *Twelfth Night* the remark he stresses is Maria's about Malvolio in Act III, Scene 2: 'He does smile his face into more lines than is in the new map, with the augmentation of the Indies.' This is an obvious reference, Pemberton believes, to the map in the second edition of Hakluyt's *Principal Navigations* (1599), which included for the first time such additions as Mount Raghley, Virginia, and the country of Guiana, of both of which Raleigh was the first English explorer. Pemberton believes that *Twelfth Night* was written *before* 1599—a debateable point—so how could either Shakespeare or Bacon have known about this map? Hakluyt would certainly have drawn it from Raleigh's own reports, and no contemporary would have been more likely to see it before publication than the valiant explorer himself (pp. 119–20).

But *Hamlet*, Pemberton thought, was the autobiographical play *par excellence*, a belief shared, as we shall see, by Lefranc, Demblon, Kent, Davis, Hore, and others—unfortunately, in support of quite different candidates for the authorship. Pemberton believed that, in the character of Claudius, Raleigh was satirizing King James, Hamlet's phrase 'Hyperion to a satyr' referring to the contrast between the magnificent Queen Elizabeth, who had showered Raleigh with honours, and the contemptible King James, who had caused his downfall at Court:

'Under cover of this character Sir Walter attacked the man who caused his great fall. . . . It was against him—against James—that the once powerful courtier in his pride and anger vented his contempt. He struck at the abject creature . . . whose enmity had caused his humiliation' (p. 143 sq.).

'Against this view,' Pemberton concluded, 'no valid argument can be presented.'

Sir Walter was arrested by the King's government in July 1603 and imprisoned in the Tower of London. He is known to have attempted his own life, and Pemberton believes that Hamlet's famous soliloquy on suicide refers to this episode. Claudio's lines in *Measure for Measure* 'find Ralegh's mind still reverting to thoughts of death'. But here the author was trying to please his royal enemy, with the hope of obtaining a pardon:

'The Duke in this play is evidently King James, and the author flatters him. . . . Certain slanderous reports current regarding James are rebuked. . . . "I never heard the absent Duke much detected for women; he was not inclined that way." ' * *Macbeth* is set in the King's native land and introduces witches, on whom James was an acknowledged authority. The reference to the 'equivocator' in the Porter's speech is 'undoubtedly an allusion to Henry Garnet . . . [who was] imprisoned in the first storey rooms of the Bloody Tower . . . immediately under the second storey rooms occupied by Raleigh' (p. 180).

Many of Sir Walter's former friends turned against him after his downfall, and Pemberton believes it to be highly significant that some of the Shakespearean plays written at this time turn on the motive of ingratitude. 'Ingratitude is the dominant note in *King Lear* . . . *Timon of Athens* . . . sounds a similar note.' In the days when Raleigh had enjoyed the Queen's favour, he had been granted many lucrative sinecures, in particular the wine-licensing patent. These had earned him corresponding unpopularity with the ordinary citizen, who naturally rejoiced at the former favourite's overthrow, which was made the subject of popular ballads. Pemberton believes that Cleopatra's fear of being hoisted up

> to the shouting varletry
> Of censuring Rome

reflects the author's own experience of unpopularity with the crowd. *Coriolanus* obviously turns on the same issue (pp. 141, 183 sq.).

Shakespeare probably never travelled farther westwards than Bristol or Barnstaple—the western limit of his company when on tour—but Raleigh was the explorer of Guiana. He was also the first colonizer of Virginia, and Caliban's remark, 'No more dams I'll make for fish', was based directly, Pemberton believed, on

---

* pp. 162–3. The slanders against James, however, were not that he was addicted to women, but that he was too fond of handsome young men. If Raleigh wrote *Measure for Measure* with the intention of flattering the King in the character of the Duke, then he would not have risked the phrase, 'he was not inclined that way'.

Raleigh's reports to the Government on the Virginian natives. In *Othello*, too, the reference to

> Cannibals that each other eat,
> The Anthropophagi, and men whose heads
> Do grow beneath their shoulders

is evidently based upon Raleigh's book *The Discoverie of Guiana*, as are the references to Indian sun-worshippers in *All's Well* and *Love's Labour's Lost*. Can we reasonably doubt, asks Pemberton, that the same man wrote both the book and the plays? (p. 106 sq.)

Last, but by no means least, there is the question of Shakespeare's 'familiarity with seamanship'. The reputed author was born in a midland county and probably was never on board ship in his life. A critic writing in *Chambers's Journal*, 20 March 1852, refers to Shakespeare's mastery of nautical terms, and ten years later a critic in the *St. James's Magazine* (July 1862) entitled his article 'Shakespeare a Seaman'. In 1910, W. B. Whall, Master Mariner, wrote a whole book on the subject: *Shakespeare's Sea Terms Explained*. He referred, for instance, to Pistol's words in *The Merry Wives*:

> This punk is one of Cupid's carriers:—
> Clap on more sails; pursue; up with your fights;
> Give fire; she is my prize, or ocean whelm them all!

and commented (p. 17): 'This is Elizabethan sailor talk pure and simple. How did the writer obtain sufficient knowledge of the sea to write *like a sailor*?'

Pemberton believes the answer to be obvious: that the writer *was* a sailor, one of the most noted seamen of a seafaring age (p. 94 sq.). It is upon this rock, as it were, of seamanship that Pemberton rests his case.

III

The politics of the Elizabethan age obtrude far more in unorthodox writings about Shakespeare than in orthodox. If Raleigh cannot be proved to have been the writer of Shakespeare's works, then perhaps his arch-enemy Robert Cecil, Earl of Salisbury, has a better title? Or, if not Bacon, why not Essex? There is a freedom from bias in the putting forward of these alternative candidates that must command respect.

Whether any reader was actually unbiased enough to consider all four candidates with equal attention may be doubted, but the opportunity certainly existed. A reader in 1905 who had reluctantly abandoned Bacon could have turned to Essex, while about two years after Pemberton's *Ralegh* there appeared a book by a fellow-countryman advocating Cecil. The reader, and particularly the American reader, had plenty of political Shakespeares to choose from.

The Essex and the Cecil cases appear to be exclusively American, and to be so exclusively the property of their pioneer advocates that nobody else was inspired to follow suit. This is not, of course, to imply that a Shakespeare in the exclusive possession of one author may not be as genuine as a Shakespeare whose face has launched a thousand pamphlets. But it means that in our History such Shakespeares have to be treated with the utmost brevity.

The claim for the authorship of Robert Devereux, second Earl of Essex (1566-1601), was put forward by Latham Davis in a book entitled *Shakespeare: England's Ulysses*, published at Seaford, Delaware, in 1905. The claim for Robert Cecil, Earl of Salisbury (*c.* 1563-1612), was put forward by J. M. Maxwell in a pamphlet entitled *The Man Behind the Mask: Robert Cecil, first Earl of Salisbury, the only True Author of William Shakespeare's Plays*, published at Indianapolis in 1916.

Cecil's dates better fit those of Shakespeare's plays; Mr. Maxwell could furthermore point to several references in the *Sonnets* which fit remarkably well both the physical defects and political career of Burghley's son. In *Hamlet* there is obvious autobiography in the scene where Polonius bids farewell to Laertes on the latter's departure for Paris. Mr. Maxwell, in fact, was so sure of his man that he took another leaf out of the Baconian book and claimed that Robert Cecil had written not only Shakespeare but a considerable amount of the other writings of the age, 'given to the world under various aliases'.

In regard to literature, however—if I may mention such a thing without impropriety—Essex has the edge. That he also had the edge of the executioner's axe as early as 1601—before most of Shakespeare's best plays were written—cannot gainsay the fact that he was a noted patron of letters who had written poetry himself. He had, too, the military experience to write the battle scenes in *Henry the Fourth* and *Henry the Fifth*, and being one of the most handsome favourites of the Queen he had, too, a personal knowledge of courtly love to enable him to write *Love's Labour's Lost, Two Gentlemen of Verona, Romeo and Juliet*, and *Much Ado About Nothing*. He had the experience of high politics, too— if not to the extent possessed by Salisbury—which no less a person than Bismarck found in Shakespeare.

We have mentioned *Love's Labour's Lost*. But in his list of Shakespeare's plays in *Palladis Tamia* (1598), Francis Meres mentions another comedy called *Love's Labour's Won*. No play of this name is known, unless it be an alternative title for *The Taming of the Shrew*, but Latham Davis put forward the ingenious suggestion that this so-called play is really an alternative title for the *Sonnets*, which he believed to consist of speeches delivered by allegorical characters such as Knowledge and Ambition.

The two cases have each their comparatively strong points. What we miss is the attempt at proof that we find in more fertile theories. Perhaps it was the lack of such attempt in both Davis and Maxwell that led to their advocacy's having no successors.

CHAPTER V

BURTON: SOUTHAMPTON: SHIRLEY
1885–1905

There's something in his soul
O'er which his melancholy sits on brood.
SHAKESPEARE: *Hamlet.*

I

The play of *Hamlet* is not only Shakespeare's most famous work, it has fascinated generations of actors and literary critics. It is not surprising to find, as we have already found, that it has fascinated also many of those who take unorthodox views upon the subject of the authorship. They have regarded it as the author's most auto-biographical work, and as the chief character is a study in melancholy it has been assumed that the author himself must have been melancholy, too. The attribution of Burton's *Anatomy* to Bacon–Shakespeare was built almost entirely on this supposition, and the world of the unorthodox would have been sadly lacking in ingenuity had it not thrown up a writer who looked at the matter the other way round. Not Bacon–Shakespeare as the author of Burton's *Anatomy of Melancholy*, because of that work's relation to *Hamlet*, but—on the contrary—because of the relation of *Hamlet* to *The Anatomy of Melancholy*, Robert Burton as Shakespeare! That was the position visualized by 'Multum in Parvo', the pseudonym of M. L. Hore, in a pamphlet entitled *Who Wrote Shakespeare?*, published at Denver, Colorado, in 1885.

American writers seem to specialize in standing the Baconian Theory on its head. The Burton case is not the only one. There are the curious theories advanced by Mr. W. C. Arensberg, in *Francis Bacon, William Butts and the Pagets of Beaudesert* (Pittsburgh, 1929) and other works. Mr. Arensberg appears to suggest that William Butts was the real author, working under the twin pseudonyms of 'William Shakespeare' and 'Francis Bacon'. His grandfather was William Butts, court physician to Henry VIII, and he seems to have been connected with Lord Paget, co-author of

Shakespeare in Delia Bacon's Group Theory. Mr. Arensberg is therefore a 'Baconian' in a very special sense.

The Burton theory was mentioned at Leipzig in 1887, in the famous *Shakespeare–Jahrbuch*, but seems otherwise to have died a natural, if somewhat premature, death. From the point of view of strictly literary advantages for the authorship of Shakespeare, this early death is surprising, however. With so many candidates— Rutland, Derby, Cecil, Essex, etc.—one has to take their literary potentialities for granted, because there is no proof that they ever wrote anything of value. Robert Burton certainly did, if only the one book. It is true that he was born rather late—in 1577—to have written Shakespeare. He was only 16 when *Venus and Adonis* was published, and younger still at the probable date of the earliest plays. But a similar discrepancy in the case of Rutland has not pre- vented the advocacy of Roger Manners from running for half-a- century and in several different countries. If a man of title could be an infant prodigy, why not the future Rector of Segrave and permanent resident at Christ Church, Oxford?

It is, of course, Burton's vast learning and classical scholarship that M. L. Hore emphasizes, as we should expect from his Latin pseudonym. A scholar himself, who assures us that his little book is the product of years of study, he sees in Burton and Shakespeare alike a fellow scholar and kindred spirit, convinced as he is that they are one and the same man. Shakespeare's apparent learning and his presumed wide acquaintance with the classical authors have always been a part of the unorthodox case; if such could be pre- dicated of Bacon and Raleigh, how much more so of one of the most learned men whom even Oxford has produced!

And there is the additional proof, Hore points out, of Shake- speare's familiarity with medicine—on which whole books have been written. A familiarity surprising in an actor, but not sur- prising at all in one who described himself as 'by profession a divine, by inclination a physician'. Two of the biggest stumbling- blocks in the path of those who adhere to the traditional author- ship, Hore believed, are removed at once if we accept this scholar– physician–divine as the real author. The 'divinity' should not be overlooked. Bishop Wordsworth once wrote a book *On Shake- speare's Knowledge and Use of the Bible*. Surprising, perhaps, in an actor; hardly so in a professional student of theology like Burton.

Such, then, was Hore's case, advanced with a prudent scholarship worthy of its subject. 'At no very distant day,' he promised, he 'may contribute something more copious'. It is to be regretted that that day seems never to have arrived. Perhaps a more copious volume would have answered certain outstanding questions. For instance, as a question of fact, not opinion, I should have been glad to know Hore's explanation of the puzzling discrepancy in Burton's spelling of the name Shakespeare. (See above, p. 21.) He appears to have been uncertain as to the correct spelling of his pseudonym; unless the actor 'Shakspere' wrote *Venus and Adonis*, while Burton himself ('Shakespeare') wrote *Much Ado About Nothing*. This would certainly remove the need for Burton to have written the former work at the tender age of 15 or 16; but, on the other hand, this poem has often been regarded by critics, especially unorthodox critics, as full of classical learning. And it is precisely upon this classical learning, and the relation of *Hamlet* to *The Anatomy*, that the whole case for Burton rests.

Perhaps I can point out here one very common misquotation made by unorthodox theorists. The famous remark by Greene in the Preface to his *Farewell to Folly* is often quoted without the word 'theological', as if Greene was referring to the difficulties of *noblemen* who had written poems or plays which their dignity did not allow them to acknowledge publicly. What he was actually referring to was the difficulties of *clergymen* who had written poems or plays which it would be against their cloth to own. Thus Greene's words do not support either the Baconian or the Rutlandian case, though often twisted to that purpose. There was no Rev. Francis Bacon, Dean of St. Albans, or Rev. Roger Manners, Bishop of Rutland, with whom Greene's words can be associated. But there was, of course, the Rev. Robert Burton, Rector of Segrave.

II

The theory that Henry Wriothesley, third Earl of Southampton (1573–1624), was the real author of Shakespeare might seem likely, at first glance, to have proved very popular. For Southampton was the only nobleman with whom the traditional author, Shakespeare of Stratford, can be shown to have had any association—though we have noted (p. 46 above), on the authority of Mrs. Stopes, that the association seems not to have been either very intimate or very lasting. That it could have been so we know from the relationship between Shakespeare's colleague, Richard Burbage, and the Earl of Pembroke. More than two months after the great actor's death, the Earl excused himself from a play given in honour of the French ambassador, which he confessed he 'could not endure to see so soon after the loss of my old acquaintance Burbage'. In a society still semi-feudal, such friendships between men of widely different origins—Burbage's father was the carpenter turned actor who built the first London theatre—were commoner than we imagine today. When class distinctions are obvious and undisputed, as they still were in many cases in Elizabethan times, a warm friendship can often spring up on a basis of complete inequality. It is more diffi-cult for such friendships to arise in a society where class dis-tinctions are blurred or disputed—and they were by no means com-pletely blurred or disputed in the late sixteenth century.

Nevertheless, the theory of Southampton's authorship has *not* been popular. The really popular unorthodox theories have always had as their candidates some aristocrat whose known relationship to Shakespeare is nil. On a foundation of utter ignorance, such theories have always been the most fertile in invention. It is be-cause we know nothing of any connection between Shakespeare and Bacon (or Shakespeare and Oxford) that so many people have be-come convinced that there was the strongest link between them. Southampton's known patronage of Shakespeare has rather queered the pitch for any invention of that sort on his behalf. Un-orthodox theories, like certain plants, thrive better in the dark.

He has been co-opted, it is true, into various Group Theories, and in Peter Alvor's Dual Theory of Southampton–Rutland he was given precisely half of Shakespeare's works. The only writer who considered that he was the author of the other half as well appears to have been J. C. Nicol, whose claim was put forward in a leaflet entitled *The Real Shakespeare*, published in London in 1905.

Mr. Nicol was a student of Donnelly and Mrs. Gallup, but he did not agree with them that the various ciphers and cryptograms discovered in the First Folio were evidence that Bacon had written the plays or even edited them. Indeed, he found clear crypto-graphic evidence that Southampton was both author and editor, that in fact he completed his life's work in the Folio volume the year before he died.

Exactly twice as popular as the case for Southampton was the case for Sir Anthony Shirley, which produced two advocates in the late nineteenth century. In a book curiously entitled *William Shakespere of Stratford-on-Avon* (Dinsdale-on-Tees, 1888), Shirley's authorship was first suggested by Scott F. Surtees, a writer no relation, I believe, of the creator of Jorrocks, though he came from the same part of England. The suggestion was taken up by C. Shirley Harris in an article, 'Sir Anthony Shirley the Author of Shakespeare's Plays', which appeared in *Notes and Queries*, 13 March 1897.

Shirley was a travelled man, whose exploits were celebrated in a play—*The Travailes of the Three English Brothers, Sir Thomas, Sir Anthony and Mr. Robert Sherley*—acted in London with no less a person in the cast than Shakespeare's colleague Will Kemp. He was a friend of the Bacons and the Cecils and had married Essex's cousin, so was well acquainted with politics and the manners of the Court. His authorship of the *Sonnets*—dismissed by Judge Stotsenburg *—rests chiefly on the references in Sonnets 76, 105, 135, and 136 to the words 'one' and 'all one'. The ancient arms of the Ferrers family, to which he belonged, had the motto 'only one'.

* In *Baconiana* (1892) and Ch. XXII of *An Impartial Study*. The dismissal was conducted in favour of another candidate, Sir Philip Sidney. See above, p. 46.

F

CHAPTER VI

THE CASE FOR DERBY
1891–1952

Another part of the field . . . Retreat and flourish.
Re-enter . . . Derby bearing the crown.
SHAKESPEARE: *King Richard the Third.*

I

The theory that the plays of Shakespeare were really written by William Stanley, sixth Earl of Derby (1561–1642), has been developed during the twentieth century largely by French writers, but it was first put forward by an Englishman nine years before the century opened. The history of the Derby case started modestly enough in the shape of three articles in *The Genealogist* by the antiquarian James Greenstreet: 'A Hitherto Unknown Noble Author of Elizabethan Comedies' (July 1891); 'Further Notices of William Stanley' (January 1892); and 'Testimonies against the Accepted Authorship of Shakespeare's Plays' (May 1892). The writer died shortly after the last of these articles had appeared, so did not have the opportunity to develop the case himself. His articles were referred to in an article in *Baconiana*, July 1897, and also in an essay by the orthodox biographer Sir Sidney Lee in the *Nineteenth Century and After*, May 1906.

The case has since been developed in France, Switzerland, and Belgium by such writers as Abel Lefranc, Jacques Boulenger, J. Depoin, and Mathias Morhardt, and in England and America by Robert Frazer, R. Macdonald Lucas, J. le Roy White, and A. W. Titherley, among others. The principal writings on the theory have been Frazer's *The Silent Shakespeare* (Philadelphia, 1915); Depoin's *L'énigme Shakespearienne* (Paris, 1919); Boulenger's *L'Affaire Shakespeare* (Paris, 1919); Lefranc's *Sous le masque de William Shakespeare* (Paris, 1919), *La réalité dans le 'Songe d'une Nuit d'été'* (Geneva, 1920), *Le Secret de William Stanley* (Brussels, 1923) and *A la découverte de Shakespeare* (Paris, 1945–50); Lucas's *Shakespeare's Vital Secret* (London, 1938); Morhardt's *A la Rencontre de William Shakespeare* (Paris, 1938); and Titherley's

82

Shakespeare's Identity (Winchester, 1952). A. J. Evans's recent *Shakespeare's Magic Circle* (1956) we have mentioned in our chapter on the Group Theories. Mr. Evans does not give Derby as sole author but believes him to have been the chief figure in a group of aristocratic authors.

The late Prof. Lefranc is the chief figure among the group of Derby theorists. For the first time, and perhaps the last, an unorthodox theory on the Shakespeare authorship question can claim to have had at its head a writer who was a professional literary scholar. Lefranc was a Professor of Literature at the Collège de France in Paris, an authority on Rabelais who had also written on Calvin, Pascal, André Chénier, and Renan. His writings on the Derby theory are distinguished from nearly all other unorthodox writings by their literary scholarship.

Having paid this deserved compliment to the leader of the Derby school, I must nevertheless confess that few of the theories seeking to prove that Shakespeare did not write his own plays appear to me to rest upon so slender a foundation. Its history started modestly enough, we have observed; its foundations also were extremely modest. The whole of the Derby case has been built from two references found by Greenstreet in the *Calendar of State Papers, Domestic Series*. We must therefore see first of all precisely what these references are.

II

Greenstreet had agreed with the Baconians and most of the other unorthodox theorists that the author of the works must have been a widely-travelled nobleman. But he did not find convincing either the Baconian theory or any of its rivals. It was while he was searching for a more suitable aristocratic author that he came across these references to the Earl of Derby.

He found them in the *Calendar of State Papers (Domestic)*, Vol. CCLXXI, p. 227. A Jesuit spy, with the name or pseudonym of George Fenner, was employed by Father Parsons to report on the possibility of persuading certain English noblemen with Catholic sympathies to join in a plot against the Queen; his letters were intercepted by the counter-espionage service of the Privy Council. Two of these letters, dated 30 June 1599, explained that the Earl of Derby's participation in any plot of this nature was not now to be hoped for—and Derby as a possible pretender to the throne was the nobleman whom Parsons and his superiors naturally wanted most. The first letter, addressed to a correspondent at Antwerp, explained that 'Therle of Darby is busyed only in penning comedies for the commoun players'; the second, to a correspondent at Venice, gave the same information but with that variation of spelling so beloved of Elizabethans: 'Our Earle of Darby is busye in penning commodyes for the commoun players.' It was upon these two references that Greenstreet built the whole edifice which led him to believe that Shakespeare's plays were written by William Stanley.

Having found his aristocrat, he needed to discover more about him. Who precisely was this Earl of Derby? Greenstreet consulted the authorities—such as Seacome's *Ancient and Honourable House of Stanley*—and discovered that William, the sixth Earl, was born in 1561, that he was the second son of the fourth Earl and younger brother of Ferdinand, Lord Strange, afterwards the fifth Earl, who was the patron of a noted company of actors who played at the Rose Theatre. He matriculated at St. John's College, Oxford, at the early age of 11, and later studied law at the Inns of Court (*Genealogist*, July 1891, p. 206). He was certainly the much-travelled nobleman whom Greenstreet was seeking, and he found out in particular that about the year 1583 Derby was probably in Navarre, the scene of *Love's Labour's Lost*, which no one has ever suggested that Shakespeare could have visited. The various parts of what Greenstreet believed to be the true solution to the authorship question were now falling into place.

He further discovered that the crest of the Stanley family was an eagle. Thus, when Spenser referred to the poet Aetion (meaning 'eagle-man') he was probably referring to Stanley. Spenser himself was related to the family, Lady Strange having been born Alice Spencer or Spenser.

An aristocrat who is known to have written comedies for the common players and who was also known by Spenser as a poet; one who had travelled extensively on the Continent, had been educated at Oxford and had also studied law: it is not to be wondered at that Greenstreet felt a mild elation at having now discovered so quickly what he had been searching for previously for so long.

He died, as has been mentioned, in 1892, before he could develop the theory further, and the continuation of the Derby case had to wait till the period of the First World War, in particular till it came under the attention of Prof. Lefranc. He was able to confirm Greenstreet's findings and add a great deal more.

It has been observed that Lefranc was an authority on Rabelais, and he became convinced that the character of Falstaff had a Rabelaisian origin. Derby knew France and her literature as intimately as any Englishman of his time, so was able, not only to create the Rabelaisian figure of Sir John, but to write the French scene in *Henry the Fifth*. (*Sous le masque*, Vol. I, p. 4 sq. Compare Morhardt, *A la recontre*, who was convinced that Shakespeare, by the evidence of the plays, '*savait le français à fond*'.) That play, and several others, also contain battle scenes and Welsh characters; and Derby, versed in the military art, knew Wales and her people very well indeed.

These, however, Lefranc considered important but subsidiary points. He based his main claim for the Derby authorship on six plays: *Love's Labour's Lost*, *A Midsummer Night's Dream*, *The Merry Wives of Windsor*, *Twelfth Night*, *Hamlet*, and *The Tempest*. He first of all noted what he considered to be the true French atmosphere of *Love's Labour*, and its relation to French history. But this was by no means all. In Act Five a pageant of the Nine Worthies is acted, and at Chester, in the Earl of Derby's home county, a similar popular play was annually performed. A version of the Chester play was published in 1584 by Richard Lloyd, Derby's former tutor, and Lefranc believed that in the character of Holofernes—a name significantly derived from that of Gargantua's first tutor—Derby was poking fun at Lloyd (*Sous le masque*, II, p. 17 sq.).

The comedy of *A Midsummer Night's Dream* Lefranc believed to have been written for Derby's own marriage to Elizabeth Vere, daughter of the Earl of Oxford and granddaughter of Lord Burghley. The celebrated interlude of Bottom's Pyramus was evidently modelled on one of the popular plays performed by the artisans of Chester. (*Le Secret du 'Songe d'une nuit d'été'*, *L'Opinion*, 16–23 October 1920, p. 423; *Sous le masque*, II, p. 104 sq; *A la découverte*, I, pp. 421–505.)

The Merry Wives and *Twelfth Night* Lefranc considered to embody certain circumstances of Derby's life and his reflections upon them. The character of Malvolio in the latter play was evidently based on William ffarrington, the steward of the Stanley family, whom Lefranc had traced in the Derby Household Books. *'Dans chacune de ces comédies, William Stanley a exprimé ses sentiments per- sonnels'* (*"A propos des 'Joyeuses Commères de Windsor'," L'Opinion*, 5–12 February 1921, p. 167.) Compare *A la découverte*, I, p. 521 sq.

Hamlet is Lefranc's *pièce de résistance* and the reason why the cover of the first volume of *A la découverte de Shakespeare* is adorned by a picture of Mary Queen of Scots and Lord Darnley. One would not immediately connect these illustrious personages with the plays of Shakespeare, any more so than the Countess of Bedford, Sir Philip Sidney, and the Earls of Southampton and Essex, whose portraits embellish the pages of Peter Alvor's *Das Neue Shakespeare-Evangelium*. But Lefranc was convinced that *Hamlet* was a kind of 'problem play', based upon the murder of Darnley and the adultery of Mary. Ophelia's original was Helène de Tournon, who died of love. (*Sous le masque*, II, Ch. IX; *A la découverte*, I, Part One: *'La fin du mystère d'Hamlet'*; *Helène de Tournon: Celle qui mourut d'amour et l'Ophèlie d' 'Hamlet', passim.*)

With regard to *The Tempest*, Lefranc considers that this play stands out in the literature of the Jacobean age for its favourable treatment of magic, and he thinks it highly significant that Derby was a friend of the magician John Dee, formerly—so to speak— Astrologer Royal. In his diary, Dee gives a formula for summoning angels, two of whom he calls Anael and Uriel. When Derby came to write *The Tempest*, he combined the two names in the character of Ariel.

Such, then, is Lefranc's case, presented with a wealth of literary and historical detail. If much of it must seem irrelevant to the authorship question which it is supposed to solve, we can at any rate admire the skyscraper built by the French professor upon the three modest bricks laid by Greenstreet in the early 'nineties.

III

The most recent book to advocate Derby as sole author is A. W. Titherley's handsome volume *Shakespeare's Identity: William Stanley, Sixth Earl of Derby*, published at Winchester in 1952. Dr. Titherley adds some more detail to the points raised by Green- street and Lefranc, and puts forward some new points of his own.

He is particularly keen to stress Derby's authorship of the *Sonnets*, a point rather neglected by Lefranc. While pointing out that the *Sonnets* 'never unequivocally betray the person', he is able to find what he considers two personal clues: in the sonnets where the author 'lets out' that his name is Will, and in the sonnet where he reveals that he is lame (*Shakespeare's Identity*, p. 5. Compare Dr. Titherley's edition of *Shakespeare's Sonnets, as from the pen of William Stanley*).

Dr. Titherley therefore gives us the following list of requirements for the author of Shakespeare's works: (1) his Christian name must have been William; (2) he must have been intimately acquainted with Elizabethan and foreign courts; (3) he must have been a patriot, feudal in outlook and Lancastrian by sympathy; (4) he must have been gifted with deep wisdom; (5) he must have had motives for concealing his personality; (6) he must have travelled extensively abroad; (7) he must have been familiar with the Welsh people; (8) he must have been able to read Latin, French, and Italian authors in the original; and (9) he must have been deeply versed in ancient classical lore and Renaissance literature (p. 5 sq.). Dr. Titherley finds all these essentials in Derby, but in no one else who has been suggested. He points out, furthermore, that long before the name 'William Shakespeare' appeared in print, certain immature poems had been published under the initials 'W.S.'—when Shakespeare of Stratford was 'a raw lad, then helping in the slaughter-house'.

That virtually completes the case for Derby, in the brief space at our disposal. A few minor points have been added to it. For example, in *Shakespeare's Vital Secret*, Mr. Macdonald Lucas suggests that the anonymous poem in the Second Folio initialled I.M.S. was written by Derby's eldest son James, who had omitted the 'a' and the 'e' to put enquirers off the scent. In *Shakespeare's Magic Circle* Mr. Evans refers to the researches of Prof. Lambin in *Les Langues Modernes*, where it was argued that the plot of *Measure for Measure* is similar to the events in Paris in 1582, when Henri III was absent from the capital and Claude Tonart was condemned to death for seduction but afterwards reprieved. Derby was in Paris about this time, and it is Mr. Evans's contention that *Measure for Measure* could only have been written by an eyewitness of these events.

CHAPTER VII

THE CASE FOR RUTLAND
1907–1947

You must call him Rutland now.
SHAKESPEARE: *King Richard the Second.*

I

If the Derby case is mostly French in its development, the case for Rutland is no less certainly both German and Belgian in its origins. In our chapter on the Group and Dual Theories, we saw that an American writer, Wilbur Zeigler, was the first to suggest Roger Manners as part author and that Peter Alvor saw him as co-author with the Earl of Southampton. The first to suggest that Rutland might have written the entire works appears to have been Carl Bleibtreu in the introduction to the third edition of his play *Der wahre Shakespeare*, published at Munich in 1907—a position which he developed in his book *Shakespeares Geheimnis*, published at Berne in 1923. Meanwhile, the American writer Lewis F. Bostelmann had brought out both a biography of Rutland (New York, 1911) and a play entitled *Roger of Rutland*, and the Belgian Rutlandians, MM. Demblon and Dessart, had published their works. Carl Schneider, too, had preceded the second volume of his fellow-countryman Bleibtreu with a volume of his own entitled *Neues Zeugnis für Rutland-Shakespeare*, published in Berlin in 1922.

The Belgian professor, Célestin Demblon, is often considered the originator of the Rutland theory and there is no doubt that he did most to publicize it. Member for Liège in the Belgian Chamber of Deputies and lecturer on the history of French literature in the University of Brussels, he had read some five thousand works on the Shakespeare authorship question—a feat mentioned in our Introduction—and had come to the conclusion that only Alvor and Bleibtreu were on the right track. He embodied the results of his findings in two lengthy books—the first contains 560 pages—entitled respectively *Lord Rutland est Shakespeare* (1912) and

L'Auteur d'Hamlet' et son monde (1914), both published in Paris. His fellow-countryman, A. Dessart, wrote a similar book, *Lord Rutland est-il Shakespeare?*, published at Liège in 1913.

Demblon was not, then, the founder of the theory, but he made it his own. In his first book he invited all Shakespeare lovers to meet on 26 June 1912 at the seat of the Rutland family, Belvoir Castle, in honour of the third centenary of the author's death. His theory, he wrote proudly, '*a fait beaucoup de bruit, dans la presse européenne, notamment à Paris, à Rome, à Milan, à Madrid, à Cologne, à Berlin, à Moscou, et quelque peu à Londres et à New-York. Ce n'est qu'un commencement*' (*Lord Rutland est Shakespeare*, 2nd ed., p. 27).

He was right: it was only a beginning. For besides the books already mentioned, the Rutland theory was to be advocated in an article by the Argentinian writer Paci, 'El misterio Shakespeare', in the journal *Nosotros* (Buenos Aires, December 1928); in the book by Prof. Porohovshikov, *Shakespeare Unmasked* (New York, 1940); and, most recently, in Mr. Sykes's *Alias William Shakespeare?* (London, 1947). Thus, although the theory has been meagre in the number of its adherents, compared with the Baconians, it can at any rate claim that no less than eight countries—Germany, Switzerland, Belgium, France, the United States, the Argentine, Russia, and England—have had a hand in its propagation.

The first thing that a stranger to the theory would ask is this: what connection had Roger Manners with Shakespeare or Shakespeare with the Rutland family? The former part of the question no one can answer, but a possible answer to the latter was suggested by Demblon. He pointed to the fact (or the apparent fact) that in March 1613, about nine months after Roger Manners's death, Shakespeare and his fellow-player Burbage performed a service for his successor, the sixth Earl, Francis Manners. In the accounts-book of Belvoir Castle there is the recorded payment for this service, dated 31 March 1613: 'To Mr. Shakespeare in gold about My Lord's *impresa* 44s; to Richard Burbage for painting and making it, in gold 44s.' This 'impresa' was a shield painted with a device and motto, to be carried in the tournament at Whitehall on the anniversary of the King's accession.

Although modern biographers (e.g. Chute, p. 267, and Harrison, *Introducing Shakespeare*, p. 42) seem to accept this as a fact, I believe that Mrs. Stopes has proved that the Shakespeare referred to was not the dramatist at all. In an article in the *Athenaeum* (16 May 1908) she demonstrated that the man referred to was probably John Shakespeare, a professional maker of bosses and emblems, who among other things is described in the Wardrobe Accounts of Charles I, both as Prince and King, as having made 'gilt bosses charged with the arms of England'. He, a professional craftsman, is much more likely to have been employed by Francis Manners in a task of this kind than the actor-dramatist of the same name. He is believed to have been a cousin of Shakespeare's, but this is not necessary to explain the connection with Burbage. For Burbage had two reputations at the time: he was not only a famous actor, he was also a well-known painter, whose 'portrait of a woman' used to hang in the College at Dulwich founded by his rival actor Alleyn. He is believed to have painted the portrait of Shakespeare which is now in the National Portrait Gallery and is reproduced in our Frontispiece.

Carl Bleibtreu discovered the more sinister facts that the burial of Roger Manners took place hastily at night and that no one was allowed to see the face of the dead man. Mr. Sykes confirms (p. 198) that it is possible that Francis may have murdered his brother to gain the Earldom, as Claudius in *Hamlet* murdered *his* brother to gain the crown of Denmark.

Among the five thousand works on the authorship question which Demblon had read was Greenwood's *The Shakespeare Problem Restated* (1908). In this book Greenwood had formulated the theory that the true author was probably neither Shakespeare nor Bacon but an unknown aristocrat, 'a busy man whose aim it was to use the stage as a means to convey instruction to the people, and to teach them a certain measure of philosophy' (p. 514). In his answer to Greenwood, which came out the same year as Demblon's first volume, Andrew Lang wittily summarized Greenwood's theory as follows:

'Conceive a "concealed poet" of high social position, contemporary with Bacon and Shakespeare. Let him be so fond of the Law that he cannot keep legal "shop" out of his love sonnets even. Make him a courtier; a statesman; a philosopher; a scholar. . . . Let this almost omniscient being possess supreme poetic genius, extensive classical attainments, and a tendency to make false quantities.

Then conceive him to live through the reigns of "Eliza and our James" without leaving in history, in science, in society, in law, in politics or scholarship a single trace of his existence. He left nothing but the poems and plays . . .' (*Shakespeare, Bacon and the Great Unknown*, p. 5).

It was this Great Unknown of Greenwood's invention whom Demblon believed he had discovered in Roger Manners, fifth Earl of Rutland. He was a courtier and a scholar, and had studied law, and Demblon further discovered that he had travelled widely, in particular that he had been to Denmark. Instead of leaving no trace of his existence, as Greenwood had surmised, Rutland in 1603 had been appointed Ambassador Extraordinary to the Court of Elsinore, to represent James I at the christening of the Danish King's son and heir. And he had made an official report of his embassy.

Hamlet is therefore the chief witness in the Rutland case as well as in the Derby and other cases. Not only was there bad blood between the brothers Manners, leading possibly to murder as in *Hamlet*, there was also Rutland's actual visit to the scene of the play, Elsinore, where he had the opportunity of adding some local colour to the 1604 Quarto. He had been in prison from 1601 to 1603, for his part in the Essex rebellion: '*il exhala sa douleur*,' explained Demblon, '*dans le premier 'Hamlet', écrit en 1602*.' Furthermore, during his embassy to Denmark he probably met again the two Danish courtiers, Rosencrantz and Guildenstern—who duly figure in *Hamlet*—who had been his fellow-students at Padua. Demblon discovered this information by going to Padua himself and searching the university records.

Like Peter Alvor, Demblon believed the plays to be autobiographical. He suggested that Rutland depicted himself, at various stages in his life, under the characters Biron, Bassanio, Romeo, Benedict, Jacques, Hamlet, Brutus, and Prospero—much as Goethe did under the characters of Werther, Hermann, Faust, and Tasso, and Balzac with Raphael, Balthasar Claes, etc. (*Lord Rutland est Shakespeare*, p. 16). Prof. Porohovshikov was to come to much the same conclusion.

II

Prof. Porohovshikov, however, is not a complete Rutlandian, as Demblon was. He believes—as we have already noted—that Bacon wrote *Venus and Adonis*, *Lucrece*, and *Love's Labour's Lost*, and also that 'of all the poets suggested as the possible author of the puzzling booklet of *Shake-speare's Sonnets*, Edward de Vere is by far the more [*sic*] probable candidate' (*Shakespeare Unmasked*, p. 263). The Professor merely gives to Roger Manners the distinction of having composed all of Shakespeare's plays except some of the earliest, though he believes that 'we find nothing to guide us to the poet's identity in *Troilus and Cressida*, *Timon of Athens*, and *King Henry the Eighth*' (p. 43).

The attribution to Bacon of some of the early work—and Porohovshikov considers the *First Part of King Henry the Sixth* to have been 'written in collaboration by three or four, perhaps even five dramatists'—certainly removes part of the most obvious criticism against the case for Rutland: namely, the age of Manners at the time. He was born in 1576, so was only 16 when the first of the history plays was produced and about 16½ when *Venus and Adonis* was published. Demblon had suggested that 'the childish erudition' of *Love's Labour's Lost* must have been the fruit of Rutland's school recollections, and Mr. Sykes was to maintain that the author was 'an infant prodigy in an age when men matured far earlier than they do in the twentieth century'. He mentions the early maturity of Raphael, Mozart, Byron, Victor Hugo, and others, concluding that 'these instances show that, although it would have been a remarkable feat to write *Henry VI*, *The Comedy of Errors*, *Richard III* and *Titus Andronicus* between the ages of fifteen and eighteen, it was not an impossible one' (*Alias William Shakespeare?*, p. 154 sq.). By giving some of the early work to other authors, Prof. Porohovshikov is relieved from much of the more obvious embarrassment to the Rutland case.

Otherwise, his advocacy follows the lines laid down by Bleibtreu and Demblon. Being himself an aristocrat, he is particularly concerned to stress the familiarity of the author with hunting, hawking, and suchlike aristocratic pursuits (*Shakespeare Unmasked*, pp. xv, 20, 94. Compare Sykes on the use of tennis terms in *Henry the Fifth*: 'Shakspere could never have learnt this expensive game'). He quotes from Miss Caroline Spurgeon's *Shakespeare's Imagery and*

What it Tells Us (1935) to the effect that Shakespeare in his works makes 260 allusions to the classics and mythology, 196 to sports and games, 192 to war and weapons, 172 to the sea and ships, 124 to the law, and 74 to the drama. The Professor concludes from these figures that the author must have had an excellent classical education, must have been devoted to an open-air life, must have done some soldiering abroad, must have studied law, and must have been interested in the theatre. It can be proved, he maintains, that Rutland *did* have a classical education (at Cambridge), that he subsequently studied law at Gray's Inn, that he was a landed proprietor devoted to the usual sports and pastimes of his class, that he took part in the Essex expedition to Ireland, and that he was a friend of theatre patrons, including the Earl of Derby. On the other hand, the 'popular London actor' had no university education, did not study law, was no landed proprietor, was never a soldier, and probably 'never saw a spoonful of salt water' in his life. His interest in the theatre would have been emphasized in the plays, if he had really written them, whereas it comes as a poor sixth to the other five interests mentioned (pp. 22, 42, 64 sq., 94 sq., 122 sq.).

The reasons for secrecy Prof. Porohovshikov sees as bound up with the writing of *King Richard the Second*, a play containing the deposition of a monarch and therefore treasonable by the standards of Queen Elizabeth:

'The simplest way to divert the Queen's suspicions . . . was to bring forth as the author a man whose social standing was too low, even too contemptible, to entertain the august apprehensions. . . . Fortunately, by a singular concurrence of circumstances, the means for the purpose were at hand. Three or four years ago the two poems *Venus and Adonis* and *Lucrece* had been published under the name of William Shakespeare. [Both poems, we must remember, the Professor believes to have been written by Bacon.] About the same time, an actor of the Curtain and the Globe [The Globe was not opened till 1599] of the name William Shakspere or Shaxper had become a sort of jack-of-all-trades around his playhouse. So William Shakespeare *the dramatist* was born and christened, who never lived in flesh and blood and never shall die in fame . . . William Shakspere the actor assumed the part of William Shakespeare the dramatist and acted it discreetly and well . . . Behind the footlights [There were no footlights on the Elizabethan stage.] . . . a few men did know part of the truth . . . but . . . not one of them would deprive his playhouse of its wealthy patron' (pp. 130–1).

All unorthodox theories have to assume some 'singular concurrence' of this kind, with or without footlights. For example, 'It was a stroke of luck for Francis Bacon that there happened to be in London the actor Will Shaksper whose name was similar to the name that Bacon had already taken as a pseudonym' (Johnson, *The Shaksper Illusion*, p. 89); ' "Shakespeare" . . . is an adopted pen-name . . . An actor had been found who bore, or who went under, a very similar name, Shaksper or Shakspere' (Kent and Another, *Edward de Vere, the Real Shakespeare*, p. 17). In Mr. Sykes's book, which is the most recent written to support the Rutland case, *King Richard the Second* figures as one of the main points.

III

We have mentioned Mr. Sykes's *Alias William Shakespeare?* in the first paragraph of this book. It was published in 1947 and had the privilege of a preface by the distinguished historian, Mr. (now Sir) Arthur Bryant. Sir Arthur gave cogent reasons for disbelieving in the case put forward by Mr. Sykes, but he claimed truly that the book was an interesting addition to the theories previously advocated. The theory, of course, was not so original as Sir Arthur supposed: the book is valuable for another reason, namely that it summarizes the evidence discovered by Bleibtreu, Demblon, and Porohovshikov, adding a few new points in turn.

Mr. Sykes's assistant in his researches was no less a person than Mr. Sherlock Holmes, who apparently had come up from his beeloud glade in Sussex at the Rutlandian's urgent request. Holmes must have been getting on in years in 1947; but though a nonagenarian at least, he had lost none of his powers of reasoning or action. Hearing that the question in hand was the authorship of the works of Shakespeare, which he had never read, he immediately borrowed a copy and read all the plays and poems straight through, with the aid doubtless of a considerable quantity of the strongest tobacco on the market. Then he joined a repertory company and toured the provinces, and after making other researches of one kind or another, he announced to the astonishment of Dr. Watson-Sykes that the author of Shakespeare's works must have possessed the following qualifications: he must have (1) been thoroughly at home in Court circles; (2) been educated at Cambridge; (3) been a qualified lawyer; (4) been able to speak fluent French and Italian; (5) been fond of hawking and other field sports; (6) travelled in France and Italy; (7) seen active service about 1599; (8) visited Denmark about 1603; (9) experienced a heavy storm at sea; (10) had a knowledge of forestry; (11) been a supporter of the Earl of Essex and a friend of Southampton and Pembroke; (12) suffered reverses of fortune; (13) been on bad terms with a brother or brothers; and (14) died young (p. 15 sq.).

Having compiled this list, Holmes was able to prove, pretty conclusively, that the actor Shakespeare did not possess any of the necessary qualifications. Besides, if he had possessed them all, he would simply not have had the time to write the plays. Holmes's experience of a repertory company on tour convinced him that an actor's is a full-time job, with little leisure for original composition.

Nor, in Holmes's considered opinion, could Bacon possibly have been the author. True, he was a qualified lawyer, but Shakespeare's plays—here Mr. Sykes agrees with the old opinion of Castle—reveal both legal training and some inaccuracies on points of law. Therefore, the author must have known *more* law than Shakespeare could possibly have known, but *less* than Bacon. Furthermore, Bacon saw no active service, and he could not possibly have been the author of *Richard the Second*. This play had a special performance in February 1601, on the day before the rebellion of Essex, being commissioned by the conspirators in the hope that this spectacle of a king's deposition would inspire the citizens of London to follow Essex against the Queen. After the failure of the rebellion, Bacon took part in the prosecution of his former friend and patron, who would surely have known that he had written the play, if he really had.

'With his life at stake [asks Sherlock Holmes] would Essex have hesitated to speak out? He had only to say that Mr. Francis Bacon, the learned counsel for the prosecution, was the author of the play *Richard II* which his friends had specially ordered to be performed on the eve of their action. Result: the ignominious collapse of the prosecution.'*

For similar reasons, neither Derby nor Oxford, nor yet Raleigh, could have been the author of Shakespeare's plays—in the considered opinion of Mr. Sherlock Holmes.

These red herrings being disposed of, Holmes next considers the case for Roger Manners, and finds that all the clues point to him. Holmes particularly stresses (*a*) the knowledge of Italy revealed in the plays, and the corresponding fact that Rutland in 1595 started his Grand Tour by going to Holland and Germany, thence proceeding to Padua, Verona, Venice, and probably Milan, returning home through Switzerland and France; (*b*) the theme of brother versus brother in *Hamlet*, *The Tempest*, *King John*, *Much Ado About Nothing*, *As You Like It*, and *King Lear*, and the corresponding fact of the strained relations between Roger and Francis Manners; (*c*) the difference in realism between the early battle scenes and those in *King Henry the Fifth*, and the corresponding fact that in 1599 Rutland saw active service in Ireland under Essex; and (*d*) the addition of local colour to the 1604 Quarto of *Hamlet*, and the corresponding fact of Rutland's embassy to Elsinore (pp. 69 sq., 97 sq., 115 sq., 150 sq.).

Such, in brief, is Holmes's case for Rutland. 'The life of William Shakespeare as revealed in the plays,' he concludes, 'is identical with the life of Roger Manners.' Mr. Sykes imagines the great detective pausing before the portrait in Belvoir Castle and saying triumphantly to Lestrade of Scotland Yard: 'There's your man, Inspector!'

---

* Sykes, p. 142. Compare Morgan: 'If Francis Bacon wrote *Richard the Second*, it was a piece of matchless effrontery for him to maintain that his own production had been displayed as a counterfeit presentment in aid of a treason in which his friend was engaged' (*Shakespeare in Fact and in Criticism*, p. 178).

CHAPTER VIII

BARNARD: DEVONSHIRE: STIRLING
1914–1930

Sit we down,
And let us hear Bernardo speak of this.
SHAKESPEARE: *Hamlet.*

I

Delia Bacon, it has been observed, was not inspired by family considerations when she put forward the theory that the plays and poems of Shakespeare were really written by a group of Elizabethan courtiers, of whom Francis Bacon was the chief philosopher. As far as is known, Delia was not a descendant of Francis, and though J. Thomas Looney was descended from an old Manx family, several of whose members had intermarried with the Stanleys, former Kings of Man, he did not on that account embrace the theory of Abel Lefranc, that William Stanley must have written Shakespeare. On the contrary, his investigations led him in another direction entirely and he was eventually to put forward a rival candidate in the Earl of Oxford. The only unorthodox theorist to have been influenced by family considerations—unless Shirley Harris was—appears to have been Mr. Finch Barnard, who in three pamphlets (*Shakespeare and the Barnard Family*, 1914; *More Light on Shakespeare*, 1914; and *Science and the Soul*, 1918) put forward the suggestion that Shakespeare's works were written by an ancestor of his who married the actor's granddaughter Elizabeth.

It is rather intriguing, after all the talk about 'the illiterate maltster of Stratford', to find a theorist who bases his claim on family connection with 'the notorious money-lender'. It is perfectly true that Elizabeth Hall, only child of Shakespeare's elder daughter Susanna, married first Thomas Nash or Nashe of Stratford, who studied at Lincoln's Inn, and secondly John Barnard or Bernard, of Northamptonshire, who was knighted by Charles II. After her mother's death, Lady Barnard became the owner of New Place and other property, according to the terms of Shakespeare's will. She died childless in 1670, the last direct descendant of Shakespeare. 'The author's manuscripts,' Mr. Barnard concludes, 'are to be found, no doubt, among the Barnard family papers.'

The case, in brief, is that Shakespeare was the actor-manager who produced the plays on the stage, but that the actual author was John Barnard, the country gentleman who was eventually to marry the actor's granddaughter. The evidence for the theory is a little meagre, except in so far as it implies the negative side of Baconianism, in respect of Sir John's greater breeding. Shakespeare, like some other actors of the time, had become officially a gentleman, or rather his father had become so and he had inherited the honour in 1601; but Barnard had been *born* a gentleman—a distinction of greater significance then than in modern times.

Mr. Finch Barnard devotes many of his pages to a consideration of the names of the characters in Shakespeare's plays. He finds that several Barnards, or similar names, figure therein. There is, for instance, the trusty soldier Bernardo in *Hamlet*, who—significantly enough—speaks *the very first line* in the most famous play that has ever been written. Bernardo's fellow-sentinel is called Francisco, who speaks the *second line* of the play, and Mr. Finch Barnard points out that the father of the author, John Barnard, was named Francis. In *Science and the Soul* Mr. Barnard brings in St. Francis of Assisi, whose relevance to the plays of Shakespeare is not so immediately apparent.

II

So far as I have been able to discover, the Barnard theory begins and ends with the three little books by Mr. Finch Barnard. We have noted similar cases of theories which have convinced their creators but have failed to convince anybody else: for instance, the Burton theory. In 1930 we come across two other theories which also apparently failed to gain a hearing.

Both theories seem to be exclusively German. The first was suggested by Peter Alvor in his book *Neue Shakespeare Biographie*, published at Würzburg in 1930; the second was referred to by the same author—but is not otherwise known to me—in *Die Shakespeare-Frage und das Ben Jonson-Problem*, published in the same city during the same year. The first gives the works, or the greater share in them, to Charles Blount, Lord Mountjoy, afterwards Earl of Devonshire (1563–1606); the second, only referred to in passing by Alvor, gives the works to Sir William Alexander (1567–1640) who in 1633 was created Earl of Stirling.

As we observed with regard to Burton, it is difficult to know what makes some theories die a natural death soon after they are first advocated, while others can claim generations of believers. On the face of it, there seems as much reason to believe that Devonshire wrote Shakespeare as that Bacon did, and the case for Stirling appears every bit as sound as the Oxfordian. But a historian must go by the facts, and the facts are that the Devonshire and Stirling theories are almost unknown outside Germany, while the Baconian and Oxfordian theories are as well known in America as in Europe.

Mountjoy was the ardent lover of Essex's sister, Lady Rich, whose husband divorced her on account of this *affaire*; he subsequently married her while Lord Rich was still alive, to the indignation of King James, who compelled him to retire from Court: in these episodes we find both the passionate lover of the early plays and the disillusioned courtier of the later. Mountjoy succeeded Essex in Ireland, so had the personal experience of war to write *Henry the Fifth*. A lover, a courtier, a soldier, one who had known reverses of fortune: the claim is by no means less considerable than others.

What we miss perhaps is any evidence of literary accomplishment, but we cannot say the same of William Alexander. The case for Stirling rests equally upon social and literary qualifications, and the latter being the rarer among unorthodox theories we must look at it briefly first.

Stirling wrote both sonnets and plays, including what are known as the *Monarchicke Tragedies*. These number four: *Croesus*; *Darius*; *The Alexandraean*; and *Julius Caesar*. The last-named has little in common with Shakespeare's, unless we count a common source in Plutarch, but *Darius*, published in Edinburgh in 1603 and in London the year after, has one speech at any rate which is faintly reminiscent of a famous speech in *The Tempest*. Karl Elze, the nineteenth-century German critic, took the reminiscence in the literal sense of the word and based on it part of his argument that *The Tempest* was written in 1604. The speech from *Darius* is as follows, and the reminiscence, if such it is, is of course in Prospero's last speech in *The Tempest*:

> Let greatness of her glassy sceptres vaunt,
> Not sceptres, no but reeds, soon bruised, soon broken;
> And let this worldly pomp our wits enchant,
> All fades and scarcely leaves behind a token.
> Those golden palaces, those gorgeous halls,
> With furniture superfluously fair,
> Those stately courts, those sky-encountering walls,
> Evanish all like vapours in the air.

That is one of the chief arguments in the Stirling theory, as it is one of the arguments in Miss Gwynneth Bowen's case for dating *The Tempest* before the death of the Earl of Oxford (*Shakespeare's Farewell* p. 8). But there are other arguments for making Shakespeare a Scotsman. Not only was Stirling a well-travelled nobleman, who had studied abroad and journeyed through France, Spain, and Italy; not only was he Keeper of the Signet and a Judge of the Court of Session; he had most of the qualifications deemed essential by earlier theorists, with one very important qualification added: he was born in, and knew intimately, the country of *Macbeth*.

It is surprising how previous unorthodox writers had passed over this problem. If a personal knowledge of Italy is deemed necessary to write *The Merchant of Venice*, how much more so a personal knowledge of Scotland to write *Macbeth*! The local colour in that play is so much greater than in any of the plays set in Italy, and who but a Scotsman could have painted it? Some of us may think this intimate acquaintance with Scottish life by far the most powerful argument for Stirling's authorship. To most of the London nobility in Shakespeare's time, the country of *Macbeth* must have seemed more distant and more strange than the country of *Romeo and Juliet*.

CHAPTER IX

THE 'OXFORD' MOVEMENT
1918–1957

O cheerful colours! see where Oxford comes!
SHAKESPEARE: *The Third Part of King Henry the Sixth.*

I

The theory that Shakespeare's works were really written by
Edward de Vere, the seventeenth Earl of Oxford (1550–1604), can
most accurately be dated from the month of November in the year
1918, when J. Thomas Looney handed to Sir Frederick Kenyon,
the Director of the British Museum, a sealed letter in which he
announced his discovery. In 1920 he published his book, *'Shakespeare' Identified in Edward de Vere*, which he had begun before
the war. Among the chief results of this publication was the
founding in London in 1922 of the Shakespeare Fellowship, whose
object is the investigation of the problem of Shakespeare's authorship, with particular emphasis on the claims of Oxford. The first
President was Sir George Greenwood, and among the original
Vice-Presidents were Looney himself, who died in 1944, and the
leader of the Derby school, the late Prof. Lefranc. At the time of
writing (1957) all the officials of the Shakespeare Fellowship—
though not all the members—are Oxfordian.

So the Oxfordian theory, like the Baconian but unlike other unorthodox theories, has a centre; like the Baconian, too, it has a
periodical, *The Shakespeare Fellowship News-Letter*. Most of the
books and pamphlets advocating the case for Oxford have been
written by prominent members of the Fellowship, as the Francis
Bacon Society has sponsored the majority of the books and pamphlets advocating Bacon. For instance, one of the founders of the
Fellowship, Col. B. R. Ward, wrote *The Mystery of Mr. W. H.*
(1923), and his son, Capt. B. M. Ward, wrote *The Seventeenth Earl
of Oxford* (1928). Past Presidents have included Lt.-Col. M. W.
Douglas, author of *Lord Oxford and the Shakespeare Group* (1952);
Percy Allen, author of *The Case for Edward de Vere* (1930); and
Rear-Admiral H. H. Holland, author of *Shakespeare through Oxford*

Glasses (1923). Among present Vice-Presidents are Miss Hilda Amphlett, author of *Who was Shakespeare?* (1955), and William Kent, part-author of *Edward de Vere, the Real Shakespeare* (1947).

Other prominent Oxfordians or 'Oxford Group-Theorists' in Great Britain have included the novelist and critic Marjorie Bowen; Dr. V. A. Demant, former Chancellor of St. Paul's; Dr. Gilbert Slater, late Principal of Ruskin College; Dr. Gerald H. Rendall, former Headmaster of Charterhouse, author of *Shakespeare's Sonnets and Edward de Vere* (1930); and the present President of the Fellowship, Mr. Christmas Humphreys, distinguished barrister and authority on Buddhism.

We noted, however, in our Introduction that the Oxfordian theory is Anglo-American, and some of the chief books on the case have come from the United States. The best edition of Looney is the New York reprint of 1949, with an introduction by William McFee and afterwords and notes by Charles Wisner Barrell, himself author of *Elizabethan Mystery Man*. Mrs. Eva Turner Clark, author of *Axiophilus* (New York, 1926), organized an American branch of the Fellowship in 1939. Its present President is Dr. Louis P. Bénézet of Dartmouth College, author of *Shakspere, Shakespeare and de Vere* (Manchester, New Hampshire, 1937).

Such, in very brief outline, is the history of the Oxfordian theory—a twentieth-century 'Oxford' Movement—from its origins in 1918 to the present time. My procedure in this chapter is now to be twofold: first, I intend to give a summary of the Oxford case as originally put forward by Looney; and secondly, a brief survey of what has since been added by Looney's successors.

II

Looney, like Greenstreet and Pemberton, accepted the negative side of the Baconian case, agreeing that the actor William Shakespeare could not possibly have written the plays. A schoolmaster at Gateshead, he was used to reading Shakespeare with his class, particularly *The Merchant of Venice*. Continued study of this and other plays convinced him that the dramatist must have travelled in Italy, and he agreed with Greenwood and the Baconians that there was a painful contrast, most embarrassing to the orthodox position, between 'the coarse and illiterate circumstances of his [Shakespeare's] life and the highly cultured character of the work he is supposed to have produced' (*'Shakespeare' Identified*, p. 21).

Over the last hundred years there has developed a kind of 'orthodoxy' among unorthodox writers, one of the chief points being that every writer has to produce a list of essential qualifications for the task of writing the plays of Shakespeare. Looney was no exception to this rule, but he divided his list into two parts: first, some general features arising from a reading of the plays; and, secondly, some special characteristics.

First, wrote Looney, we may say of Shakespeare that he was (1) a matured man of recognized genius; (2) apparently eccentric and mysterious; (3) of intense sensibility, a man apart; (4) unconventional; (5) not adequately appreciated; (6) of pronounced literary tastes; (7) an enthusiast for the drama; (8) a lyric poet of recognized talent; and (9) of superior, classical education, the habitual associate of educated people (p. 92; compare Kent, p. 21).

Secondly, Looney wrote, to these nine points we may add the following: Shakespeare must have been (1) a man with feudal connections; (2) a member of the higher aristocracy; (3) connected with the House of Lancaster; (4) an enthusiast for Italy; (5) a follower of sport, including falconry; (6) a lover of music; (7) loose and improvident in money matters; (8) doubtful and somewhat conflicting in his attitude to women; and (9) of probable Catholic leanings, but touched with scepticism (p. 93 sq.; compare Slater, p. 50).

Contrary to the opinion of the Rutlandians, Looney laid special stress on the maturity of Shakespeare's works, including the very earliest. Demblon had thought the actor from Stratford far too old to have written the early works; Looney thought him far too *young*:

'We are asked to believe that a young man—William Shakspere was but 26 in the year 1590 which marks roughly the beginning of the Shakespearean period—began his career with the production of masterpieces without any apparent preparation, and kept pouring out plays spontaneously at a most amazing rate. He appears before us at the age of 29 as the author of a superb poem of no less than 1,200 lines and leaves no trace of those slight youthful effusions by means of which a poet learns his art and develops his powers' (p. 76).

Looney had as sound a reason for stressing the maturity of the early works as Demblon had for emphasizing their immaturity. The reason in both cases was the age of their respective candidates. We have seen that Rutland, born in 1576, was only 16 when the First Part of *King Henry the Sixth* was acted and not yet 17 when *Venus and Adonis* was published by Shakespeare's Stratford contemporary Richard Field. Oxford had been born as far back as 1550, and so was 43 when 'the first heir of my invention' was brought out. The fact that he died in 1604, before many of Shakespeare's best plays were written, is the most obvious point against the Oxfordian theory; how Looney and his successors get around this embarrassment will concern us in the corresponding chapter of the second part of this book.

In *The Unlifted Shadow* (1954), Miss Katharine E. Eggar observes:

'When he [Oxford] died in 1604, he left behind him not glory, but what was considered a stain on the family name: not fame, but an oath of concealment. What a struggle those in the secret were faced with! How to keep the young son and the great name isolated from the contamination of the public stage? How to be faithful to the Dead and yet preserve the inestimable treasure? It took nearly 20 years of love and toil to effect the rescue of the works— that is, to keep the secret and to give us the First Folio' (p. 8).

What concerns us more directly here is Looney's belief that *Venus and Adonis* was *not* the 'first heir' of Shakespeare's invention, that in fact it had been preceded by many lyric poems. Looney was not only a student of *The Merchant of Venice*; he had also studied Palgrave's *Golden Treasury*, and it was while doing so that he came across the lyric beginning 'If women could be fair, and yet not fond', the only poem Palgrave had included from the pen of Edward de Vere. This was the first time Looney had thought of Oxford as a possible candidate for the Shakespearean authorship, but now everything seemed to fit in, as closely and inevitably as Bacon to Baconians or Roger Manners to Rutlandians. This early poem and others like it—in 1921 Looney edited *The Poems of Edward de Vere*—were a sign, he believed, that the first productions of Shakespeare were not in reality the first fruits of their author. He further discovered that Oxford was well known as an amateur dramatist in London some years before Shakespeare arrived. He quotes Creizenach's *English Drama in the Age of Elizabeth* about the poet John Lyly,

'who found . . . effective patronage at the hands of the Earl of Oxford, who himself practised the dramatic art. By him Lyly was entrusted with the management of the troupe known as the "Oxford Boys", which was under his protection. It is probable that the players who had named their company after this nobleman publicly acted the plays written by their patron' (Quoted by Looney, p. 265.)

Compare this other quotation from the same German authority:

'Side by side with the poets who earned their living by composing dramas we may observe a few members of the higher aristocracy engaged in the task of writing plays for the popular stage, just as they tried their hands at other forms of poetry for the pure love of writing. But the number of these high-born authors is very small and their appearance is evanescent. Edward, Earl of Oxford, known chiefly as a lyric poet, is mentioned in Puttenham's *Art of English Poesie* as having earned, along with Edwards the choir-master, the highest commendation for comedy and interlude. Meres also praises him as being one of the best poets for comedy' (Quoted by Looney, pp. 265–6).

It is difficult for non-Oxfordians to reconcile this evidence of Oxford as a known writer for the public stage, which all Oxfordians consider one of their main points, with their equal insistence that he had to keep his 'great name isolated from the contamination of the public stage', as Miss Eggar has written. Whether Edwards the choir-master has ever been considered the author of Shakespeare's plays I have been unable to discover.

A lyric poet writing verse suspiciously like *Venus and Adonis*, and furthermore a patron of the stage whose company probably acted comedies of his own composition. And known in London some years before Shakespeare set foot there! Looney could hesitate no longer: after years of labour, he had found the true Shakespeare and he must announce the discovery to the world.

All the other 'qualifications' needless to say, Oxford had in abundance. His family 'traced its descent in a direct line from the Norman Conquest' and had connections with the House of Lancaster; he had the best education available, both privately and at

Cambridge; he was a well-travelled man, lampooned even as the 'Italianate Englishman'; he was noted in the State Papers at Rome as one of the English nobility 'of Catholic leanings'—in fact, as Looney is moved to exclaim: 'Everything fits in, in a most extraordinary manner.' A similar exclamation was made by Dr. Watson-Sykes when Mr. Sherlock Holmes proved conclusively that Shakespeare's works were written by Rutland.

Besides these general points, Looney believed he was able to prove Oxford's authorship by several points of detail. For instance, the plot of *All's Well That Ends Well* closely parallels a contemporary story about Oxford; * the story of *Hamlet*, of course, parallels the life of Oxford as closely as other theorists believe it to follow the lives of Raleigh, Derby, Rutland, etc.; and the *Sonnets* are not only autobiographical, their form was one which Oxford himself had invented. The sonnet by de Vere called *Love thy Choice* may be regarded, says Looney, as the first 'Shakespearean' sonnet (pp. 386-7).

Oxford assumed the mask of Shakespeare in 1593, compensating the actor very liberally for the use of his name. Will Shakspere, concludes Looney,

'might, if he were capable of apprizing the work justly, have felt honoured in being trusted by "Shakespeare" in furthering his literary purposes. But that he was himself the author of the great poems and dramas stands altogether outside the region of natural probabilities, and he must now yield for the adornment of a worthier brow the laurels he has worn so long' (p. 292).

Such, in brief, was the theory maintained by J. Thomas Looney. It remains for us to find out what additions have been made by his successors.

III

The chief supplementary point undoubtedly refers to Oxford's claim to have written the *Sonnets*. Several Oxfordians have made a special study of the question: the late Col. Ward in *The Mystery of Mr. W. H.* and Dr. Rendall in *Shakespeare's Sonnets and Edward*

---

* Looney, pp. 233-4, quotes Wright's *History of Essex*, Vol. II, p. 517: 'He [Oxford] forsook his lady's bed, [but] the father of Lady Anne by stratagem contrived that her husband should unknowingly sleep with her, believing her to be another woman, and she bore a son to him in consequence of this meeting.'

de Vere, books already mentioned; Charles Wisner Barrell in articles in the American Fellowship *News-Letter*; and G. W. Phillips in *Shake Spears Sonnets* (1954).

We observed in our Introduction that the Oxfordians have gone one better than the other theorists in their deductions from the fact that the name 'Shakespeare', like most other Elizabethan names, was spelt by contemporaries in a variety of different ways (see above, p. 19 sq.). Where Baconians and others have simply divided the actor-dramatist into two, the followers of Looney have found *three* Shakespeares, almost as many as King Richard found Richmonds at the Battle of Bosworth. The first, and least important, is Shakspere, the man from Stratford, whom the Oxfordians regard as a mere business man about the theatre, much as Cuthbert Burbage was in real life. The theory is advanced that the actor-gentleman Shakespeare was Sir Edward Vere, illegitimate son of the poet and dramatist Oxford (Shake-speare) by Anne Vavasour, Gentlewoman of the Queen's Bedchamber. This Sir Edward was himself the father of Sir William D'Avenant by a similar adventure on the wrong side of the blanket.*

It may be asked: what has all this to do with the *Sonnets*? To Oxfordians the connection is clear: they believe that it was to this illegitimate son that Oxford addressed them. Dr. Bénézet writes:

'A great many Shakespearean scholars are now convinced that Oxford's illegitimate son [was] the fair youth of the *Sonnets*, was an actor in his father's company of players, and furthermore they are practically certain that he passed under the name of William Shakespeare' (*Shakspere, Shakespeare and de Vere*, p. 25).

Col. Ward accepted Lee's opinion, first suggested by Mrs. Stopes, that the 'Mr. W. H.' of the publisher's dedication to the *Sonnets* was William Hall. He further discovered that this Hall was 'joyned in matrymonye' to Margery Gryffyn at Hackney Church about nine months before the *Sonnets* were entered on the Stationers' Registers (*The Mystery of Mr. W. H.*, pp. 20–1). In the year which saw the publication of the *Sonnets*, King's Place,

---

* For this last point, see the pamphlet by Phillips: 'I suggest that he was father of Sir William D'Avenant: for it seems clear that an illegitimate son of Mistress Davenant, wife of a vintner in Oxford, by Mr. William Shaksper, could never possibly have been received in high society. Mrs. Davenant, then, must have been only foster-mother to William, called D'Avenant—son to "mellifluous Shakespeare", grandson to De Vere' (p. 23).

Hackney, was sold by the widowed Countess of Oxford (the Earl's second wife) to Fulke Greville, later Lord Brooke. Col. Ward's contention was that Hall procured the manuscripts of the *Sonnets* from King's Place, before the transfer of the property, and sold them to the publisher Thomas Thorpe, who acknowledged the receipt by dedicating the poems to 'the onlie begetter'—that is, 'procurer', not 'inspirer', as so many have thought. The inspirer of most of the *Sonnets* was the author's illegitimate son; the inspirer of the 'dark lady' sequence was not Mary Fitton—who was, in any case, a blonde—but the author's mistress Anne Vavasour, who in her son 'called back the lovely April of her prime' (*The Mystery of Mr. W. H.*, p. 22 sq. Compare Allen, p. 140; Kent, p. 14).

There is some minor evidence also for Oxford's claim to the *Sonnets*, in particular the first line of Sonnet 125: 'Were't aught to me I bore the canopy', which Oxfordians believe is a reference to the duty of Oxford as hereditary Lord Great Chamberlain (a ceremonial office not to be confused with the government office of Lord Chamberlain) to bear the canopy, with the Earl Marshal, over the head of the Queen (See Slater, p. 184; Allen, p. 177; Bénézet, p. 24).

Col. Ward's son, Capt. B. M. Ward, followed the Oxfordian trail in a different direction. He made the discovery that Oxford was paid a salary of £1,000 a year, from the Secret Service Fund, from 1586 to his death in 1604. No information is given in any official document as to the services rendered by the Earl for this imposing salary, but Capt. Ward in his biography of Oxford suggests that it was payment for directing war propaganda, including the composition of Shakespeare's history plays. He developed the suggestion in several articles contributed to reviews in London and Paris.

It might be thought at first glance that a member of the ancient nobility like Oxford would be incapable of the warm sympathy for all classes and sorts of people that is so evident in Shakespeare's plays. But Capt. Ward points out that this is by no means the case. He quotes some lines written by the Earl in 1573, containing the stanza:

> The idle drone, that labours not at all,
>   Sucks up the sweet of honey from the bee;
> Who worketh most, to their share least doth fall,
>   With due desert reward will never be.

These lines, according to a remark by Capt. Ward to Gilbert Slater (*Seven Shakespeares*, p. 187 *note*), have convinced the Soviet Government that Oxford was Shakespeare.

The leader of the American Oxfordians, Dr. Bénézet, sums up the case by means of one of those lists which have become so 'orthodox' a proceeding for unorthodox theorists. He believes that the author of the Shakespeare plays and poems must have been (1) a student of the classics; (2) an aristocrat; (3) a soldier; (4) a student of law; (5) a musician; (6) one who had travelled in Italy; (7) connected with a Red Rose family; (8) careless in money matters; (9) known as a poet apart from 'the works of Shakespeare'; (10) interested in the theatre; (11) a man whose life fits the story in the *Sonnets*; (12) known as a playwright apart from 'the works of Shakespeare'; (13) a bearer of the canopy; and (14) a close associate of the Earl of Southampton.

Dr. Bénézet then proceeds to check various Shakespeare claimants—including Shakespeare himself—against these fourteen points, with the following not entirely unexpected results. Oxford comes out top of the class, gaining all 14 marks; then comes Derby with 8 (possibly 9); the Countess of Pembroke 7; Rutland and Marlowe 6 each: Raleigh 5; Bacon 4; and lastly Shakespeare 0 (possibly 1). The possibility in regard to Shakespeare refers to 'interested in the theatre'. I believe that in this instance Dr. Bénézet is on the right track.

CHAPTER X

FLORIO: MARLOWE: ELIZABETH

1927–1957

Ah good old Mantuan, I may speak of thee as the
traveller doth of Venice:
*Venetia, Venetia,
Chi non ti vede non ti pretia.*
SHAKESPEARE: *Love's Labour's Lost.*

I

Up till now the various candidates put forward as the real author
of Shakespeare's plays have all been as English as Shakespeare himself. The sole exception is the Earl of Stirling, who was born
across the border. But we are now confronted with the suggestion
that the real Shakespeare must have been an Italian.

The dramatist's apparent knowledge of Italy has always been
one of the chief cards in the unorthodox pack. Sometimes even
orthodox writers have become convinced that he must have known
the country at first hand. Brandes, for example, believed that his
knowledge was 'closer than could have been gained from oral
description and books'. In three articles in the *Nineteenth Century
& After*, Sir Edward Sullivan pointed out that what had been
hitherto taken as evidences of Shakespeare's ignorance of Italy
showed really the ignorance of his critics.[1]

Italian critics themselves have not, of course, been backward in
stressing Shakespeare's knowledge of their country. In his book
L'Italia nella Dramma inglese (Milan, 1925) Piero Rebora asserted
roundly that the poet 'possessed a profound knowledge of Italian
language and culture, of which he made an astonishing use in his
plays'. More recently, a book entitled *Shakespeare and Italy* has
been collected from the writings and lectures of the late Ernesto
Grillo, former Professor of Italian Language and Literature in the
University of Glasgow. Grillo says:

'It seems as if Shakespeare must somehow or other have learned
enough Italian to read and understand our writers. . . . It has been
argued that in Elizabethan England translations of Italian books

abounded, but certainly Shakespeare's knowledge of life and customs in Italy was not entirely derived from them.'

Grillo believed it possible that Shakespeare visited Italy in person, perhaps in the train of some nobleman between the autumn of 1592 and the summer of 1593, when the plague was in London.[2]

But the Italian professor thought it ridiculous to say that Shakespeare himself must have been an Italian. He refers to a group of writers who have

'arrived at the absurd conclusion that his dramas must have been written by men more learned than himself, and, in support of their theory, have put forward the name of Francis Bacon, without considering that this essayist could never claim to be either a poet or a dramatist.[3] More recently, other critics have asserted that most, if not all, of Shakespeare's plays were the work of Giovanni Florio, the translator of Montaigne and a teacher of Italian in London, the son of a Florentine reformer, who [the son, not the father] was a professor at Oxford during the latter part of the sixteenth century. But to anyone in the least familiar with the works of our English poet the opinions of these critics are without justification and utterly ridiculous' (p. 89).

'The son, not the father,' I have ventured to interpolate, in the interests of clarity. But in truth both Florios have been advanced as the real author of Shakespeare's plays. The first to put forward a claim for John Florio appears to have been Erik Reger, in an article entitled 'Der Italiener Shakespeare' contributed during 1927 to the *Deutsche Allgemeine Zeitung*. The elder Florio, Michele Angelo, was first suggested by Santi Paladino in his book *Shakespeare sarebbe il pseudonimo di un Poeta Italiano*, published at Reggio in 1929. It is the latter theory, not the former, which has been taken up recently by Dr. Carlo Villa of Trieste in a book not yet published.*

The case for John Florio is, of course, based upon his connections with the Earl of Southampton, Shakespeare's first patron; on his well-known role as interpreter of Italian life and culture to Oxford students and Londoners of the upper and middle classes; and on the apparent intimacy with that life and culture revealed in the

---

* This book by Dr. Villa has been announced in advance to the Italian and world Press. See a short article, entitled 'Signor Bard', in the *Daily Telegraph*, 12 October 1956.

Shakespeare plays. The case for the elder Florio is less obvious and must be summarized at greater length. Let us take first the theory put forward by Signor Paladino in 1929.

The Italian critic gives to Michele Angelo Florio not only all the works of Shakespeare but also *I secondi frutti* (1591), the collection of Italian phrases and proverbs—from which Shakespeare may have quoted in *Love's Labour's Lost* and *The Taming of the Shrew*—which had hitherto been regarded as the work of John Florio. The elder Florio died as early as 1605, and perhaps it was Signor Paladino's contention that the manuscripts of such plays as *Antony* and *Coriolanus* were edited for the stage by the younger Florio, who lived till 1625. To this limited extent Signor Paladino's is a Dual Theory.

Dr. Villa's theory is more ambitious, the product, he assures us, of thirty years' work. Compared with Dr. Villa, the Oxfordians are cautious in their attempts to alter the chronology of Shakespeare's plays in order to fit an author who died too soon. The Italian critic goes the whole hog, maintaining that *Molto Traffico per Niente*—better known in England as *Much Ado About Nothing*—was performed at Messina in 1572, when Shakespeare of Stratford was a child of eight.

Not that Dr. Villa ignores Stratford in the manner of the Baconians. On the contrary: he believes that when Michele Angelo Florio fled to England in 1576, after his father, a Calvinist minister, had been killed by the Catholics, he went to live with his late mother's family, the Crollolanzas of Stratford-on-Avon, who had already taken the English version of their name—Shakespeare. They had lost their own son, whose name was William, and so were only too glad to adopt in his place the young dramatist Michele Angelo, who was eventually to adopt the son's English name as the author of the plays.

The complications are rather difficult to grasp. But Dr. Villa thinks them nothing beside the difficulties of the traditional case, which sees as the author of plays so intimately Italian as *Romeo* and *Othello* an actor who cannot be proved to have ever left England in his life. I await Dr. Villa's book with great interest and hope that it will eventually be translated into the great dramatist Florio's foster-tongue.

II

The title of the present work reflects the urge of most un-orthodox theorists to give the plays and poems commonly attri-buted to Shakespeare to some member or group of members of the Elizabethan nobility. When we come to one of the most recent attributions, however—that which gives Shakespeare to Christo-pher Marlowe (1564-93)—we seem to have come back to where we started from. For Marlowe was born into much the same social class as Shakespeare himself, being the son of a master shoemaker of Canterbury who, like Shakespeare's father, had married above his station. But whereas Shakespeare and Jonson, so far as is known, never attended a university,[4] Marlowe was certainly at Benet College, Cambridge—now Corpus Christi—from 1580 to about 1587. A portrait recently discovered at Corpus—the only probable portrait of Marlowe in existence—embellishes the jacket of Calvin Hoffman's book.

This book, *The Man Who Was Shakespeare* (1955), is the first attempt to prove that Marlowe wrote all the works credited to Shakespeare, though Mr. Hoffman's fellow-American Zeigler in *It was Marlowe: A Story of the Secret of Three Centuries* (1895) had given him the leading role in a Group Theory (see above, p. 44). He was also one of Slater's *Seven Shakespeares*, and other critics, both orthodox (like Robertson) and unorthodox (like Standen), had given him a share in the works.

Slater wrote:

'It is an old suggestion that Christopher Marlowe might have been Shakespeare. The reasons are obvious. Marlowe disappears mysteriously in 1593, various stories obtaining currency with re-gard to his real, supposed or alleged death; in the same year the name of "Shakespeare" first appears . . .' (*Seven Shakespeares*, p. 127).

Mr. Hoffman makes the hypothesis which Slater also had declared to be a reasonable one. 'The only hypothesis which still remains open is, it seems to me, that it was not the manner of Marlowe's death that was faked, but the death itself.' So wrote Slater, and Mr. Hoffman's book stands or falls by this argument.

Fundamentally, that is to say. Naturally Mr. Hoffman has some minor points in support. He refers, for instance, to the strong

resemblance between Marlowe's acknowledged plays and those of
Shakespeare's earliest period and to the fact that several times
Shakespeare quotes Marlowe; he also refers to an article by
Thomas Corwin Mendenhall, a professor in Ohio who had devised
a method by which the style of authors could be detected by
mechanical means. He was asked by a wealthy Baconian to prove
by this method that Bacon wrote Shakespeare. But the result
proved the opposite. It was found that Shakespeare's vocabulary
consisted of words averaging four letters and that the words used
with greatest frequency were also four-lettered. Bacon's graph
showed constant use of much longer words. But, Mr. Hoffman
adds, Marlowe's vocabulary agreed with Shakespeare's (*The Man
Who Was Shakespeare*, p. 158 sq.). I must say that this result was
only to be expected, as both Marlowe and Shakespeare wrote
mainly plays for public performance, whereas Bacon wrote mainly
learned philosophical and legal works for private reading by a small
minority of scholarly people.

I have not myself made any special study of the circumstances
of Marlowe's death—fully documented in such books as Dr.
Hotson's *The Death of Christopher Marlowe* and John Bakeless's
The Tragicall History of Christopher Marlowe. I am more interested in discovering the reasons why—*supposing* Marlowe's
death to have been faked—Mr. Hoffman thinks that he, rather than
Shakespeare, must have written the plays.

It seems to be primarily a question of the university education
we have referred to. Mr. Hoffman believes that 'The public
supply of books . . . was meagre . . . Books and free access to
books were an impossibility for the average Elizabethan' (p. 25).
Jonson, of course, was not a university man either, but he was
under the great scholar Camden at Westminster School—and Mr.
Hoffman, in any case, does not think very highly of Jonson. He
asks: 'Was Jonson sincere when he wrote of the First Folio author?
It is my belief that he was not . . . Jonson's hypocrisy was truly
odious . . . [He] was a literary mercenary, hired to commend . . .
Jonson would have written anything for money' (p. 214 sq.).

There is also the question of travel. Mr. Hoffman agrees with
previous theorists that Shakespeare's plays show an acquaintance
with French and Italian life that the dramatist could not have derived from books, even if they were more accessible than he believes they were. There is no evidence that Marlowe travelled

on the Continent during the commonly-accepted short duration of his life, but if, as Mr. Hoffman believes, he was not really killed in 1593, then it is reasonable to assume that he must have fled from his enemies abroad. That he had enemies is a fact, and Mr. Hoffman believes he had also powerful friends, in particular Sir Thomas Walsingham, cousin of Sir Francis.

Sir Thomas Walsingham, Mr. Hoffman believes, was Marlowe's lifelong patron, friend, and lover: the subject of the *Sonnets*, dedicated to 'Mr. W.H.'—that is, Walsing-ham (p. 139 sq.). And here we get the solution to a mystery that must have puzzled many readers of the Press during the spring of 1955. It was reported that the Walsingham tomb at Chislehurst, Kent, was about to be opened, at Mr. Hoffman's instigation, to see if any documents concerning Marlowe's authorship of Shakespeare might possibly have been buried there. In the event, the tomb was found empty; but what many people must have asked themselves was this: what connection had the Walsingham family with Shakespeare? None at all, of course, if we hold the opinion that Shakespeare was Shakespeare, but a most intimate connection, Mr. Hoffman believes, if we hold that he was Marlowe. It was to Sir Thomas Walsingham, on this ingenious theory, that Marlowe not only dedicated the *Sonnets* but entrusted the 'Shakespeare' plays which he had written abroad.

III

In this History section of our book I believe we have proved what we wrote in the Introduction: that few members of the Elizabethan nobility have not been credited with at least a share in the works of Shakespeare.

But it may be objected that one august name, the greatest of all, is missing. If the courtiers around the throne were capable of writing Shakespeare, why not the Queen herself? It is true we have the word of Slater that among the hypothetical Shakespeares the name of Queen Elizabeth has indeed been suggested, but I have failed to find any evidence for this theory before 1956 or for that other theory, mentioned by M. Connes, that gives Shakespeare to Richard Barnfield (except in an article on the secret ciphers of this minor poet which appeared in *Notes and Queries*, 14 September 1901). I accept, of course, the word of Slater and Connes that both theories have been advanced.

So far as I am concerned, therefore, the year 1956 is the year of
the Elizabethan Theory, and it comes remarkably apt as the fitting
conclusion to this History section of our book. If the advocates of
this theory had known I was writing this History, they could not
have managed their publication at a more convenient time.

It is an Anglo-American theory, put forward in two books, one
a serious study, the other a very entertaining novel. The serious
study is *Shake-speare the Mystery* by George Elliott Sweet, published at Stanford, California. The novel is *The Stuffed Swan* by
John Appleby, published in London.

The Queen died in 1603, but her name is still given to the period
of literature which lasted until about 1610–20. Mr. Sweet could
not, of course, similarly extend the Queen's lifetime to fit those
plays of Shakespeare that were written under King James, so he is
forced, like Dr. Villa and the Oxfordians, to alter the chronology
as well as the author. He postulates a Shakespeare period running
from 1579 to 1603, with *Hamlet* as the last play to be written. This
is also the theory advanced by Mr. Appleby, with his tongue firmly
in his cheek. The heroine in his novel comes into possession of a
sheet of manuscript written by the Queen; it is part of a letter to
William Shakespeare, and runs in modern spelling:

'. . . the remembrance of the public favour should not be forgotten.
Therefore on Sunday night our messenger will deliver to you most
secretly the play which has long been near to our heart and which,
as heretofore, is to be made public by you under your own hand.
We therefore look to you, Master Will, to copy it with all diligence
and present it to Master Burbage. The title is *Hamlet, Prince of
Denmark*, a tale much tinged with melancholy, for which reason it
may soon be forgotten. It is surely . . .' (p. 31).

The case for the Queen's authorship of Shakespeare is, of course,
as fundamentally sound—or as fundamentally unsound—as any
of the previous cases that have been advanced. Which may have
been the intended moral of Mr. Appleby's novel. Mr. Sweet can
certainly point to the Queen's mastery of politics and profound
acquaintance with courtly life; her interest in the stage, her love
and knowledge of music, her Renaissance culture in general.
That she was never a soldier is as evident as the fact that Shakespeare of Stratford was never a woman, but the feminine parts of
the plays are at least as extensive as the military, and it would surely

have been easier for the Queen to gather some details of the military art from Essex or Raleigh than for Shakespeare to imagine himself a member of the opposite sex. . . .

And so we come to the end of this History section of our book. We can go no higher in the social scale than Queen Elizabeth, but this is not to say that the year 1957 sees the end of all our Shakespeares. I do not think for a moment that this will be so. It is not for the author of *A Short History of the Future* to attempt to prophesy on his own account, but I hold the opinion that one Shakespeare often leads to another. We have been given a Shakespeare Regina; why not a Shakespeare Rex? King James was even more interested in the stage than Elizabeth was, and in fact made the company to which Shakespeare belonged the King's Men; why should it not have acted the King's Plays? James, furthermore, was an authority on witches, so who more likely to write *Macbeth*, set in his native Scotland? He was of pronounced homosexual tendencies, so who more likely—on one reading of these poems—to write the *Sonnets*? He was a scholar and a theologian, his name being immortalized in the Authorized Version of the Bible—as perhaps it will one day become immortalized in the First Folio as well. In fact, for ten guineas per thousand words, payable in advance, I will undertake to prove to all but the hopelessly prejudiced that King James—or, alternatively, Fulke Greville or Sir Thomas North—was the real author of the works erroneously attributed to William Shakespeare of Stratford-on-Avon.

NOTES

1. See 'Shakespeare and the Waterways of North Italy' and 'Shakespeare and Italy' in the *Nineteenth Century and After*, August 1908, January–February 1918. Compare Karl Elze, '*Italienische Skizzen zu Shakespeare*'; Theodore Elze, '*Bellario und die Studenten in Padua*'; Julius Zuputza, '*Ueber die Fabel in Shakespeare's "Two Gentlemen"* '; and G. Sarrazin, '*Shakespeare in Mantua*'; in *Shakespeare-Jahrbuch*, Leipzig, 1873, 1878, 1888 and 1894 respectively.

2. *Shakespeare and Italy* (Glasgow, 1949), pp. 125 sq., 132 sq. Compare Connes: 'Shakespeare's Italianism has recently had much light thrown upon it by Mme. de Chambrun's study of John Florio, the Earl of Southampton's Italian tutor, and author of dictionaries, collections of proverbs and guides to conversation, for the use of English noblemen [and others], in common use in England about 1600. The fact of the existence of these books by Florio, and their general use, is sufficient to dissipate the illusions of those people who would have us believe that Shakespeare must have visited Italy in person' (*The Shakespeare Mystery*, p. 277).

3. Compare the exclamation of Peter Alvor: '*Bacon, der Philosoph, ein Dichter! Der Dichter König!*' (*Das Neue Shakespeare–Evangelium*, 2nd ed., p. 1.)

4. Mr. Sykes observes: 'He [Shakespeare] might have gone to Cambridge. Lack of means was no bar to a university education. All Europe was full of poor scholars, and if Ben Jonson, the bricklayer's son, and Kit Marlowe, the cobbler's son, could study at Cambridge, why not Will Shakespeare, the butcher's son?' (*Alias William Shakespeare?*, p. 47). Jonson was not a bricklayer's son but a minister's son whose widowed mother married a bricklayer. There is no evidence that he studied at Cambridge; on the contrary, his step-father put him to his own trade after he left Westminster School and as late as 1598 he was still officially listed as 'citizen and bricklayer of London' (Marchette Chute, *Ben Jonson of Westminster*, p. 37; *Shakespeare of London*, p. 176).

PART TWO

CRITICISM

There is, I fear, a prosaic set growing up among us, editors of booklets, book-worms, index-hunters, or men of great memories and no imagination, who *impute themselves* to the poet, and so believe that *he*, too, has no imagination, but is for ever poking his nose between the pages of some old volume in order to see what he can appropriate. They will not allow one to say 'Ring the bell' without finding that we have taken it from Sir P. Sidney, or even to use such a simple expression as the ocean 'roars' without finding out the precise verse in Homer or Horace from which we have plagiarized it.

TENNYSON: Letter to FitzGerald

It is not in his personal emotions, the emotions provoked by particular events in his life, that the poet is in any way remarkable or interesting. His particular emotions may be simple, or crude, or flat. The emotion in his poetry will be a very complex thing, but not with the complexity of the emotions of people who have very complex or unusual emotions in life . . . The business of the poet is not to find new emotions, but to use the ordinary ones and, in working them up into poetry, to express feelings which are not in actual emotions at all. And emotions which he has never experienced will serve his turn as well as those familiar to him.

T. S. ELIOT: *Tradition and the Individual Talent*

CHAPTER I

THE GENERAL THEORY CONSIDERED

A third is like the former . . . A fourth? . . .
What, will the line stretch out to th' crack of doom?—
Another yet?—A seventh?—I'll see no more:—
And yet the eighth appears, who bears a glass
Which shows me many more.
                              SHAKESPEARE: *Macbeth.*

I

Those who have read the first part of this book will have become
aware that neither the four Shakespeares of Connes nor the seven
Shakespeares of Slater exhaust the full possibilities of the unorthodox approach. Not four Shakespeares only, nor yet seven,
have been advanced by the ingenuity of the unorthodox, but more
than fifty different Shakespeares—or more than one Shakespeare
for each of the plays and poems. If we can believe the writers
whose views have been summarized in the preceding pages, the
works of Shakespeare were written by the following people, either
singly or in various combinations: Francis Bacon, Lord Verulam;
Anthony Bacon; Sir John Barnard or Bernard; Barnabe Barnes;
Richard Barnfield; Richard Burbage; Robert Burton; William
Butts; Robert Cecil, Earl of Salisbury; Henry Chettle; Samuel
Daniel; Thomas Dekker; William Stanley, Earl of Derby; Lord
Mountjoy, Earl of Devonshire; John Donne, Dean of St. Paul's;
Thomas Sackville, Lord Buckhurst, Earl of Dorset; Michael
Drayton; Sir Edward Dyer; Queen Elizabeth; Walter Devereux,
first Earl of Essex; Robert Devereux, second Earl of Essex; Henry
Ferrers; John Fletcher; Michele Angelo Florio; John Florio;
Robert Greene; Bartholomew Griffin; Thomas Heywood; Ben
Jonson; Thomas Kyd; Thomas Lodge; John Lyly; Christopher
Marlowe; Thomas Middleton; Anthony Munday; Thomas
Nashe; Edward de Vere, Earl of Oxford; Henry, Lord Paget;
George Peele; Mary Sidney, Countess of Pembroke; William
Herbert, Earl of Pembroke; Henry Porter; Sir Walter Raleigh;
Roger Manners, Earl of Rutland; Elizabeth Sidney, Countess of
Rutland; Sir Anthony Shirley; Sir Philip Sidney; Wentworth

Smythe; Henry Wriothesley, Earl of Southampton; Edmund
Spenser; Sir William Alexander, Earl of Stirling; William Warner
or Walker; Thomas Watson; John Webster; Anne Whateley;
Robert Wilson; Cardinal Wolsey; the Ancient, Mystic Order
Rosae Crucis; and the Jesuits.*

It is an impressive list, both in its length and in the high society
in which many of the candidates moved. A super-Group-Theorist
might claim that each candidate wrote either one of the plays or
poems or else half-a-dozen of the *Sonnets*. He would doubtless
give *Hamlet* to Rutland, *The Tempest* to Raleigh, *Richard the
Second* to the second Earl of Essex, *The Merchant of Venice* to
Michele Angelo Florio, *Measure for Measure* to Anne Whateley,
Henry the Eighth to Queen Elizabeth, *Macbeth* to Stirling, *The
Rape of Lucrece* to the Jesuits, and so forth. But those of the unorthodox who do not see that way out of their difficulties must
admit that the list is a little *too* impressive, a little *too* lengthy, to be
altogether convincing. If the unorthodox have quarrelled amongst
themselves to such an alarming extent, then the thought must arise
that perhaps Shakespeare wrote his own plays after all.

Consider for a moment some of the remarks that have been
made by one set of theorists about another. We have quoted some
examples of the abuse bestowed by the unorthodox upon William
Shakespeare of Stratford (see above, p. 51), but this is entirely
perfunctory compared with the irritation felt by the advocates of
one hypothetical Shakespeare for the advocates of another hypothetical Shakespeare. It must, indeed, be rather hard, after you
have successfully undermined the Stratfordian position in favour
of the Earl of A., to find that another writer has blown up Shagsper in order to place in the niche of fame Lord B. or the Countess
of C. In these matters, as in some others, it is easy to love our
enemies, but so difficult to forgive our friends.

'The Oxford case, no less than the Stratford one, rests on a
series of impossibilities and improbabilities that verge on the
miraculous' (a Baconian, Alfred Dodd); 'Unfortunately, what

---

* One single Rosicrucian theory, it should be added, brings in almost as many.
According to Dr. W. M. Cunningham, the distinguished American economist,
the works of Shakespeare were written by a group of Freemasons including
Bacon, Sir Tobie Mathew, Sir Miles and Sir Thomas Bodley, Sir Henry Wotton,
Sir Thomas More, Sir Francis Drake, Edmund Spenser, Sir Walter Raleigh, and
Lancelot Andrewes, Bishop of Winchester. (See *The Tragedy of Sir Francis
Bacon, Prince of England:* Los Angeles, 1940.)

should have been a scientific inquiry fell into the hands of un-disciplined and emotional lunatics. They were known generically as Baconians' (an Oxfordian, William McFee); 'Bacon's author-ship becomes yet more wildly impossible when we come to the group of political plays' (a Rutlandian, Claud W. Sykes); 'Of other hypothetical Shakespeares who have been put forward, a certain Earl of Rutland would have deserved serious consideration, had he been as able a writer as was his father-in-law, Sidney' (a Baconian, E. W. Smithson); 'The Derby theory arose from the fact that in 1599 the Earl of Derby had been occupied in "penning" plays, whilst nothing is known of his composing them' (the instigator of the Oxfordian case, J. Thomas Looney); 'The facts of incom-patibility which exclude him [Oxford] are decisive' (a Derbyite, A. W. Titherley).[1]

Judging by such remarks as these, it might be thought that those of us who believe the traditional authorship to be correct have nothing to do but wait upon the sidelines till the battle of the un-orthodox amongst themselves is over. When they have finally adopted one single candidate, or one group of candidates, by unanimous vote, there will be time for us to listen to what they have to say. . . .

Yet this is not altogether the case. For among all the quarrels of unorthodoxy, one voice is very nearly unanimous already. And that is the voice which asserts that the works of Shakespeare could have been written only by an aristocrat or with aristocratic assist-ance. In that illusion the Baconian rests contentedly with the Oxfordian, the Rutlandian with the supporter of Derby or Raleigh or Lord Knows Who, the advocate of a single candidate with the supporter of a group. The great majority of all unorthodox theories rest upon this aristocratic assumption, and where it is absent its place is usually filled by the equally invalid assumption that the works could only have been written by a university graduate. Many theories, as we have seen, combine the two.

My procedure in this critical part of my book will, therefore, be as follows. In this first chapter I shall discuss the aristocratic assumption, because that seems to me the central issue. Once prove—as it is very easy to prove—upon what false notions this aristocratic assumption rests, and the way is clear for a considera-tion of the comparatively minor issues. Some of these will be con-sidered in relation to a particular candidate, as the question of law in regard to Bacon; but what I shall say in these chapters about one theory will, of course, apply to a good many others. If we are to avoid needless repetition, some such procedure must be adopted.

II

The aristocratic assumption is based upon a false view of the English Renaissance, a view which is bound up with a misreading of the relations between noble patronage and professional genius. To anyone who is aware of the true relations, some of the remarks made by unorthodox theorists must seem rather extravagant.

For instance, Dr. Bénézet, one of the leading Oxfordians, informs us that the young Edward de Vere was 'endowed with musical, poetic and dramatic powers beyond those of any Englishman of his time' (*Shakspere, Shakespeare and de Vere*, pp. 16–17). Such a statement is truly breath-taking. Passing over the 'poetic and dramatic', as being the question about to be discussed at length, what can we possibly say of that claim for Oxford's musical powers save that it betrays an ignorance of music which is regrettable in a university don? The Elizabethan–Jacobean period was the greatest period of English music, an age in which composers like Byrd, Dowland, Farnaby, Weelkes, Wilbye, Bull, Campion, and Gibbons were all working. Wilfrid Mellers, composer and music critic, says that 'the achievement of the Elizabethans and Jacobeans in music is strictly comparable with their achievement in literature . . . The Elizabethan and Jacobean age is . . . one of the greatest epochs in the history of European music' ('Words and Music in Elizabethan England', *Pelican Guide to English Literature*, Vol. 2, p. 386). Compare the same author's *Music and Society*, and Eric Blom's *Music in England*. Mr. Blom calls the Elizabethan era 'England's most glorious musical period' (p. 41).

William Byrd, usually considered the greatest Elizabethan composer, was born seven years before Oxford but was still a young man when Oxford was young. He was a distinguished composer during the period when Dr. Bénézet claims that de Vere was 'endowed with musical powers beyond those of any Englishman of his time'. If this is the case, then Dr. Bénézet has performed a notable service: he has discovered an Elizabethan composer greater than Byrd, greater than Dowland, greater than Bull. He has only to continue, and tell us exactly which of Oxford's compositions he is thinking of, and we shall all be able to share in the discovery. . . .

That Oxford, like many nobles of the time, was a distinguished amateur in music there is no doubt; but this is a very different thing from implying that he was superior in this field to professional composers. In a list of Elizabethan–Jacobean composers, neither Oxford nor his son-in-law Derby [2] would figure in the first fifty names; and they occupy, I believe, a similar lowly position in any list that might be drawn up of Elizabethan poets and dramatists.

Do I, therefore, deny the contribution of the aristocracy to the English Renaissance? I do nothing of the kind. In fact, it seems to me that it is the Oxfordians and other theorists who are in danger of denying the very real contribution of the Court and nobility to our Golden Age of Music and Poetry in their uncomprehending attempts to claim the entire credit on their behalf. *If* the aristocratic contribution had been the only one, then the summit of our Elizabethan music would not have been the compositions of Byrd and Dowland and their fellow-professionals, it would have been the amateur efforts of noblemen like Derby. Leaving Shakespeare aside for the moment, the summit of our Elizabethan literature would not have been the plays of Marlowe and Jonson, nor even Spenser's *Fairie Queene*—for Spenser, while connected with the nobility, was not an aristocrat himself but a civil servant—it would have been Sidney's *Arcadia*.

Music and literature are the products of individual genius, but also of certain circumstances in national and international life. It is when we consider the social and cultural circumstances of the Elizabethan age that we can give full credit to the Court and nobility. Not, however, to the Court and nobility alone; for it is a misreading of cultural history to assume that their contribution was the only one or even that it was the most important. The culture of the age was fed by three sources, each being as important as the others.

The contribution we can consider first was made by the Court, the Church, and the nobility—the upper ranks of government, clerical and lay.[3] Byrd became a gentleman of the Chapel Royal in 1569; many other professional composers owed part of their opportunity to similar Court or Church offices, or to private patronage as tutors in great nobles' houses. These nobles also had their own libraries, and many a poor scholar was grateful for being permitted to use them. A great part of the nation's money found its way into the pockets of the nobility, sometimes by legal robbery, such as the Queen's granting of monopolies and patents to her favourites of the moment. But some of this money was returned to the nation in other ways, by the expenditure of the nobility on cultural and educational pursuits. The greatest architect of the age, the former joiner's apprentice Inigo Jones, son of a cloth-worker, came under the patronage of the Earl of Pembroke, who sent him to study in Italy. Many other examples could be mentioned.

In regard to dramatic literature, the chief contribution of the Court and nobility lay in their protection of professional players and playwrights against the opposition of the City of London. There were, of course, many amateur productions, as well as professional, at Court, in country houses, at the universities and Inns of Court; but these amateur efforts, while being important in the development of the English drama, were not so important as the popular and professional side.

The greatest works of the age, in music and literature alike, were the result of a combination of continental with native culture. Our second contribution, therefore, is at the other end of the social scale, in such things as folk-songs and dances, and in that vigour of common speech which makes the best plays of the professional dramatists so much more potent an artistic experience than the best of the university and country-house dramas. In a play by Marlowe or Shakespeare or Jonson, the metaphorical life of the language comes directly from the speech of the common people, as actually spoken in farm and street, as 'folk-songs could be used by learned composers in their motets and masses without any feeling of selfconsciousness' (Mellers, *loc. cit.*, p. 387). Languages are not suddenly 'invented', as the Baconians seem to imagine;[4] they are the product of traditional use, of centuries of actual speech by ordinary people. Behind the Shakespearean drama there lies, not only the aristocratic and classical drama of the Court and universities, but—and much more important—the popular and religious dramas of the fifteenth century.

The third contribution I speak of is the contribution of the professionals, the people who actually composed the music, who wrote the literature, who painted the pictures, who designed the buildings, and carved the sculptures on them. They owed much to the patronage of Court and Church, much also to the folk-culture of the time, allied as it was with the more humble of the arts and crafts. Who, then, were these professionals?

They appear to have come from every class in society, with the exception of the nobility. Particularly did they come from the middle classes, both the more prosperous upper ranks of this class —the merchants, the lawyers, and so on—and the more humble lower-middle class of small masters and craftsmen, such as were the fathers of Marlowe, Shakespeare, Webster, Harvey, Greene, Stow, Burbage, Chettle, Alleyn, Speed, Walton, and Chapman, and the step-father of Jonson. Biographical details of the Eliza-bethan composers arc unfortunately lacking in most cases: we know that the greatest of the madrigal composers, John Wilbye, was the son of a tanner, but we know little or nothing of the personal background of Byrd, Dowland, and most of the others. But the very fact that we know nothing proves that they could not have been of noble birth, for records of great families are extant. Presumably some of the Elizabethan composers, like composers in every age and country, sprang from families of professional musicians. Music runs in families to a much greater extent than literature: we have a Bach, a Mozart and a Haydn family but not a Shakespeare or a Molière family.

Three contributions, then, all of equal importance, and the nobility playing the greatest part in only one: that is surely the truth, so far as it can be summarized in a brief space, about Eliza-bethan culture. If it seems disappointing to those modern people who would prefer to believe that Elizabethan culture was pre-dominantly aristocratic, they must remember that no nobleman of the age ever claimed to have composed the masses of Byrd, the madrigals of Wilbye or the plays of Shakespeare. Some of them could have claimed with truth that they *protected* the public stage against its Puritan and commercial enemies, that they *aided* archi-tects like Jones to study abroad, that they *recommended* Spenser and many others to posts under Government, that they *helped* the professionals in every way they could and to a degree that has justly won them the acclaim of succeeding generations. But they did not claim to be professionals themselves. It was left to Dr. Bénézet to claim for Oxford that he possessed greater musical powers than Byrd or Dowland, it was left to Durning-Lawrence to claim that Bacon wrote most of the literature of the age. Such claims would have been regarded with derision by those on whom they were foisted.

The 'social handbook' of the sixteenth century—so we can call it—was Count Baldassare Castiglione's *Il Cortegiano*, published in 1528 and translated by Sir Thomas Hoby under the title of *The Book of the Courtier* (1561). That useful manual instructed the nobility of Europe in the proper way to behave, including the proportion of time and attention they should give to various pursuits. It was particularly stressed that they should not devote too much attention to any one pursuit, lest they be mistaken for a professional —like Titian or Byrd or Shakespeare. The ideal aimed at was to have a smattering of everything, but not too much of any one. (See a witty article by the late Dr. Wilhelm Schenk, 'The *Cortegiano* and the Civilization of the Renaissance', *Scrutiny*, Cambridge, June 1949.)

This manual, which had a great influence in England on Italianate courtiers like Oxford, helped to form the cult of the dilettante. But we must remember that this had its better as well as its sillier side. The culture of the Elizabethan aristocrat, at its rare best— such as we see in Sir Henry Wotton—was truly universal. While the courtier could not hope to rival the professional in his own field, even if he had wanted to, he often knew more about the other arts than a professional who had devoted his life to one. What did the Earl of Pembroke know about architecture? Probably not as much as Inigo Jones's little finger. But he may well have had the acquaintance which Jones lacked in many other matters.

It was on this better side of the dilettante cult that the seed of patronage sprouted. Those noblemen who were cultured were cultured in many different fields, and thus were ideally suited to become the patrons of professional men in all the arts. They could not themselves compete with Jones or Byrd or Shakespeare, any more than the Medicis or the Popes had competed with Michelangelo and Raphael, or François I had done Jean Clouet's work for him. But their cultural range was wide enough, their sympathies were sufficiently broad, for them to appreciate what the professionals had to offer—whether it was a building by Jones, a song by Dowland, or a play by Shakespeare. They themselves practised most of the arts, with professional assistance, but they did not foresee a time when they—the kindly patrons, the enthusiastic amateurs—would be credited with the masterpieces of their 'servants', the professionals. I believe it is as well for the officials of the Shakespeare Fellowship that the Earl of Oxford is safely dead, for they would be in some danger of being run through if they insulted the Earl in person by suggesting he had written Shakespeare's plays. For a courtier brought up on Castiglione, a greater insult could hardly be imagined.

II

What, then, has persuaded so many people, not all of them in the ranks of the unorthodox, that Shakespeare's plays were either written by a courtier or by someone else with an intimate knowledge of Courts and upper-class life? The first answer is given by Henry Pemberton, a writer who—as we have seen—supported Sir Walter Raleigh for the authorship:

'Every one of his plays *The Merry Wives of Windsor* excepted—is either placed immediately in the Court, or else portrays Court life through the introduction of Lords, Dukes, and other noblemen. I doubt if there can be found in any instance a breach of what may be termed the technical etiquette of Court life, as depicted in these dramas . . . and invariably the language given to these Kings, Princes and noblemen is peculiarly appropriate' (*Shakspere and Sir Walter Ralegh*, pp. 4–5).

Dr. Titherley agrees: 'No author ever moved so easily among Kings, Princes, Dukes and Noblemen' (*Shakespeare's Identity*, p. 4). A whole host of unorthodox opinion concurs, including books already cited by Alvor, Durning-Lawrence, Sykes, Standen, Greenwood, Bénézet, Stotsenburg, Johnson, and numerous others.

The immediate question we must naturally ask these critics is: how do they know? What intimate acquaintance with sixteenth-century Court life did Pemberton possess, that led him to be so certain that Shakespeare also possessed it? Dr. Titherley was formerly Lecturer in Organic Chemistry at the University of Liverpool, and in anything to do with his own field of science I would accept his opinion unhesitatingly. But I cannot accept his opinion on Shakespeare's intimate acquaintance with Court life until I know what acquaintance with Elizabethan Court life he himself possesses. He must have a standard of intimacy by which to

I

measure Shakespeare's intimacy; what I want to know is how on earth he has got hold of it. It must be a miraculous laboratory indeed in which Dr. Titherley is enabled to make such measurements.

The truth is, of course, that Dr. Titherley, like Pemberton and the rest, knows as much as I know about Court life in Shakespeare's time—which is very little, as little as was known by the orthodox scholar, Prof. Herford, when he once wrote that 'Shakespeare was the first master of the language of polished and astute debate, of high-bred conversation, of courtly ceremony'. A few memoirs have come down to us; we can read the official documents and also idealistic portrayals of Court life like Castiglione's. But when we have explored the entire field, our knowledge will remain very meagre. How kings and queens spoke among themselves, what was the behaviour of great nobles in off-duty moments: these are matters on which the most learned historian must confess his almost total ignorance. And these are just the matters in which Shakespeare excels—or seems to excel.

What standard of comparison, then, have critics like Pemberton and Dr. Titherley taken? Where have they drawn their seemingly intimate knowledge of Elizabethan Court life by which they have measured Shakespeare's seeming intimacy? There can be only one answer: they have drawn their knowledge—*from Shakespeare's plays*. It is by the standard of the plays of Shakespeare themselves that they have measured Shakespeare's intimacy with Court life! We can all agree that by *theatrical* standards Shakespeare's knowledge of Court life was reasonably great, if not so great as Webster's.

John Webster was the son of a tailor, and it is doubtful whether he ever left England in his life. Yet his most famous plays, *The White Devil* and *The Duchess of Malfi*, deal exclusively with Italian Court life. Dukes and duchesses and cardinals move through these plays as to the manner born; but no one really knows what relation these characters bear to the realities of Court life in Italy. We can make a guess, of course, on the basis of our limited knowledge; we can guess that Webster's picture of Court life is as theatrical and as conventional as Shakespeare's, if more detailed and sophisticated.

There is no greater authority on Elizabethan social life than Miss St. Clare Byrne. Though she would not claim to know very much about the Court life of the period, for the simple reason that most of the evidence is lacking, it is safe to say that no scholar knows any more. Here is part of what she has written about Shakespeare's dealings with Court life:

'The etiquette and ceremonial complications of regal life find but little reflection in the plays. What Shakespeare either did not know, or else deliberately rejected for dramatic purposes, was the circumstance and order of life in a royal household. . . . Messengers should not burst into the royal presence without being announced by gentlemen-ushers. But they rush in gaily in *Cymbeline* (II, iii), in *Hamlet* (IV, vii), in *Antony and Cleopatra* (II, v), in *Richard III* (II, iv), and *Henry V* (II, iv), when no particular dramatic purpose save economy is thereby served. In *Richard II* Aumerle—a man already suspect—rushes wildly into the presence (V, iii), to be pursued to the door a moment later, first by his father, and then by his mother, both of whom shout and clamour for admission until the King unlocks the door . . . [In *Macbeth*] the murder of Duncan . . . is almost completely "romantic" in its disregard of contemporary circumstance' (M. St. Clare Byrne, 'The Social Background', in *A Companion to Shakespeare Studies*, p. 199 sq.).

Compare Dryden, *Essay on the Dramatic Poetry of the Last Age* (1672): 'I cannot find that any of them [the Elizabethan dramatists] had been conversant in courts, except Ben Jonson; and his genius lay not so much that way as to make an improvement by it.' The common complaint of Restoration critics like Dryden about their predecessors in drama, especially Shakespeare, was that they were ill-bred, ungentlemanly, unused to polite society. Dryden's well-known praise of Shakespeare was arrived at in spite of his regrets for his predecessor's 'barbarism'.

We need not go to the other extreme and suggest that Shakespeare knew no more about courtly life than the average member of the Globe audience. Evidently a professional actor, belonging to one of the leading companies, must have known *something* about the life of the Court before which he sometimes had to appear; particularly under James, when the company Shakespeare belonged to became the King's Men, must the actor-dramatist have grown acquainted with the external side of Court life, though he could have known little, except through rumour and gossip, about what went on behind. If Dryden was not misinformed, Ben Jonson was the one dramatist of the age who did mix, for a time, with Court circles, and he was the one who wrote least about them. The others set most of their courtly interiors in ages and countries conveniently remote—to the satisfaction of their audience, who knew even less about the contemporary reality.

It is essential in these matters not to consider Shakespeare in isolation. His name was spelt in a variety of ways; so were the names of the majority of his fellow-Elizabethans—as we noted in our Introduction. His plays are often set in palaces—like the majority of other plays of the period. If the fact in regard to Shakespeare means that he was a nobleman himself, then the fact in regard to Webster, Tourneur, Middleton, Chapman, and the rest, must mean that all these other dramatists were also noblemen —or all pseudonyms for Bacon, as some Baconians actually believe! The unorthodox have been misled by one of the simplest dramatic conventions of the age.

It is complained by some theorists that Shakespeare, if he really was Shakespeare, should have written *The Shoemaker's Holiday*, or some such piece, instead of plays about kings and queens. The complaint should be directed to the proper quarter, that is to Marlowe, who knew more about shoemakers than Shakespeare. By the same argument, too, Webster should have written about tailors, not cardinals, Chapman about farmers, not dukes, Jonson about bricklayers, not alchemists.

IV

There is a second seeming proof that Shakespeare was an aristocrat, and this concerns what is alleged to be his aristocratic sympathies. Many orthodox critics have fallen into this error, together with virtually the whole of the unorthodox. Even Sir Arthur Bryant, in his very rejection of the Rutlandian case, seems to take it for granted that Shakespeare's outlook was aristocratic, though he does not think he was an aristocrat himself. 'As for Shakespeare's aristocratic political outlook,' Sir Arthur writes, 'this does not seem to me to prove that Shakespeare must necessarily have had an aristocratic background. Such an outlook is extremely common in those who have risen in the social scale' (Introduction to Sykes, *op. cit.*). May I remind Sir Arthur, with every respect, that there is no evidence at all that Shakespeare's sympathies were aristocratic—or, for that matter, that his sympathies were democratic? We simply do not know.

As Baconians and others are never weary of telling us, there is not in existence a single letter written by Shakespeare—though they conveniently forget to add (if they are aware of the fact) that there does not exist, either, a single letter written by Webster, Marlowe, Tourneur, Beaumont, Fletcher, or most other dramatists of the age. After the lapse of more than three centuries, this is not surprising: most of the Elizabethan letters extant are, naturally, those of statesmen or great noblemen, preserved either in government offices or country houses. Shakespeare's illiteracy is no more proved by the absence of surviving letters than the illiteracy of other dramatists is proved by a similar absence.[5]

What *is* proved by the non-survival of letters (or other manuscripts expressing private opinions) is our entire lack of information regarding Shakespeare's personal opinions on any subject. Can we not derive these opinions from the plays? Evidently not, for plays consist of a number of speeches and actions by different characters, and any dramatist who knows his job—and we may presume that Shakespeare knew his—naturally puts into the mouth of an individual character the opinions and reflections appropriate to his personality and situation. Only if we knew what Shakespeare's private opinions were, could we attempt to identify the dramatist with any of his creations; as we do not know this, there is no evidence to suggest that he himself agreed with the opinions of any particular character. We can easily guess which of Bernard Shaw's characters were most and least sympathetic to him, but we do not derive our guess-work from the plays; we derive it from the prefaces and from what we know, which is considerable, about Shaw's personal opinions on politics and society.

It is claimed that Shakespeare shows his scorn for the common people by the words of his character Coriolanus when going into exile:

> You common cry of curs! whose breath I hate
> As reek o' the rotten fens . . .

What Shakespeare does show by this and similar passages is his profound insight into the nature of his character Coriolanus. Apart from the fact that he was closely following Plutarch in North's translation, how could Shakespeare or anyone else write a play

about a Roman general notorious for his pride without indicating
by his speeches his contempt for his social inferiors? There is
nothing to show that Coriolanus was a character personally admired by Shakespeare; that the dramatist identified himself with
his creation. The play is a very objective one, Coriolanus being
studied as dispassionately as the people and the Tribunes. The
point of the tragedy is surely missed if we take Coriolanus's view
of the citizens, or the citizens' of Coriolanus, to be the truth, or the
whole truth.

The other quotation always dragged out of its context in support of the aristocratic argument is Ulysses's speech about 'order'
in *Troilus and Cressida*. It is assumed by many orthodox scholars,
as well as by all unorthodox theorists, that this represents Shakespeare's own view—which I will believe when a letter or a diary by
Shakespeare is discovered indicating that this is so. I do not
believe it could possibly have been so, unless Shakespeare was a
consummate hypocrite. If he had personally shared Ulysses's
opinions, he must have regretted that his father had married his
mother. His father was a self-made man, a poor farmer's son who
married the daughter of his father's landlord and reached the
highest civic office in Stratford.[6] By the standards of Ulysses, such
a rise in the world was to be deplored.

Nor could Bacon have possibly agreed with this speech of
Ulysses, unless he also was a consummate hypocrite. For Bacon's
father, too, was a self-made man, 'son of the sheepreeve to the
Abbey of Bury St. Edmunds' (Trevelyan, *English Social History*,
p. 115) who became Lord Keeper under Elizabeth. The reeves in
early Tudor times, as in the fifteenth century, were sometimes
prosperous men, but according to Skeat (quoted by Pollard in his
edition of Chaucer's *Prologue*, p. 89) they were all originally serfs
of the manor. I am talking, of course, of real life; in Baconian
romance, Francis Bacon is the son of Queen Elizabeth by the Earl
of Leicester.

Such nobles as Oxford and Derby could have agreed with
Ulysses without disparaging their origin. For such men belonged
to what we commonly (though in fact erroneously) call 'ancient'
families: that is, they traced their ancestry to one of William the
Conqueror's followers. But that means they really belonged to
families who only settled in England in the eleventh century, and
thus were newcomers compared with the majority of English people

who were (and are) descended from mainly Anglo-Saxon stock.
People who talk, except by convention, of the 'ancient' families of
1066 are confusing William the Conqueror with Robinson Crusoe.
England was not a desert island when William conquered it, but a
country of some million or so inhabitants, from whose loins the
majority of us are mainly descended. Those whose blood is mainly
Celtic go back further still. I am talking, again, of real life; in the
romances of Burke and Debrett, the only people who are credited
with having possessed two parents, four grandparents, eight great-
grandparents, etc., are those who are in possession of docu-
mentary proof of such rare acquisitions.

The greatest poet writing in English at the present time is Mr.
T. S. Eliot, and he is also one of our best critics. In one of his
essays on Shakespeare, after mentioning the different and conflicting views that have been taken of the poet's personal opinions,
he suggests that he 'may have held in private life very different
views from what we extract from his extremely varied published
works'. Mr. Eliot goes on:

'I admit that my own experience, as a minor poet, [as the greatest
poet in English since Yeats, many of us would say] may have
jaundiced my outlook; that I am used to having cosmic sig-
nificances, which I never suspected, extracted from my work (such
as it is) by enthusiastic persons at a distance . . . and to having my
personal biography reconstructed from passages which I got out
of books, or which I invented out of nothing because they sounded
well; and to having my biography invariably ignored in what I
did write from personal experience; so that in consequence I am
inclined to believe that people are mistaken about Shakespeare
just in proportion to the relative superiority of Shakespeare to
myself' ('Shakespeare and the Stoicism of Seneca', *Selected Essays*,
p. 127).

V

Those who believe Shakespeare to have identified himself with
any particular character in his plays seem to me to hold a very poor
notion of the dramatist's art. They point to the convincing way in
which Shakespeare has entered into characters like Coriolanus,
Hamlet, Lear, Cleopatra, Timon. Quite so; but it is the dramatist's task—and also the novelist's—to enter convincingly into the

nature of his characters, particularly of course his main characters. Dickens entered so convincingly into his creation of Pecksniff that a lady who had read the monthly parts wrote to him in protest, and the great novelist was forced to add a footnote to the book edition of *Martin Chuzzlewit*, explaining that he himself did not share Mr. Pecksniff's hypocritical views! Many would be the footnotes Shakespeare would have had to write had he lived to see the remarks of some of his critics.

Particularly, of course, over *Hamlet*. The scene which the un-orthodox stress is that showing Hamlet with the players. This is supposed to be based upon the noble author's own relations with his player-servants. But this view can hardly be substantiated. That Hamlet was not Shakespeare himself can be proved by the sort of drama Hamlet liked. The speech of the First Player (II, ii) represents this:

> Anon he finds him,
> Striking too short at Greeks. His antique sword,
> Rebellious to his arm, lies where it falls,
> Repugnant to command: unequal match'd,
> Pyrrhus at Priam drives, in rage strikes wide:
> But with the whiff and wind of his fell sword,
> Th' unnerved father falls . . .

Magnificent, of course, in a way—but that way was not Shake-speare's. This speech is a *parody* by Shakespeare—one of the most skilful parodies ever written—of the sort of drama which the more learned of courtiers and university men most esteemed, the sort of drama written at Wilton by the Countess of Pembroke and her band of tame poets, drama observing the Unities, with practically no action at all, with a limited number of characters, and with speeches by messengers hundreds of lines long. That was the sort of thing esteemed by the more learned people at Court and at the universities, the sort of plays which Bacon would have written had he turned to the drama seriously, the sort of plays which Lady Pembroke translated and the Earl of Stirling composed. This sort of drama is known to us today as 'closet drama', as distinct from plays like *Hamlet* and *Lear* and *Antony*, where the Unities are shattered, where there are many characters (to the disgust of Voltaire among others) and where most of the action, instead of being reported by 'classical' messengers, takes place on the stage itself, even to the blinding of Gloucester in *Lear* and to that famous stage-direction in *The Winter's Tale*: 'Exit, pursued by a bear'. As Miss Chute says: 'It is a sobering thought that Hamlet the playgoer would not have approved of *Hamlet* the play.'[7]

But there is, of course, as Miss Chute implies, no earthly reason why Hamlet should have approved of *Hamlet*. Hamlet the character is the creation of a dramatist, not the dramatist himself, either as he was or as he would have liked to be. A man like Hamlet could no more have written *Hamlet* than a man like Coriolanus could have written *Coriolanus*—or than a man like Pecksniff could have written *Martin Chuzzlewit*. Shortly before *Hamlet* was written—or adapted from Kyd—Shakespeare and his company had been made the butts of a good-humoured piece of buffoonery, *The Return from Parnassus*, written by some undergraduates at Cambridge. The speech of the First Player was Shakespeare's way of saying that he could write the sort of drama admired at Cambridge as well as anyone if he liked—and if he lowered himself to do so. Luckily, he gave us only the one speech, admired by Hamlet as it would have been admired by Sidney, and then continued with his own art, leaving the stage at the end of the play—in defiance of all the classical rules—littered with corpses like a battlefield.

NOTES

1. Dodd, *Who Was Shake-speare?*, p. 13; McFee, Introduction to Looney, *'Shakespeare' Identified*, p. xv; Sykes, *Alias William Shakespeare?*, p. 140; Smithson, *Baconian Essays*, p. 119; Looney, *op. cit.*, p. 333; Titherley, *Shakespeare's Identity*, p. 138.

2. Part of a *pavane* composed by Derby and published in 1624 is proudly illustrated in Lefranc's *A la découverte de Shakespeare*, Vol. I. It was published in a collection by Francis Pilkington and was probably composed by Derby with Pilkington's assistance.

3. Some of the great churchmen of the age, like Wolsey in an earlier period, were not upper-class by origin. Edmund Bonner, Bishop of London in 1540, is described as 'of obscure and doubtful parentage'; Sir John Mason, Dean of Winchester in 1549, was the son of a cowherd; John de Feckenham, Abbot of Westminster in 1556, was 'of humble origin'; Matthew Parker, Archbishop of Canterbury in 1559, was the son of a clothworker; Thomas Cooper, Bishop of Winchester in 1584, was the son of a tailor; George Abbot, Archbishop of Canterbury in 1611 and one of the translators of the Bible, was the son of a clothworker; his brother Robert became Bishop of Salisbury in 1613.

4. 'In Bacon's plays, known under the pseudonym of Shakespeare, there are 15,000 different words, nearly half of which he invented' (Advertisement for

Durning-Lawrence's book *Bacon is Shake-speare*, on last page of *The Bacon–Shakespeare Controversy*, by a Barrister). Compare Durning-Lawrence, *The Shakespeare Myth*, pp. 27–8: 'We owe our mighty English tongue of today to Francis Bacon and to Francis Bacon alone. The time has now come when this stupendous fact should be taught in every school.'

5. There are letters in verse surviving, such as the one from Beaumont to Johnson quoted on p. 209 below; but these survive, of course, because they were printed.

6. Marchette Chute, *Shakespeare of London*, Chap. 1. Shakespeare's paternal grandfather, Richard Shakespeare of Snitterfield, was one of the tenant farmers of Shakespeare's maternal grandfather, Robert Arden. When John Shakespeare had married Mary Arden, become High Bailiff of Stratford and through that office had become eligible for a coat-of-arms (according to the rules of the Office of Heralds), 'the son of the tenant farmer of Snitterfield', as Miss Chute truly observes, 'had come a long way' (p. 10). It seems to me equally false to claim, with the Baconians, that John Shakespeare had no right to a coat-of-arms or to claim, with Dr. G. B. Harrison (*Penguin Shakespeare*), that the coat-of-arms purchased in 1596 'was the official recognition that he [Shakespeare] and his family were gentlefolk'. The truth surely is that John Shakespeare was eligible for a coat-of-arms solely by reason of his office of High Bailiff; his own family were certainly not gentlefolk and his wife lost that dignity when she married him. 'Just what connection Mary Arden may have had with the Warwickshire Ardens is not clear. When the Office of Heralds in London was obliged to wrestle with the problem they finally linked her with another branch of the family and the actual genealogy has never been straightened out to anyone's satisfaction' (Chute, p. 6). What is certain is that the office of High Bailiff of Stratford was one of the 'divers offices of dignity' which made its holder eligible in Elizabethan times for admission into the ranks of the gentry.

7. Chute, p. 198. A Baconian, Roderick Eagle, observes: '*Antony and Cleopatra* has no less than 42 scenes (one of 10 lines being followed by one of 5!). No professional playwright wrote that' (*Shakespeare: New Views for Old*, p. 91). On the contrary it was the professional playwrights like Shakespeare who delighted in swiftly changing action; it was courtiers like Sidney and his followers who thought plays should abide by the rules of Aristotle which had been revived at the Renaissance. *Antony* and *Lear* and *Hamlet* are three of the supreme achievements of the popular, rather than the learned, drama. There was no scenery to speak of on the Elizabethan stage and therefore no limit to the number of scenes: a scene ended when the characters left the stage.

CHAPTER II

THE CASE AGAINST THE GROUP THEORIES

... unless I err (a thing
Easy in such simplicity), deluded
By dearly beloved Delia ...
w. CLARK: *Polimanteia* (1595).

I

On the face of it, the Group Theory in its variety of forms appears the most reasonable of all the unorthodox theories of the authorship of Shakespeare's works. That plays of the period were often written in collaboration is a fact known to everybody; what more reasonable, therefore, than to assume that Shakespeare's plays, if not his poems, come into this category?

Yet I believe the assumption to be almost as illusory as the aristocratic assumption. The main source for our knowledge that often Elizabethan plays were put together by two or three or more playwrights is the diary and papers of the theatre manager Philip Henslowe, father-in-law of the great actor Alleyn. Unfortunately, Shakespeare wrote almost exclusively for the rival company, the Chamberlain's (afterwards the King's Men), not for the Admiral's Company, which was the one run by Henslowe. So, apart possibly from some of the very earliest plays attributed to Shakespeare, such as *Titus Andronicus* and the three parts of *Henry the Sixth*, the evidence afforded by Henslowe is completely irrelevant to Shakespeare's career. 'The Silence of Henslowe', about which unorthodox theorists are always so triumphant, is in fact no support at all for the opinion that Shakespeare was unknown as a playwright; it only supports the opinion that, unlike other dramatists of the time, he wrote exclusively—from the spring of 1594 onwards—for the company he had joined as an actor (see Chute's biography, p. 105 sq.). If, before the plague years, he was one of the many dramatists who wrote in collaboration, that is the utmost we can say. The enormous advantage which he had over rival dramatists was not because he was the blind for some nobleman or group of noblemen, but because he was not dependent on his writing for his living. He was a professional actor who shared in the profits of his company; his plays belonged to his company, and his company 'belonged' to his plays: the advantages were mutual.

Henslowe's evidence being irrelevant, we have no reason to believe that Shakespeare's plays were the result of collaboration, except possibly for the very earliest—which are also the weakest. That he adapted some of his plays from earlier plays written by others is extremely likely, however; he seems to have written *Hamlet* from an earlier version of the story, possibly by Kyd. But adaptation from earlier versions of *stories* is not the same thing as collaboration. The plots of Shakespeare are unimportant: he got them from a variety of sources, including older plays by others, histories like Holinshed and Plutarch, and collections of stories from the Italian such as Painter's *Palace of Pleasure*. What matters is what he made of the stories and the characters and the setting, not these things in themselves.

I see no collaboration, then, only adaptation—except possibly for the very earliest plays. Some would add: except also for some of the latest. There is a widespread idea that Fletcher wrote most of *Henry the Eighth*. This was first suggested by Tennyson to Hallam while they were undergraduates at Cambridge in the early 1830's (F. J. Furnivall, *Introduction to Gervinus*, p. xxvii), and has no other backing beyond the feeling that the play, or most of it, is more in Fletcher's style than Shakespeare's. This may be so, but it is dangerous to go against contemporary opinion. As Miss Chute says: 'John Heminges and Henry Condell brought out the First Folio while Fletcher was still alive, and *Henry VIII* appears in the First Folio as the work of William Shakespeare' (*Shakespeare of London*, p. 270 *note*). The omission of *Pericles* from the Folio has never been explained, and in this case the Group Theorists are at liberty to conjecture that Shakespeare had agreed to a collaboration. I think it more likely, though, that he had adapted an earlier play and that his part in it was so small—and the principal author still alive?—that Heminges and Condell decided against its inclusion.

I have said that the earliest plays, the ones most likely to have been written in collaboration, are also the weakest. This may also be considered true of *Pericles*. Most readers will agree, at any rate, that of the four last comedies or tragi-comedies—and they all have much the same theme—*Pericles* is the weakest; it is not, it will be agreed, such a masterly achievement as *The Winter's Tale* or *The Tempest*, and contains little that is truly comparable with *Cymbeline*. I will go further: the Elizabethan plays which are acknowledged to be the best are the work of one man; the plays which are known to have been produced by collaboration are comparatively poor.

Let us consider this in more detail. Beaumont and Fletcher are the obvious exception, but are they, after all, such a great exception? Scholars are not so certain nowadays that the output of these two dramatists was mostly in collaboration. Chambers in *The Elizabethan Stage* gives the partnership only seven plays: *Philaster*, *The Maid's Tragedy*, *A King and no King*, *Four Plays in One*, *Cupid's Revenge*, *The Coxcomb* and *The Scornful Lady*. The first three of these are probably the best, but hardly comparable with a dozen or more of Shakespeare's, half-a-dozen of Jonson's, Marlowe's *Dr. Faustus*, Webster's *White Devil* and *Duchess of Malfi*, or Tourneur's *Revenger's Tragedy*, to name the most obvious examples that spring to mind. The one great play of the period that was probably the result of collaboration seems to me to have been *The Changeling*, the best part of which—almost entirely separable from the rest—is usually credited to Middleton. The comic scenes in *Faustus*, too, may have been later additions by an inferior hand.

This critical section of my book may be regarded as a series of variations on a single theme: *you cannot treat Shakespeare in isolation*. That is invariably what unorthodox theorists try to do, and the Group and Dual Theorists are no exception. If Shakespeare's plays were written by a group, why not Jonson's or Webster's plays also? It is up to the Group Theorists to explain precisely what other dramatists besides Jonson contributed to *Volpone* or *The Alchemist*. That Jonson did work sometimes in collaboration is a fact, but it is also a fact that when he came to collect his own plays together, shortly after Shakespeare's death, he omitted most of these pieces.

What other dramatists combined to produce Jonson's *Alchemist* or Webster's *Duchess*? No Group Theorist tells us this, and yet we are asked to assume, without any proof, that such plays as *Lear* and *Antony* were the result of collaboration between Raleigh, Bacon, Paget, and others, or by a group headed by Oxford (who died before these plays were written) or by some other group headed by Derby! It does not appear very likely.

Without any proof . . . . But, of course, most Group Theorists imagine they have ample proof of their contention. We must, therefore, examine some of these alleged proofs before we proceed any further.

II

I celebrated the centenary of Delia Bacon's original Group Theory by doing a thing which very few people have done: I read her book.* This is a most difficult proceeding for anyone who cares for the English language; with the possible exception of Mrs. Henry Pott, Delia Bacon is the most eloquent illiterate in the whole wide range of unorthodox literature—which is saying a great deal. Hawthorne's Preface is written in good English, but after that Delia Bacon herself takes over for the next seven hundred pages, with a fluent disregard of thought which defies analysis. So far as she offers any proof of her theory, it is found in the parallels she draws between the 'philosophy' of Shakespeare and the philosophy of Bacon. She refers at one point (p. 139) to 'the new science he [Bacon] was introducing upon this Globe theatre'; at another (p. 520) to 'this great Educational Association . . . for the culture and instruction of the masses'; and, again, 'this great firm in letters'— by which she evidently means Raleigh, Bacon & Co. Only those unfamiliar with unorthodox literature will dare to add 'Ltd.'

I agree with Delia Bacon and her followers to this extent: that *if* Bacon had written or helped to write the plays, they would probably have been plays with an instructional purpose. I think all of us, whatever our opinions, can safely say this, from what we know of Bacon's views upon the drama—in, for instance, the famous passage in *De Augmentis Scientiarum* (1623), the Latin expansion of *The Advancement of Learning*:

'Dramatic poetry, which has the Theatre for its world, would be of excellent use if well directed. For the stage is capable of no small influence both of discipline and corruption. Now of corruptions of this kind we have enough; but the discipline has in our times been plainly neglected.'

* That is, *The Philosophy of Shakespeare's Plays Unfolded*, completed in 1856 and intended to be published in America. But only a small part of it appeared that year, in the form of an article in *Putnam's Magazine*, and the whole book was eventually published in London the year after. See above, p. 37 sq.

This was written some time after Shakespeare's death, and when almost the whole of the greatest period in our drama had been written and performed. Bacon's failure to appreciate it springs inevitably from his philistine notions of dramatic art; the only kind of drama either he or most of his followers can approve of is plays with an instructional, didactic purpose, comparable with the religious pamphlets and stories of Hannah More. To associate plays like *Lear* and *Antony* with any such low artistic purpose is revolting. Those who think it sublime should keep away from Shakespeare altogether.

The quotation from Bacon is typical of his general attitude to poetry. As Dr. L. C. Knights, Professor of English Literature at Bristol University, has written:

'In the short section on poetry, included in the general survey of the branches of learning with which the second Book of the *Advancement* opens, the formal eulogy is less significant than the oddly limited function assigned to imaginative works. . . . When Bacon descends from general encomium to an enumeration of the specific virtues of poetry he confines himself entirely (as elsewhere in the *Advancement*) to the explicit moral lessons and illustrations of human temperament that it affords. . . . There is never any indication that Bacon has been *moved* by poetry or that he attaches any value to its power of deepening and refining the emotions. . . . Bacon in fact sanctions that divorce between imagination and reason, emotion and intelligence, that . . . was to have a bad effect on English poetry; and he passes with evident relief from the "theatre", where "feigned histories" are enacted, to "the judicial place or palace of the mind, which we are to approach and view with more reverence and attention" ' ("Bacon and the Seventeenth-Century Dissociation of Sensibility", *Scrutiny*, Summer 1943; reprinted in Prof. Knights's *Explorations*).

Is there the parallel which Delia Bacon claimed to have found, between the 'philosophy' of Shakespeare's plays and the philosophy of Bacon? Certainly there is, for Shakespeare's plays can be fitted into any philosophy that has ever existed, including Bacon's. But Shakespeare is not exceptional in this respect: any dramatist or novelist who has created a great number of reflective characters can be fitted into any philosophy, including Bacon's. All that is required is to extract those portions of the literary artist's work

which conform, more or less, to the philosophy favoured—and
ignore the remainder. Shakespeare has been called a Puritan and a
Papist, an Anglican and an Agnostic, a Reactionary and a Pro-
gressive, and scores of other conflicting things, just as Dickens has
been called a Tory, a Marxist, and practically everything else under
the sun. But Bacon was a real philosopher, not a dramatic poet (or
a novelist) whose characters naturally speak the emotions relevant
to their personality and situation. No one could confuse the
philosophy of Bacon with that of Pascal or Spinoza, but Shakespeare's plays can be adapted to any philosophy, or any prejudice,
you care to mention.

The supposed close relation between their 'philosophies' was
the only proof attempted by Delia Bacon for her Group Theory.
In all her loosely-reasoned 700 pages, no proof of any kind was advanced for the crediting of Sir Walter Raleigh as the leading poet
of the group; no proof of any kind was advanced for the claim that
the works of Shakespeare were written by a group at all. She
shared the common illusion that the Elizabethan Court was composed of great professional poets; it was mostly composed, in fact,
of great professional politicians, of whom the greatest perhaps was
the Queen herself. The fact that some of these politicians were also
distinguished amateurs in letters is no proof that they wrote the
plays of Shakespeare or of any other professional dramatist. It must
be acknowledged that Delia Bacon never once suggested that any
proof of her theory was needed; so perhaps we can leave it at that.

Her followers have been more circumspect. They have realized
that mere assertion of a claim can convince no one save those already convinced, and they have cast about for proofs. Thus, Peter
Alvor found a proof that the Earl of Rutland wrote *The Two Gentlemen of Verona* and *The Merchant of Venice* in the fact that Roger
Manners had travelled in Italy, and proof that the Earl of Southampton wrote *Macbeth* in the fact that Henry Wriothesley had once
visited Scotland:

'*1. War Shakespeare in Italien? Jawohl, der Verfasser der Veroneser
und des Kaufmanns von Venedig war in Italien. Graf Rutland, 'der
Student von Padua', war 1596 in Padua, Venedig, Rom. 2. War
Shakespeare in Schottland? Jawohl! Der Verfasser des Macbeth,
Graf Southampton, war mit Jakob I. in Schottland . . .*' (*Das Neue
Shakespeare-Evangelium*, 2nd ed., pp. 35–6).

The connection between these facts of travel and the authorship of the plays may seem somewhat tenuous, but if we point out the extreme vagueness of the 'proof' we are met with the assertion, particularly common among Baconians but found in most unorthodox writings, that the *cumulative value* of scores of similarly tenuous connections is surely considerable. This seems to me faulty arithmetic. The proof that because Southampton once visited Scotland, therefore he wrote *Macbeth*, is worth—in round figures, as my physics master used to say—precisely nought; scores of similar proofs are each worth precisely nought; the *cumulative value* of all these noughts is not a considerable figure, as the unorthodox suppose, but again precisely nought.

III

Perhaps the most favoured of recent Group Theories is the Oxfordian one which suggests that the Earl of Oxford was the leader of a government committee which wrote Shakespeare's historical plays as patriotic propaganda in the war against Spain. This theory had its origin, as we have noted, in the discovery by Capt. Ward that Oxford was the recipient of £1,000 a year from the government for services unspecified.

The theory, I should imagine, is one most popular with those who have either never read Shakespeare's historical plays or have forgotten the nature of them. *Henry the Fifth* can be regarded as a patriotic play, though it is much else besides; and there are certain brief passages in *King John* and *Richard the Second* which lend themselves to patriotic interpretation. But if a government committee led by Oxford really wrote Shakespeare's histories for propaganda purposes, then it was hardly worth £10 a year, let alone £1,000. For it made practically every elementary blunder it possibly could have made, and would have been in serious danger of being executed *en masse* by an irate Queen.

Consider, to begin with, the reigns this committee chose to handle. Not Edward III, with the glorious patriotic battles of the Black Prince; nor Richard I, with the heroic Coeur de Lion in the title-role; but John, with the revolt of the Barons and the surrender to Rome; Richard II, with the revolt of Bolingbroke and the deposition of the King; Henry IV, with the revolt of Percy; and Henry VI and Richard III, with the Wars of the Roses! In fact,

K

in eight out of ten of Shakespeare's history plays the audience have
to watch Englishmen fighting or intriguing against other Englishmen—the very subject which a patriotic committee would have
avoided like the plague.

And what was—and still is—the favourite character in these
historical plays, the character who makes all the dull battle scenes
worth while? His name is Falstaff—and the mere mention of this
character is enough to dispel the illusion that he was created as
part of a patriotic play by a government committee. Falstaff as a
character in a piece of patriotic propaganda! Falstaff, with his
cynical 'food for powder, food for powder; they'll fill a pit as well
as better' and with his reflections upon honour—'What is honour?
a word . . . Who hath it? he that died o'Wednesday'—Falstaff is
about as likely a creation by a patriotic committee as Don Quixote
by a committee for the encouragement of chivalry.

Falstaff, Pistol, Justice Shallow, Mistress Quickly, Doll Tear-
sheet, Bardolph, Master Silence . . . these are creations of individual and professional genius, and of a subtle and far-reaching
comic spirit equalled in English literature only by Jonson and
Dickens. Such figures could not possibly have been created by a
group of noble amateurs commissioned by the government to work
up hatred against Spain. (To say nothing of the misreading of
Elizabethan policy such a theory involves.) If the sponsors of this
theory could get around Falstaff, around 'that huge bombard of
sack, that stuft cloakbag of guts, that roasted Manningtree ox with
the pudding in his belly', then there might possibly be something
to be said for it. But I do not see how they *can* get around Falstaff
—unless they regard him as a sort of naughty sweet to soften the
patriotic pill. But Englishmen are not usually in need of encouragement before they give three cheers for Englishmen, any
more than Frenchmen before they give three cheers for Frenchmen.

Slater believed that the authorship of all Shakespeare's works,
not simply the historical plays, was a State secret:

'Who was the organizer of the group? The Earl of Oxford. How
was it that the membership of the group . . . and indeed the mere
fact that the plays were the work of the group . . . was never
allowed to become a matter of general knowledge? Because it was
a State secret, and the State was at war . . . Why was a "Shake-

speare Mask" sought out? To stop enquiry. Why was the secret kept up to the very end, and the deception perpetuated in the publication of the First Folio? To spare the susceptibilities of the surviving members of the group, and their friends and relatives' (*Seven Shakespeares*, p. 32).

Compare Gilbert Standen:

'The name [Shakespeare] would seem to have been chosen partly on account of its similarity to the name of the actor, William Shakspere, who replaced Marlowe in the group immediately after his murder in 1593, and partly because the Director of War Propaganda [Oxford] could be fittingly described as a spear shaker . . . No doubt it also came to include later on all the members of the group' (*Shakespeare Authorship*, p. 27 sq.).

A State secret . . . I realize the advantages of the argument. No proof is available that Shakespeare's works were written by a group, government-sponsored or otherwise. But if the matter was a State secret! Well, no proof is obviously to be expected, and the way is open to romance. Gilbert Standen even drags the Queen in. He believes that the plays of Shakespeare and his fellow-dramatists were 'accomplished by means of a national organization receiving its original impulse from the Queen herself' (*op. cit.*, p. 18). If we ask for evidence of this organization, we are told—it was a State secret.

The argument of this Group Theory, like other Group Theories old and new, proceeds through a number of assumed relations between unconnected facts. The fact of Shakespeare's works (*c.* 1590–*c.* 1612) is not in dispute; neither is the fact that Oxford received a State pension of £1,000 a year for services unspecified (1586–1604). But any relation between these two facts, the plays on the one side and the pension on the other, is entirely conjectural.

It is not disputed, either, that England, despite the government's efforts to keep the peace, was at war with Spain during part of the time that Shakespeare's plays were being written. But any relation between these two facts, the war on the one side and the plays on the other, is entirely conjectural.

It is not disputed, either, that there was such a person as the Earl of Oxford (1550–1604) and such persons also as Bacon,

Raleigh, Rutland, Derby, Essex, Southampton, Queen Elizabeth, the Countess of Pembroke, etc., but any relation between these persons and the writing of Shakespeare's plays is entirely conjectural.

Why, then, have so many of the unorthodox favoured the Group or Dual Theory in one of its many forms? For an entire century now, some people, at any rate, have believed in it. I suggest that the main attraction is its simplicity. There are some awkward questions to answer if you favour any single unorthodox candidate; but if you favour them all, then the difficulties apparently vanish and you can concentrate on the 'strong points'—which are really no stronger than the weak points—of each candidate in turn. Thus, you can explain Shakespeare's apparent intimacy with legal matters by bringing in Bacon, a professional lawyer, as a member of the group; you can explain Shakespeare's apparent intimacy with the Court of Navarre by bringing in Derby, who probably knew it; you can explain Shakespeare's apparent intimacy with Italy and Denmark by bringing in Rutland, who had visited both countries; you can explain Shakespeare's apparent knowledge of the sea and the New World by bringing in Raleigh, one of the most valiant explorers of the age; you can explain Shakespeare's knowledge of the female heart—as evident in *Troilus and Cressida* and *Antony and Cleopatra* as in Middleton's *Women Beware Women* or Heywood's *Woman Killed with Kindness*—by bringing in Lady Pembroke, who undoubtedly was a woman born and bred; you can explain Shakespeare's apparent intimacy with Court life by bringing in all these and others like them. In fact, the attraction of the Group Theory is that by its means you can explain all the apparent discrepancies between Shakespeare's work and his life.

But how if these discrepancies are more apparent than real? We have seen already that Shakespeare's apparent intimacy with Court life does not really bear examination; that his treatment of Court life on the stage was entirely conventional in the theatrical sense and bore little relation to the actual conventions of life at Whitehall; that he had no more intimate acquaintance with Courts, English or foreign, than John Webster, the son of a tailor. In the next few chapters I shall be pointing out that the other apparent 'intimacies' of Shakespeare do not stand examination, either.

CHAPTER III

THE CASE AGAINST THE BACONIANS

I will not do them wrong; I rather choose
To wrong the dead, to wrong myself, and you,
Than I will wrong such honourable men . . .
You will compel me, then, to read the will?
SHAKESPEARE: *Julius Caesar.*

I

The Baconian Theory, as we saw in the first part of this book, has both a negative and a positive side. Since most Baconian works begin with the negative and then go on to treat of the positive, I shall adopt the same procedure here.

The negative side consists in brief of a denial that Shakespeare could have written the plays and poems attributed to him. As it was succinctly stated in one of the early proceedings of the Bacon Society:

'The contention of the Baconians is that William Shakspere had no hand whatever in the production of either the plays or the poems—that he was an uneducated man, who could just manage to write his own name; that there is not a particle of evidence that he ever wrote, or could write, anything else.'

Many Baconians go so far as to call him an illiterate: for example, 'The most unlearned of men, William Shakespeare of Stratford, who never seems even to have attempted to write a single letter of his own name'; 'There is no proof that he could write at all'; 'There is no evidence to show that Will Shaksper could either read or write' (Durning-Lawrence, *The Shakespeare Myth*, p. 32; Walter Ellis, *The Shakespeare Myth*, p. 4; Edward D. Johnson, *The Shaksper Illusion*, p. 48).

The evidence for this presumed illiteracy falls under several heads, each of which we must examine in turn. First, it is (quite correctly) stated that there is not a single letter in existence which is known to have been written by Shakespeare. As we have already noted (p. 133 above), there is not a single letter surviving from the pen of Marlowe, Webster, Fletcher, Beaumont, Tourneur, or

149

most other dramatists of the period. So if Shakespeare is to be presumed illiterate for this reason, these other dramatists must also be considered illiterate. (There are letters by Jonson in existence, also one letter by Kyd.)

Secondly, the Baconians state (again quite correctly) that Shakespeare's father and mother, on documents that exist, did not sign their names, but made their marks. This is deduced as evidence of their illiteracy, and the presumption is advanced that Shakespeare was brought up in an illiterate household. Neither argument can stand examination. In the twentieth century, for a person to make his mark rather than sign his name is rightly regarded as evidence of illiteracy. But it was not so in the sixteenth century. When Lady Jane Gordon, daughter of the Earl of Huntly, married the Earl of Bothwell in 1566, she signed her name with a cross (Connes, *The Shakespeare Mystery*, p. 278). It is improbable that this great lady was illiterate.

'The use of a mark as a signature [writes Miss Chute] does not mean anything one way or the other. A close friend of Shakespeare's, Adrian Quiney, made his mark in the Council records on the same page as John Shakespeare and he occasionally used an inverted capital Q for his signature; but there are letters of Adrian Quiney's extant to prove that he could have written his name if he wanted to. Christopher Marlowe's father signed his will with a mark, although he was a clerk in Canterbury with his signature still extant in the church register' (*Shakespeare of London*, p. 5. Marlowe's father, a master shoemaker, was Clerk to the Church of St. Mary's, Canterbury; he married the daughter of the Rector of St. Peter's).

It is chiefly on the presumed illiteracy of Shakespeare's father that the Baconians have built up their case that Shakespeare could not possibly have been educated at the local free Grammar School. They point out (again quite correctly) that the condition of entry to the Grammar School was an ability to read and write, maintaining that the illiteracy of Shakespeare's father does not suggest that his son would have been able to qualify. If indeed John Shakespeare *had* been illiterate, then there would be much to be said for their suggestion; but the presumed fact happens to be an error of history, arising from a confusion of modern customs with those of the sixteenth century.

The earliest biography of Shakespeare—Rowe's *Life* prefixed to his edition of the plays (1709)—tells us that when John Shakespeare fell upon less prosperous times he was forced to withdraw his son from school because he wanted his help at home:

'He had bred him, 'tis true, for some time at a Free-School, where 'tis probable he acquired that little Latin he was master of. But the narrowness of his circumstances, and the want of his assistance at home, forced his father to withdraw him from thence, and unhappily prevented his further proficiency in that language.'

The third of the Baconians' supposed proofs of Shakespeare's illiteracy is founded upon a study of his last will and testament. They state (again quite correctly) that this detailed document contains no mention of any books. The assumption they (and others) draw from this is that Shakespeare possessed no books. 'Bookless in life and bookless in death,' declares Alfred Dodd; 'No one ever saw Shakspere with a book in his hand,' confirms Prof. Porohovshikov. What the Professor means is that no document exists, signed and witnessed, stating that Shakespeare was seen reading a book. No such document exists in the case of any other Elizabethan dramatist, either. It would be very curious if it did. . . .

To return, however, to the will. Baconians and others make much of this strand in their argument, pointing out that Shakespeare's son-in-law, Dr. Hall, when he came to make *his* will in 1635 *did* mention the books he possessed. The assumption is that all persons of the period who possessed books mentioned them in their wills.

But this assumption is not correct. The most learned theologian of the age was Richard Hooker, author of *The Laws of Ecclesiastical Polity*. He must have possessed books, yet none is mentioned in his will.

A Derbyite, Dr. Titherley, mentions the absence of books in the will of Hooker, but says illogically of a similar absence in the will of Shakespeare: 'It may be inferred from this that he had none' (*Shakespeare's Identity*, p. 107). All that may correctly be inferred from the absence of books in the will of Shakespeare, *because* of a similar absence in the will of Hooker, is that it was not always the custom of Elizabethans to mention books in their wills. It is to be presumed that when Dr. Titherley was a lecturer in chemistry at

Liverpool, he conducted his experiments more carefully; otherwise, he would have blown himself across the River Mersey.

No book is mentioned in the will of another learned contemporary, Reginald Scot, author of *The Discoverie of Witchcraft*. The son of Sir John Scot, educated at Oxford, and one of the most enlightened men of his time, he must obviously have possessed books; yet none is mentioned in his will. And we find the same absence in the will of the poet Samuel Daniel, one of the poets who came under the wing of Lady Pembroke and who wrote closet dramas according to the rules of Aristotle. 'Shakespeare's library is a figment of the imagination,' exclaims Dr. Titherley. Can the libraries of Hooker, Scot, and Daniel be also considered figments of the imagination?

Shakespeare appointed Thomas Russell, Esquire, to be overseer of his will. Now who was this Thomas Russell? It is safe to say that no one knew precisely who he was before Leslie Hotson published his '*I, William Shakespeare* . . .' in 1937. Dr. Hotson discovered that Russell was the son of Sir Thomas Russell and was educated at Queen's College, Oxford; he was a brother of Sir John Russell, to whom the father of Samuel Butler, author of *Hudibras*, was servant. This country gentleman was 'above all the other legatees and Shakespeare himself in social rank' (Hotson, pp. 15, 21, 41, etc.). Greenwood calls Russell a 'Stratford worthy' (*The Shakespeare Problem Restated*, p. 41). This mistake is natural, as he was writing in 1908, many years before Dr. Hotson published his researches. What is sad is that future Baconian pamphlets will inevitably follow Greenwood, instead of Hotson, on this and similar points.

Did Russell possess any books? One would naturally suppose so, a country gentleman educated at Oxford. Yet, on Baconian principles, he can be proved to have possessed no books and therefore to have been illiterate. Dr. Hotson gives in full his last will and testament (p. 274 sq.). It is an extremely detailed document, but no books are mentioned. By Baconian–Titherley standards of evidence, Thomas Russell's library must also be a figment of the imagination.

What about Bacon's library? Is that a figment of the imagination, too? The truth is that Bacon had so scanty a respect for the susceptibilities of Baconians that he entirely forgot to mention his library in his will. He mentioned his wife; indeed, he mentioned her twice, for he added a codicil revoking the legacies he had previously bequeathed her: 'Bacon, in his last will, left large gifts to his wife, and afterwards "utterly revoked them", as he said, for "just and good causes", and left her to her legal rights' (Donnelly, *The Cipher in the Plays*, p. 370). But he forgot to mention his library—which, therefore, on Baconian principles, ceases to exist.

'Where is Bacon's library?' asks Mrs. Pott, more in sorrow than in anger. 'It is observable that in neither of his wills (elaborate and detailed in particulars though they be) does he mention his library.' Mrs. Pott admits he mentions his own writings and manuscripts: 'But of *books* there is not a word' (*op. cit.*, p. 227). Adapting Mark Twain, we can say: "Many philosophers have died poor, but this is the only one in history who has died *this* poor!'

Yet that Bacon had books and could read them there is no doubt. There is no doubt, either, that Russell, Daniel, Scot, Hooker and Shakespeare also possessed books and could read them. I am not accusing the Baconians of dishonesty; lack of knowledge accounts for most of their errors, and an inability to assess evidence accounts for the rest. Copying down their pamphlets from earlier pamphlets, which were themselves copied down from still earlier pamphlets, they have never come into contact with either literary criticism or scholarship. Consequently, their picture of 'Shaksper of Stratford' is a wholly romantic one, a product entirely of their own imagination. Mr. Johnson, for example—the present President of the Francis Bacon Society—has a chapter in his book *The Shaksper Illusion* entitled 'The Testimony of Mrs. Susanna Hall', in which he imagines a Baconian lawyer examining Shakespeare's daughter, who is presumed illiterate. I will give a short extract, typical of the whole:

'*Counsel:* I suppose that he also spent a considerable part of his time in his study.
Mrs. Hall: In his what, Sir?
Counsel: In his study—the room where he kept his books.
Mrs. Hall: Father had no books, Sir.
Counsel: . . . How was that?
Mrs. Hall: Father could not read, Sir.
Counsel: You swear on your oath, Mrs. Hall, that your father could not read?
Mrs. Hall: Yes, Sir.

Counsel: Could your father write?
Mrs. Hall: No, Sir . . .
Counsel: Can you yourself read?
Mrs. Hall: No, Sir . . .
Counsel: '. . . I take it, Mrs. Hall, that even if your late father had
   written the plays you yourself would not have been able to read
   them?
Mrs. Hall: No, Sir.
Counsel: Thank you, Mrs. Hall. I have no further questions to ask
   you' (pp. 164–5.)

Some of us will have some questions to ask Mr. Johnson. Like
all the Baconians, he has been misled, as we have seen, into thinking Shakespeare himself illiterate. But what has misled him into
thinking Mrs. Hall illiterate? The truth is that Mr. Johnson is out
of date; he has not kept up with unorthodox literature; he does not
know which of the anti-Shakespearean positions have been
abandoned and which are still hotly defended. The fallacy of Mrs.
Hall's illiteracy is one which has long been abandoned. Dr.
Titherley, who would have adhered to it if he could, is forced to
admit that 'his eldest daughter Susanna who married Dr. Hall . . .
could not only sign her name but must have been generally well
educated' (*Shakespeare's Identity*, p. 108). When she died, the
following epitaph was placed over her grave:

'Here lyeth ye body of Susanna, wife to John Hall, Gent., ye
daughter of William Shaksperc, Gent. She deceased ye 11th of
July, A.D. 1649, aged 66.

> Witty above her sexe, but that's not all—
> Wise to salvation was good Mistress Hall.
> Something of Shakspere was in that, but this
> Wholy of Him with whom she's now in blisse.'

'Wise to salvation' was a Puritan expression, and it was not pre-
tended that she inherited that vein of piety from her father, who
had been a professional man of the theatre. What she did inherit
from Shakespeare was her 'wit', and this word in the seventeenth
century meant 'intelligence' or 'understanding'.
   The Baconian invention of Shakespeare as a 'money-lending
maltster' comes from a typical misreading of the evidence. The

correct view of these matters is given in Miss Chute's biography. As regards the 'malt':

'For the past few years there had been an alarming succession of bad harvests in England and the Privy Council was keeping a close eye on the local price of wheat and barley, or, as the Elizabethans called it, corn and malt. To offset any tendency toward profiteering, the Privy Council ordered a survey of every barn in England . . . The survey showed that everyone in Stratford was being illegal . . . William Shakespeare . . . had about ten quarters of malt. . . . Alexander Aspinall, the schoolmaster, had eleven quarters. . . . Thomas Dixon had seventeen . . . everyone in Stratford had as much barley stored away as possible and held on to it as long as he could' (*Shakespeare of London*, p. 165).

As regards the 'money-lending':

'In 1604 he sued an apothecary named Philip Rogers who had run up a debt of over thirty-five shillings on some purchases of malt. . . . In 1608 he sued a member of the gentry named William Addenbrooke over a debt of six pounds. . . . This is an abnormally low number of lawsuits . . . since there was no machinery for the monthly or quarterly collection of bills . . . a suit . . . had come to be regarded as a normal way to collect a debt' (pp. 261–2).

II

The methods of the President of the Francis Bacon Society are, of course, important in our enquiry. One other example must suffice us here. Mr. Johnson wants to make the common Baconian point that Shakespeare was unknown to the men of letters of his time; and this, incredible as it seems, is how he makes it:

'Will Shakspere's residence in London extended over a period of more than twenty years. The men of letters, his contemporaries, were Raleigh, Sidney, Spenser, Bacon, Cecil, Walsingham, Coke, Camden, Hooker, Drake, Hobbes, Inigo Jones, Herbert of Cherbury, Laud, Pym, Hampden, Selden, Walton, Wotton and Donne. No record has come down to us of Will Shakspere being known to or holding any conversation with any of these men or any other writer or poet' (*Will Shakspere of Stratford*, p. 52. Compare *The*

Shaksper Illusion, p. 42, where a shorter list, including Drake and Jones and Walsingham, is described as a 'brilliant band of authors').

It is truly an impressive list. Scholars must be grateful to Mr. Johnson for giving them so many new poets and men of letters. No one before Mr. Johnson had ever supposed that the greatest seaman of the age, Drake, or the politicians Cecil, Walsingham, Pym, Hampden, etc. were men of letters, a 'brilliant band of authors'. How has this list come about, then? How could even the President of the Francis Bacon Society make so many blunders in so short a space?

The answer, as it happens, is simple. Ninety years ago the orthodox scholar Richard Grant White gave a list of contemporaries of Shakespeare eminent in various fields, in order to prove his assertion that 'Shakespeare left no trace upon the political or even the social life of his era'. This list was copied out by a Baconian and used in a pamphlet, whence it was copied out by another Baconian and used in a book; and so on and so forth, through the past ninety years. Somewhere in the long series of unacknowledged transcription, the original list of contemporaries eminent in various fields became transformed into a list of eminent contemporary poets and men of letters—without changing the names except by the addition of one or two. And so it reached Mr. Johnson, who did not apparently think it odd that the valiant seadog Francis Drake or the secretary of state Francis Walsingham should have been credited with the writing of poetry or other literary works.

Passing over this confusion, we must ask ourselves what truth there is in the contention that Shakespeare was unknown to the literary men of the time. There is no truth in it. The most distinguished dramatist of the age, with the single exception of Shakespeare himself, was Ben Jonson, and his remarks upon his friend and rival are on record. Baconians imagine that because in Baconian romance they have disposed of Jonson's testimony to their own satisfaction, they can therefore ignore him. But they cannot do this, for their dismissal of Jonson's testimony is itself based upon faulty reasoning.

A charge made by most of the unorthodox, not simply the Baconians, is that Jonson's epigram on Poet-Ape was directed against Shakespeare. It is much more likely to have been directed against Dekker, the 'Demetrius' of *The Poetaster*. In his reply, *Satiro-Mastix*, Dekker makes the character Crispinus (representing himself) say ironically to Horace Junior (Jonson):

> That fearful wreath this honour is your due,
> All poets shall be poet-apes but you.

The famous lines in the First Folio—'To the memory of my beloved, the author, Master William Shakespeare, and what he hath left us'—are not disputed by the Baconians to have been written by Jonson. They simply say that he was referring to the author (by which they mean Bacon), not the man Shakespeare. That Jonson knew Bacon is a fact, and it is also a fact that in his volume of *Discoveries* (not printed till 1640) he used the self-same expression about Bacon's eloquence that he had used (or was to use) about Shakespeare's poetry: in both cases, quoting from the same classic source, he said he would not look for comparisons to anything produced by 'insolent Greece or haughty Rome' (Vitzthum, *Shakespeare und Shakspere*, pp. 145–6).

But you cannot treat these facts in isolation. Jonson's lines in the First Folio were preceded by some others, 'To the memory of the deceased author, Master W. Shakespeare', written by Leonard Digges. Now Digges was a Stratford contemporary of Shakespeare and stepson to Thomas Russell, overseer of Shakespeare's will; he had spent his youth in the parish of Aldermanbury in London, where he had been a friend of the actors Heminges and Condell, the editors of the Folio (Hotson, *op. cit.*, p. 215 sq.). His lines in the Folio contain a reference to Shakespeare's 'Stratford monument'. This, of course, is also the answer to the theory of Gilbert Slater about Lady Pembroke: certainly there is more than one Avon in England, but there is not more than one Stratford-on-Avon. One poem prefacing the Folio refers to 'Avon', another poem to 'Stratford': the two must be taken together, they cannot be separated.

Nor can Baconians treat Jonson's repetition of a phrase as if it were the only case on record. Jonson was fond of repeating himself; for example, in his *Ode on Bacon's Birthday* he wrote of him as one

> Whose even thread the fates spin round and full,
> Out of their choicest and their whitest wool.

In *The Hue and Cry after Cupid*, he wrote of King James as

> A prince that draws
> By example more than others do by laws . . .
> That was reserved until the Parcae spun
> Their whitest wool; and then his thread begun.

He was also fond, as we all are, of his own opinions. We have mentioned that, generally speaking, it was the Court and universities who most esteemed the learned drama, and the professional dramatists like Shakespeare who maintained the popular dramatic tradition. But there were naturally exceptions on either side: some of the Court, notably King James, seem to have preferred the popular to the learned drama, and Jonson, a professional man of the theatre, was a determined classicist. Though he acknowledged in the Folio verses that Shakespeare, a 'natural' writer, nevertheless owed something to artistic skill:

> Yet must I not give Nature all; thy art,
> My gentle Shakespeare, must enjoy a part . . .
> For a good poet's made, as well as born:
> And such wert thou . . .

in his conversations with Drummond he had asserted, more frankly, that 'Shakspeer wanted arte'. By Jonson's standards of 'art', by which he meant the classical or pseudo-classical theories of the Renaissance, he was, of course, quite right: as we saw when discussing *Hamlet* (p. 136 sq. above), there were few dramatists of the age less 'artistic' in this sense than Shakespeare.

The stress should lie, therefore, not where the Baconians put it: on the difference of opinion between Jonson's remarks to Drummond and his lines in the Folio; but on something that enhances our opinion of both Shakespeare and Jonson. The two men were rivals in more than a personal sense; they were the supreme embodiments of rival attitudes to the drama, which we have called for brevity the 'popular' and the 'learned'. What is so magnificent about Jonson's eulogy in the Folio is precisely that it comes from the pen of the chief opponent of the kind of 'natural' drama in which Shakespeare excelled. If Jonson had been a mere follower of Shakespeare, his lines would not have had the same force.

We must remember that he claimed to be a lover of Shakespeare 'on this side idolatry'—plainly inferring that some of his contemporaries had taken their admiration to the point of idolizing everything Shakespeare had written. We can admire his common sense as much as his generosity—remembering too that his praise came at a time when the rival was safely dead and he himself the undisputed monarch of English literature.

Is there no truth at all, then, in the Baconian legend? There is a little truth in it, but it does not bear the Baconian interpretation. It is perfectly true—and was part of Grant White's original point—that Shakespeare was not known in high political circles. Hence Baconians can find no mention of him among political memoirs and documents, but much mention of Bacon. As Bacon was a politician himself, this is hardly surprising. There is no reason to believe that Shakespeare ever wanted to move in political circles, high or low. We should expect to find him moving among his fellow-professionals, and this is where we do find him moving. He was the friend and rival of the second greatest dramatist of the age, being himself the greatest; he was the friend and colleague of Richard Burbage, one of the two greatest actors of the age, the other being Alleyn of the rival company; and he was almost certainly the friend of one of the leading publishers of the age, his fellow-Stratfordian Richard Field. Whether he was acquainted personally with any of the professional composers is not known: all that is known is that Robert Johnson set the songs in *The Tempest* and that earlier Shakespeare 'was in touch with Morley, though perhaps not personally' (Blom, *Music in England*, pp. 62, 86–7).

III

The positive side of the Baconian case consists largely of the assumption that the author of Shakespeare's plays must have been an aristocrat, a lawyer, and a scholar. We have seen that the aristocratic assumption of the unorthodox is founded upon a series of illusions (p. 124 sq. above); is there any more truth in the assumption that Shakespeare must have been a lawyer?

The Baconian case would hold good providing two conditions were observed: first, that all lawyers who have studied the question agree that Shakespeare must have been a lawyer; and, secondly, that the legal allusions in Shakespeare's plays and poems are more common, and show a more intimate acquaintance with the law, than in other works of the period. In fact, neither of these conditions is observed.

The Baconians rightly say that some lawyers who hold that Shakespeare wrote his own plays nevertheless insist that he must have had some training in a lawyer's office. The eighteenth-century scholar, Malone, thought this, so did the eminent Victorian lawyer Lord Campbell in his book *Shakespeare's Legal Acquirements Considered* (1859). On the other hand, a Recorder of Carlisle, E. J. Castle, thought that Shakespeare wrote some of his plays with expert legal assistance but not others; he found law in plays where Campbell found none, no law at all in plays where Campbell found some, and 'laughable mistakes' in plays where Campbell declared there was no deviation from strict legal procedure (Robertson, *The Baconian Heresy*, Ch. III).

Campbell confessed that he himself remained rather 'sceptical' concerning the extent of Shakespeare's legal knowledge (*Shakespeare's Legal Acquirements Considered*, p. 110), and that his argument was 'worthy of Serjeant Eitherside'. In no less than fourteen plays he found no legal knowledge that 'must be supposed to come from one who has been a professional lawyer'. Although he is often called as chief witness for the Baconian case—by means of carefully selected quotation—Campbell was so far from being a Baconian himself that his biography of her hero was described by Mrs. Pott as 'Lord Campbell's odious little Life of Bacon' (*Francis Bacon and his Secret Society*, p. 39).

The trial in *The Merchant of Venice*, thought Campbell, 'is duly conducted according to the strict forms of legal procedure'. On the other hand, as Robertson points out (p. 60), 'Mr. Devecmon [in his book *In re Shakespeare's "Legal Acquirements"*, 1899] and other lawyers have been so struck by the disregard of equity in Portia's rulings as to be unable to refrain from severe censure of Shakespeare's conception of justice.'

In more recent times we find the same difference of opinion between men equally qualified in law. On the one hand, Mr. Edward D. Johnson thinks that the trial scene mentioned is more according to contemporary Italian law than to English:

'The trial scene in *The Merchant of Venice* is in exact accordance with the rules of procedure that formerly obtained in the courts of Venice, but of course Lee [in his *Life of Shakespeare*, which Mr. Johnson had quoted] would not know this, being under the erroneous impression that English and Italian law was the same.

Lee was not a lawyer and knew nothing whatever about the practice of the law, so his opinions are of no value' (*Francis Bacon of St. Albans*, 1955, p. 45).

On the other hand, George W. Keeton thinks that an Elizabethan audience would have been struck by the general accuracy of this trial scene to the law as it then stood in England:

'The broad principle had not yet been established that an English law court may look behind the seal of the bond and examine the nature of the consideration. For the leading case of illegality of object invalidating a contract under seal, we have to wait for *Collins v. Blantern* in 1766 . . . [But] Portia . . . practises on the Chancery side as well as at the common law. She is fully versed in equitable remedies. . . . To the Elizabethan it [her speech about mercy] was a not inapt description of the Court of Chancery' (*Shakespeare and his Legal Problems*, 1930, p. 16 sq.).

The book last quoted is one of the most recent devoted exclusively to a study of Shakespeare and the law. George W. Keeton, Ll.M., Barrister-at-law, held the Bacon Scholarship at Gray's Inn and became Senior Lecturer in Law at Manchester University. Lord Darling, in a foreword, observed:

'It is greatly to the credit of an author who has gained the Bacon Scholarship at Gray's Inn that he makes no allusion to those who attribute to the greatest lawyer that learned society has produced the works generally attributed to England's supreme poet.'

But, as a matter of fact, Mr. Keeton does make one reference to the Baconians. He is speaking of the trial scene in *The Winter's Tale*:

'It is, indeed, an exceedingly irregular trial. Leontes is sole judge, as well as accuser, and neither he nor Hermione is represented by counsel. In Shakespeare's day, of course, persons accused of treason had no right to representation, nor to see a copy of the indictment before the trial, but one would at least have expected a formidable array of counsel for the Crown; yet none appears' (p. 151).

To this passage Mr. Keeton appends a footnote:

'This is a strong reason for demolishing the Baconian heresy. Bacon played a leading part in the trial of his former patron, Essex,

L

for treason. His trained mind could never have produced the dramatic irregularities of this scene.'

I accept the Baconian argument on one point: that only qualified lawyers have a right to be heard on this particular matter of legal allusions in Shakespeare. But I cannot accept what appears to be the Baconian corollary: that only those lawyers who are Baconians or whose words can be made to fit the Baconian case have a right to be heard. In *Shakespearean Studies in Baconian Light* (1904), Dr. R. M. Theobald tells us that 'all law critics admit' that such language as that used in Sonnet 46 'is not the writing of an amateur but of an expert' (p. 19). As Robertson points out, he cites only Campbell for the 'all' and does not mention Devecmon's contrary opinion.

Robertson proved by quotation, and at great length (*The Baconian Heresy*, pp. 31–177), that lawyers have in fact held widely differing views upon this matter. His book was published as long ago as 1913, but his argument still holds. Mr. Keeton, barrister-at-law of Gray's Inn, evidently sees nothing in the Baconian case but a 'heresy'; and what did Herbert Morse, barrister-at-law of Lincoln's Inn, say in a book published two years after Robertson's?

'Indications of some legal training are to be found in his plays, and many of his law terms and allusions are applied with much technical exactness and propriety. But this of itself hardly warrants the assertion that Shakespeare was ever an Attorney's clerk; at the best it is but a surmise. . . . The position he held as playwright and stage manager would have brought him into contact with many business transactions affecting his profession—and what more likely than that he should pick up some technical legal terms? . . . Once admit that because a man is a master of a few technical terms, he must therefore be a member of the profession to which those terms apply, and you can prove Shakespeare to have been a tinker, tailor, ploughboy, or sailor, or anything you will' (Morse, *Back to Shakespeare*, pp. 31–2. The supporters of Raleigh do, of course, prove by the first scene in *The Tempest*, etc., that Shakespeare was a sailor. He has also been proved to have been a printer, a soldier and a doctor of medicine).

Morse goes on to deal more directly with the Baconian case:

'And on whose head do these doubting and undiscerning critics wish to place Shakespeare's crown? On the head of no less a person than Lord Bacon, one time Lord Chancellor of England, about the very worst and most improbable selection that could be made, and the most improbable of all improbabilities' (p. 43).

It is a professional man of law who is speaking. Who am I, a layman, to question his opinion?

The truth of the matter, then, is the opposite to that claimed by Mr. Johnson: 'The legal profession, so far as it has expressed its views, is unanimous in declaring most emphatically that the author of the Plays was a trained lawyer' (*The Shaksper Illusion*, p. 57).

The second point against the Baconians is that Shakespeare's plays exhibit no more legal knowledge than is found in other plays of the period. This was proved conclusively by Robertson, who gave literally hundreds of examples of legal expressions from other Elizabethan writers, and we must observe that once again the unorthodox have been misled by treating Shakespeare in isolation. I do not propose to repeat what Robertson has written, but I will cite just one example from the many he gave and will summarize his conclusions.

Portia's phrase, 'Charge us there upon inter'gatories', was alleged by Lord Campbell to contain 'a palpable allusion to English legal procedure':

'It does [comments Robertson]; and so do the four other instances of the word in the plays. And so does Ariosto's 'What should move you Put forth that harsh inter'gatory?' in Webster's *The Devil's Law Case* (II, iii). And so does Gelaia's 'Slight, he has me upon interrogatories' in Ben Jonson's *Cynthia's Revels* (IV, i). And so does Andelocia's phrase in Dekker's *Old Fortunatus*: 'Are you created constable? You stand so much upon interrogatories.' And so does Black Will's 'You were best swear me on the inter'gat'ries' in *Arden of Feversham.* . . . And so does the question 'What are you, sir, that deal thus with me by interrogatories, as if I were some runaway?' in Greene's *Menaphon*. What then? Were these writers all lawyers?' (p. 61).

What are Robertson's conclusions? That 'the entire conception' of Shakespeare's professional knowledge of law 'is a hallucination. Shakespeare, like his corrivals, made his characters talk law as they

talked Euphuism, because it was the fashion of the age; and we
have only to compare his legal phraseology with theirs to see that
he was no more a lawyer than were Jonson, Chapman, Heywood,
Greene, Peele and Dekker in his own day, and Massinger after
him. . . .'

'Most of the champions of the 'legal' theory—orthodox, Baconian
and anti-Stratfordian alike—simply ignore the evidence for the
general currency of legal phrases in the Elizabethan and Jacobean
period. . . . They pervade all Elizabethan literature, and they tell
of a general litigiousness which is at once the cause and the explanation' (Robertson, pp. 127, 140).

The Rev. T. Carter pointed out that John Shakespeare went to
law no less than sixty-seven times (*Shakespeare : Puritan and Recusant*, p. 166). Robertson comments that this brings out 'the
normality of litigation in Stratford as in Elizabethan England in
general' as well as 'the abundant share of the Shakespeares in
legal experience' (p. 146). He goes on: 'The natural result of such
a general preoccupation is that not merely the phraseology but the
procedure of the law-courts everywhere obtrudes itself in literature
. . . Not only does the drama swarm with trials and trial scenes
[though less in Shakespeare than in some other dramatists of the
period, as Mr. Keeton was to point out], lawsuits, advocates,
judges . . . but the judicial procedure and the legal terminology
are alike constantly resorted to in poetic and polemical literature'
(pp. 149–50). There follow scores of examples (pp. 150–7) from
Greene, Nashe, Spenser, Peele, Jonson, Chapman, Rowley,
Dekker, Lodge, Massinger, Middleton, and Webster.

'Legal phrases flow from his pen as part of his vocabulary and
parcel of his thought. . . .' Every Baconian quotes these words of
Richard Grant White, but none of them quotes what White went
on to say:

'. . . But the use of such phrases is by no means peculiar to Shakespeare. The writings of the poets and playwrights of his period—
Spenser, Drayton, Greene, Beaumont and Fletcher, Middleton,
Donne, and many others of less note—are thickly sprinkled with
them. In fact, the application of legal language to the ordinary
affairs of life was more common 250 years ago than it is now [1866];
though even nowadays the usage is far from uncommon in the
rural districts. There law shares with agriculture the function of

providing those phrases of common conversation which, used figuratively at first, and often with poetic feeling, pass into mere thought-saving formulas of speech.'

I see, therefore, no logical middle position between an entire rejection of the Baconian case and all-out Baconianism. No one would claim that all the dramatists of the Elizabethan age were professional lawyers; so the only logical alternative, on the legal evidence, to a rejection of Bacon as the author of Shakespeare is the claim that he was the author of the entire Elizabethan–Jacobean drama. This will not cause the President of the Francis Bacon Society to bat an eyelid, because Mr. Johnson already believes Bacon wrote most of it. Neither I nor anyone else can prove the contrary. The claim that Bacon wrote virtually the whole of the drama of Shakespeare's time is, on the legal evidence, perfectly logical—and on the literary evidence perfectly absurd. What is not logical—on the legal evidence—is the claim that he wrote Shakespeare only.

IV

An aristocrat, a lawyer, and a scholar. . . . The aristocratic assumption, as we have seen, is founded upon an illusion; the legal assumption is one where lawyers disagree and where it has been proved that Shakespeare's plays contain no more familiarity with the law than other plays of the period. Now what of the scholarly assumption? I shall be discussing in a later chapter the particular point of *classical* scholarship; in regard to Bacon, the question is rather one of learning in general.

That Bacon was a learned man there can be no doubt, though Baconians are under some illusion as to the extent of his knowledge. All of them quote a single phrase, out of its context, from a letter he wrote to his uncle, Lord Burghley, in 1592: the single phrase, 'I have taken all knowledge to be my province.' And they have assumed that this was Bacon's way of saying that he was desirous of knowing everything—even that he *did* know everything! But what Bacon really wrote was this:

'Lastly, I confess that I have as vast contemplative ends as I have moderate civil ends; for I have taken all knowledge to be my province; and if I could purge *it* [my italics] of two sorts of rovers, whereof the one with frivolous disputations, confutations and verbosities, the other with blind experiments and auricular traditions and impostures, hath committed so many spoils; I hope I should bring in industrious observations, grounded conclusions, and profitable inventions and discoveries; the best state of *that province* [my italics]. This, whether it be curiosity, or vainglory, or nature, or, if one take it favourably, philanthropia, is so fixed in my mind that it cannot be removed.'

Now what was 'that province', that particular branch of learning, which Bacon was so determined to study with a view to improving it? It was the province of natural philosophy, or, as we should call some of it today, science: the study of the nature of all things—'all knowledge', as Bacon put it, quoting Aristotle. That was the province to which Bacon devoted the best part of his life, and it would be difficult to think of anything further removed from the writing of dramatic poetry. The study of the drama as a means of *education* (not as an art) comes into philosophy, of course, on its social side; and Bacon, as we have noted (p. 142 above), found the drama of his own age—the plays of Shakespeare and other professional dramatists—sadly lacking in the qualities he esteemed. He expressed this view in 1623, the very year of the Folio publication of the plays Baconians believe him to have written! Nothing would more have aroused his anger than to be told he had written just those plays of the public theatre whose educational deficiencies he had condemned.

One man, sixty years later, would have been grateful had Bacon really written Shakespeare. His name was Nahum Tate, afterwards Poet Laureate, who in 1681 wrote an adaptation of *King Lear*, giving the tragedy a happy ending. Now if Bacon had written *Lear*, Tate's trouble would not have been necessary, for the author would already have given the play a happy ending. On Bacon's philistine notions of dramatic art, *Lear* should show 'the masses' that virtue is triumphant in the end, that crime does not pay, and other original observations of the same nature. Therefore, as in Tate's version, Bacon's *Lear* would have ended with the King restored to his throne and Cordelia married to Edgar; the Fool would not have existed at all. Tate's version of *Coriolanus*, significantly entitled *The Ingratitude of a Commonwealth*, would likewise have been more to Bacon's liking than the original.

Bacon's enormous influence on Restoration culture coincided, as it was bound to do, with Shakespeare's lowest degree of esteem. Samuel Pepys, a President of the Royal Society, where Bacon's portrait hung in the place of honour, thought *Twelfth Night* 'a silly play' and *The Tempest* 'better in Dryden'—that is, the version by Dryden and D'Avenant (1667) in which Prospero is given another daughter and Caliban is provided with a sister, all in the interests of 'logic' and 'consistency'. Evelyn saw *Hamlet* acted, but noted in his diary that 'now the old plays begin to disgust this refined age'. Dryden himself, though too great a poet and critic to disparage Shakespeare, wrote that his style 'is so pestered with figurative expressions that it is as affected as it is obscure'.

I cannot, then, see anything in the artistic genius of Shakespeare on the one hand, and the scientific or philosophical genius of Bacon on the other, which should lead any reasonable person to assume that the two men were the same. Failing to find a single contemporary allusion connecting Bacon with Shakespeare,[1] Baconians were forced back upon secret ciphers and other things of that sort, persuading themselves that Bacon acknowledged his authorship by means of ciphered messages in the First Folio— that famous volume so mysteriously referred to by Mark Twain as 'the Quarto'. The truth is that any authorship of any book can be 'proved' by means of ciphers. Rev. R. B. Nicholson, in *No Cipher in Shakespeare: A Refutation of the Hon. Ignatius Donnelly's 'Great Cryptogram'* (1888), discovered that Donnelly's cipher could be made to prove the opposite of what he had maintained. Nicholson found the following message in the Folio: MASTER WILLIAM SHAKESPEARE WRIT THIS PLAY AND WAS ENGAGED AT THE CURTAIN. Later on, the Rev. Ronald Knox (the late Mgr. Knox) proved conclusively by means of ciphers that Tennyson's *In Memoriam* was written by Queen Victoria. The last link in his chain of evidence was the cryptographic message contained in the line 'A potent voice of Parliament'. This is obviously an anagram for 'Alf, poet-pen to Victoria. Amen' ('The Authorship of *In Memoriam*', *Essays in Satire*, p. 234). Most illogically, Baconians continue to believe in the orthodox authorship of Tennyson's poem.*

---

* Since this chapter was written, there has appeared a full-length study of Baconian and other ciphers entitled *The Shakespearean Ciphers Examined* (Cambridge, 1957). The authors, William F. and Elizebeth S. Friedman, are professional cryptologists. They examine in detail the ciphers of Donnelly and others, coming to conclusions similar to those of Dr. Nicholson.

In 1867 a box of manuscripts was discovered at Northumberland House in the Strand, and to the delight of Baconians this contained not only the complete version of Bacon's masque *The Conference of Pleasure* but on the outside cover of the collection a list of contents scribbled over with the names of 'Bacon' and 'Shakespeare' several times repeated. Among the missing manuscripts, according to this list of contents, were *Richard the Second*, *Richard the Third*, and a play by Nashe. For the first time Bacon and Shakespeare were together in one box.

Yet I believe that it is altogether the wrong box for Baconian comfort. No one knows who scribbled the names, and I am more interested in the manuscript of the masque, *The Conference of Pleasure*, dated 1592. This was Bacon's most considerable dramatic effort, and we are asked to believe that the same man wrote, a few years later, such plays as *Romeo and Juliet* and *A Midsummer Night's Dream*. Even Baconians are unenthusiastic about the merits of this masque, and yet Bacon never wrote anything higher in the dramatic field. On the evidence of this and the few other masques Bacon wrote or helped to write, the great philosopher was one of the worst dramatists of the age; on the evidence of his translation of some of the Psalms,[2] he was one of the most minor of Elizabethan minor poets, scarcely worthy to be called a poet at all. That he *has* been called a poet is a fact—and by no less a person than Shelley. But Shelley was referring to the poetical (or, more truly, the Elizabethan) qualities of his prose style, not to his actual poetry: 'Bacon was a poet,' he wrote. 'His language has a sweet and majestic rhythm, which satisfies the sense, no less than the almost superhuman wisdom of his philosophy satisfies the intellect.'

I agree that Bacon's prose style, at its best, has the true 'Elizabethan' qualities, if not so apparent as in the prose of Donne and Walton and in the Authorized Version of the Bible. But on the evidence we possess, Bacon the great prose philosopher was incapable of writing the plays of Shakespeare, the great dramatic poet. The two men inhabited different worlds of the spirit, different countries of the mind, and only came together in the Northumberland Manuscript. And it is in that very manuscript, containing *The Conference of Pleasure*, that the proof of Bacon's poetic and dramatic inability lies.

NOTES

1. The one always trotted out by Baconians rests upon a simple mistake in reading. It is found in a postscript to a letter to Bacon by Sir Tobie Mathew: 'The most prodigious wit that ever I knew of my nation on this side of the sea is of your Lordship's name, though he be known by another.' It was assumed by Nathaniel Holmes (*The Authorship of Shakespeare*, Vol. I, p. 172 sq.) and by numerous later Baconians, including Vitzthum (*Shakespeare und Shakspere*, p. 110), that this is a covert reference to Bacon's pseudonym of 'Shakespeare'. But Mathew was writing from abroad to Bacon in England, so the reference cannot be to Bacon at all. Probably Mathew was referring to Anthony Bacon, Francis's brother, who was abroad—'on this side of the sea'—on secret service work and therefore passing for the moment under an assumed name. This was pointed out by Mrs. Stopes as long ago as 1888 (*The Bacon–Shakspere Question Answered*, p. 193). But the President of the Francis Bacon Society is not aware of this: he writes in *The Shaksper Illusion* (1951): 'Here we have a perfectly clear statement that Bacon had been writing under a pseudonym; indeed it cannot bear any other interpretation, and no Stratfordian has ever made any attempt to explain the meaning of these words *with their deadly significance*.'

2. Bacon's biographer Spedding observed: 'These are the only verses certainly of Bacon's making that have come down to us, and probably, with one or two slight exceptions [such as the lyric included by Palgrave in *The Golden Treasury*], the only verses he ever wrote.'

CHAPTER IV

THE CASE AGAINST DERBY

It shall be called Bottom's Dream, because it hath no bottom.
SHAKESPEARE: *A Midsummer Night's Dream.*

I

The case for the authorship of William Stanley, Earl of Derby, is distinguished among unorthodox theories, we have observed, by having had as its main propagandist a professional literary scholar. After reading the works of the Baconians, it is refreshing to turn to the late Prof. Lefranc, whose scholarship is apparent on every page and whose learning is revealed in every footnote. Yet I have also observed that few unorthodox views seem to me to have less validity than this one concerning Derby. Which point of view I intend to follow up in the present chapter.

The origins of the Derby case, in Greenstreet's discovery of 'A Hitherto Unknown Noble Author of Elizabethan Comedies', need not detain us very long. It is an interesting addition to our knowledge about nobles who occasionally amused themselves—and perhaps their audience—by writing amateur comedies for public performance, and that is the most we can say. To leap from that scrap of knowledge to the contention that therefore Derby wrote the plays of a professional dramatist like Shakespeare is as illogical as it is absurd.

And it must be admitted that the Derby theorists do not rest for long on that assumption. Greenstreet himself was seeking a noble, travelled author when he came across these references. So it is in a combination of the two assumptions that the strength, such as it is, of the Derby case lies. The first assertion is that the plays of Shakespeare must have been written by an aristocrat acquainted with foreign Courts, as Derby was; and then, if we ask what connection Derby had with dramatic composition, we are referred to the discovery of Greenstreet.

The aristocratic assumption has been discussed in the first chapter of this critical part of our book. I observed there, among other things, that there is no more evidence to show that Shakespeare was an aristocrat than Webster—whose most famous plays deal with Italian nobles and cardinals. I do not believe there is any more reason to suppose that Shakespeare—and if Shakespeare, why not Webster and other professional dramatists?—must personally have visited the different countries in which his plays are set.

The Derby case is concerned above all in this connection with *Love's Labour's Lost*. It is maintained that this play could only have been written by someone who had actually visited the Court of Navarre, as Derby probably had, and furthermore by someone intimately acquainted with French politics.

The 'probably' is rather amusing when we remember the scorn poured by unorthodox theories upon the 'probably's and 'must have's in Lee's *Life of Shakespeare*. I have been through Dr. Titherley's *Shakespeare's Identity* to see what he has to tell us about Derby's life. He first of all admits that it is not even certain where he was born (pp. 20–1); 'it is possible partly to reconstruct his movements during the next few years' (p. 22); 'there seem to be no records' (p. 29); 'during the next few years little or nothing is heard of the 6th Earl, but presumably' (p. 31); 'the facts are not very clear' (p. 33). Similarly, Baconians have to admit that 'The greater part of Bacon's life is unaccounted for. The first 40 years of his life are unaccounted for' (Eagle); 'What was he doing . . . from the age of 20 to 44? What could he not have done had he been so minded? He could at least have founded Freemasonry and written the Plays' (Dodd). The difference, of course, is that the blank periods in Shakespeare's life are construed as evidence against his authorship, whereas the blank periods in the lives of Derby, Bacon, etc. are seen as significant places in which to hide the secret writing of the works.

Does *Love's Labour's Lost* show an intimate acquaintance with French politics? We consulted the lawyers in regard to Shakespeare's supposed knowledge of the law, and found that they disagreed. I have to report the same disagreement here. Evidently it is to French scholars that we must go in order to find out whether this comedy does reveal a direct knowledge of French politics. What do they say? Prof. Lefranc is confident that it does; Prof. Connes is equally certain that it does not:

'Is this the way nobles and kings talk to one another? Are these vulgar jests, even in the mouths of women, the habitual language of Courts? How can we talk of refinement in such a case? Evidently it is all derived from Lyly's Comedies, five of which were printed between 1584 and 1592. And in this very play, which we are told [by Prof. Lefranc] is inspired by a direct knowledge of France, we find nothing which indicates direct relation with French politics, no more foreign proverbs than can be found in well known English collections of the time, but on the other hand a surfeit of affectations, of puns and of Euphuism, in the worst taste of the time' (*The Shakespeare Mystery*, p. 276).

I have no doubt that the view of M. Connes is the correct one. Nevertheless, there are certain passages in this play and other plays by Shakespeare which would lead a superficial observer to maintain that the dramatist must have visited the Court of Navarre and other places in which his scenes are set. How did Shakespeare get hold of the names of the characters in *Love's Labour's Lost*, for instance? How did he manage to pick up some small items of information about contemporary French politics? These, and similar questions about this play and others, are not completely covered by the opinion of M. Connes, and they deserve an answer.

My own answer falls into two parts. First, I would remind the reader of the relation between North's translation of Plutarch and several plays by Shakespeare. In *Antony and Cleopatra* particularly, Shakespeare follows North closely, in some passages almost word for word. Unfortunately, this is a historical play, and no one has ever suggested that the dramatist could have visited the Egypt of Cleopatra in person. But is the assumption justified that Shakespeare followed his source closely only when his theme was historical? The majority of his plays *are* historical, and their sources are mainly in Plutarch and Holinshed, with the probable addition of earlier plays upon the same subject, such as *The Troublesome Reign of King John*, *The Famous Victories of Henry the Fifth*, and *The True Chronicle History of King Leir and his Three Daughters*. But a few of his plays are contemporary or near-contemporary, notably *Love's Labour's Lost*, and my contention is that he followed his sources as closely with these plays as with his historical plays. What, then, are the sources from which he worked?

The main sources for *Love's Labour's Lost* I shall be mentioning in the second part of my answer. But I would like first of all to remind the reader that we possess, not 100 per cent of Elizabethan literature, but more like 10 per cent. What is missing is not merely the printed books that have been lost, but the manuscripts—particularly of plays—that were never printed. A leading company of actors, such as the one Shakespeare belonged to, must have received hundreds of plays during its career, and they had to be read and accepted or rejected. We know from the survivals that there were favourite themes; if all were extant, we might find, not one earlier *Hamlet*, but half-a-dozen, and perhaps a translation of a French play which provided some of the material for *Love's Labour's Lost*.

Fortunately, in this particular case, we do not need to rely upon conjecture. The second part of my answer concerns Shakespeare's reading and his relationship with his Stratford contemporary Richard Field. We have seen that the assertion of Shakespeare's illiteracy is based upon a series of misapprehensions; and indeed the notion that an actor, of all people, could possibly have been illiterate is one that has largely been given up by unorthodox theorists. It survives now only in the most old-fashioned circles of unorthodoxy, such as the Francis Bacon Society.

Shakespeare, then, could read. What was the extent of his reading? This question is bound up with the extent of literary production in his time. And we shall have to go into it at some length.

II

It is still assumed by the unorthodox, in spite of the facts that scholars have made known to us, that books were scarce in Shakespeare's time, that 'facilities for reading must have been very limited' (Ellis, *The Shakespeare Myth*, p. 7), that 'Books and free access to books were an impossibility for the average Elizabethan' (Hoffman, *The Man Who Was Shakespeare*, p. 25).

Nothing is further from the truth. Shakespeare's lifetime coincided with a tremendous development of the publishing business, in which his Stratford-born contemporary Richard Field played a part. There were books published on all matters, and to suit every purse. Particularly was this development centred on the middle classes, upper and lower, to which classes indeed most of the publishers, and many of the writers, themselves belonged. There were easy introductions published to every branch of knowledge; languages, travel books, pamphlets on contemporary foreign politics, in fact books and pamphlets, some more accurate than others, on every subject that could possibly interest the enquiring mind. For a comparable burst of publishing activity, we have to look as far forward as the Victorian age.

This development is recorded in detail in a notable work of American scholarship: Louis B. Wright's *Middle-Class Culture in Elizabethan England*, published by the University of North Carolina in 1935. I quote part of the opening to Part I, Chapter IV (pp. 81–3):

'From the mid-sixteenth century onward, the number of average citizens who were buying and reading books was steadily increasing . . . Behind this extension . . . lay something more than the mere increase in the ability to read and write. There had come . . . an increase in the appetite for printed works, a fixed habit of book-buying among citizens whose fathers, if they read at all, had been content with an almanac and the Bible . . . London, of course, was the centre. . . . At the heart of the business and political life of England . . . where every day brought news of explorations and adventures in foreign lands . . . not even the dullest apprentice could fail to feel something of the excitement around him . . . And with booksellers flaunting, under his very eyes, wares that often bore the most alluring titles, neither the tradesman nor his apprentice could resist the temptation to stop and read. . . .
. . . The appetites of the populace grew by what they fed on, and the booksellers were shrewd enough to realize the value of encouraging readers. In the open stalls of Paul's Walk, any loiterer with time to spend was free to snatch the sense of a book or pamphlet without laying out a coin; and if his fancy led him to make a purchase, pamphlets could be bought for as little as a penny [about 2/- or 2/6 in terms of modern currency, on my own rough estimate]. The multiplication of printers and booksellers [who were also publishers in those days] . . . led to cheaper books . . . One has only to scan the titles in the *Short Title Catalogue* to gain some idea of the extent and variety of works produced . . . This huge outpouring of books could not have been printed if there had not been an enormous demand from the generality of citizens. The publishers of Elizabethan England could no more live by the

custom of learned and aristocratic readers alone than can modern followers of their trade.'

There was plenty to read, therefore, when Shakespeare came to London, and more and more books were published during every year of his living there. To what extent did he avail himself of his opportunities?

We must remember that there were no public libraries till the early seventeenth century (the first examples cited by Wright, *op. cit.*, p. 76 sq., were not in London but in Norwich, 1608, and Bristol, 1614) and that Shakespeare's means were limited. Pamphlets were cheap enough, and a person restricted only to pamphlets could pick up a good deal of knowledge, accurate and otherwise (like the information in Shakespeare's plays). But there is evidence that Shakespeare either bought some books or borrowed them: he must have had a Plutarch in North's translation and an Ovid in Golding's, to give the two most obvious examples. From whom, then, did he borrow such books, assuming that he was unable to buy them or to buy them all? The answer, I believe, lies in his probable friendship with Richard Field.

Before the unorthodox seize on that word 'probable' and mangle it in their customary pleasant fashion, let me give the facts. Richard Field was the son of a tanner at Stratford, who is known to have been a neighbour of the Shakespeare family. He came up to London in 1579 and was apprenticed to the Huguenot bookseller and publisher Vautrollier, one of the leading men in the London trade; he subsequently married his employer's widow and took over the business. It was to him that Shakespeare, with plenty of publishers to choose from, took the manuscript of *Venus and Adonis*, which Field published in 1593 (Stopes, p. 241 sq.; Chute, pp. 97–8).

These are the facts. The friendship is a probable deduction from them. What, then, follows?

In the centuries when books were plentiful but public libraries rare or non-existent, there were only two courses open to an author who could not afford to buy all the books he needed. He could either get permission to use the private library of some aristocrat, or he could borrow books from his publisher. Jonson made use of Bacon's library, and we know from Boswell that his eighteenth-century namesake used to borrow books from his publishers. A letter from Dr. Johnson to Edward Cave (given in Boswell's *Life* under year 1738) has the characteristic postscript: 'Pray lend me Topsel on Animals.' And presumably Topsel on Animals was duly lent.

Shakespeare may possibly have made use of some nobleman's library; but what is much more probable is that he borrowed any books he needed from his publisher Field. The probability is increased to near-certainty when we learn what books and pamphlets were on Vautrollier and Field's list.

Mrs. Stopes gives some examples of their publishing activity (*The Bacon-Shakspere Question Answered*, Note 8) and I believe it will be agreed that the following are particularly interesting. I begin with the pamphlets which were the probable main source of the characters' names and the political allusions in *Love's Labour's Lost*:

Le politique reformé . . . contre les Calomnies de la Ligue: in French and English (1588).

Declarations of the French King and the King of Navarre upon the truce concluded . . .: in French and English (1589).

Vray Discours sur la Diffaicte des Duc d'Aumalle et Sieur de Battagny avec leurs troupes, par le Duc de Longueville et autres seigneurs (1589).

Lettre du Roy Navarre . . . (1589).

Discours brief . . . monstrant clairement qu'il est loisible . . . et nécessaire au Roy de s'allier au Roy de Navarre (1589).

Le vray Agnus Dei pour désarmer le peuple François . . . dédie au Roy très-chrestien Henry IV Roy de Navarre (1589).

Life of Gaspard de Coligny, Admiral of France.

These are not the only interesting examples on their list, bearing in mind Shakespeare's other plays. There are three popular books on medicine and psychology:

A Treatise of Melancholie; by Timothy Bright (1586).

The Method of Phisick; by Philip Barrough (1590).

The Haven of Health; by Thomas Cogan (1593).

All three are mentioned also by Wright (pp. 585–9), who observes that 'Bright's learned dissertation on abnormal psychology . . . was drawn upon by Robert Burton in his more famous *Anatomy of Melancholy* (1621)'. Not that Shakespeare needed to have borrowed Timothy Bright from Field in order to write *Hamlet*. The melancholy of Hamlet, which the unorthodox believe to be so singular, was in fact a fashionable, *fin-de-siècle* mental disease at the close of the sixteenth century. Hence the popularity of books like the one on Field's list and, later on, of Burton. Cogan's work was based on Hippocrates and was meant for the general public as well as students of medicine. So was *The Method of Phisick*: 'Barrough realized', comments Wright, 'that physicians would attack him for discovering the mysteries of medicine for every citizen to read in English', and wrote a preface anticipating their objections. All three books were widely popular and went through several editions.

Like most other publishers, Vautrollier and Field fed the popular market for foreign languages. Among their publications in this direction were the following:

An Italian Grammar, written in Latin by M. Scipio Lentulo and turned into English by Henry Grantham (1578).

Campo di Fior : the flowery field of four languages, for the further-ance of learners in the Latin, French, English, but chiefly of the Italian, tongues (1583).

The French Lyttleton, set forth by Holiband (1590).

The last-named is also mentioned by Jusserand (*Shakespeare en France sous l'ancien régime*, p. 23 *note*), who gives the sub-title as 'a most easy, perfect and absolute way to learn the French tongue' and adds that it went through many editions. This popu-larity shows that it was widely read by *untravelled* Londoners; those who knew France and the language at first hand would not have needed it.

I will cite, lastly, a more miscellaneous list of books published by the same firm:

Plutarch's *Lives*, in English.

Eusebius's *History*, in English.

De Beau Chesne's *A Booke containing divers sortes of handes*, translated by John Baildon.

A Brief Introduction to Music (1574).

A Brief Discourse of the Spanish State (1589).

Ariosto's *Orlando Furioso*, translated by Harington (1591).

A True Discourse of Sir Francis Drake's West Indian Voyage, by Walter Bigg (1593).

M

Cicero's *Orations* and *Offices*, in English (both 1594).
Guicciardini's *History of Italy*, translated by Fenton.
Phrases Manutii (1594).
Art of English Poesie, by Thomas Campion (1594).
The Metamorphosis of Ajax, etc. (1596).
Du Bartas's *Divine Weeks and Works*.
Giordano de Bruno's *Philosophy*.
Jacques Bellot's *Jardin de Vertu et Bonnes Moeurs*.
Ovid's *Metamorphoses*.

These are selections only from the list of the man who was Shakespeare's Stratford contemporary, publisher of his first poem, and probable personal friend. All these books and others could have been borrowed by Shakespeare if he had needed them, quite as easily as Dr. Johnson borrowed Topsel on Animals from his publisher Cave. My contention is that Shakespeare derived most of his information, accurate and otherwise, either from earlier plays on the same subject or from books and pamphlets borrowed from Field. The only exceptions I believe we are entitled to make are in those instances where the knowledge displayed would obviously have been known to him by his upbringing in the country or by his career as an actor in London. The metaphor in *Antony and Cleopatra* (III, x), for example—'The breeze upon her, like a cow in June'—is one that would more likely have occurred to a man brought up in a community engaged in farming and the allied crafts than to a nobleman like Derby. The word 'breeze', meaning gadfly, still exists, I believe, in the Warwickshire dialect.

Does this mean that Shakespeare was a learned man? It means nothing of the sort. It simply means that he was able to lay his hands on the books he required, if and when he required them. 'Treat him as a learned man,' wrote Farmer in his *Essay on the Learning of Shakespeare* (1767), 'and what shall excuse the most gross violations of history, chronology and geography?' What, indeed? 'Treat him as a *travelled* man', also, and how does one account for his ignorance of the fact that the Mediterranean Sea, unlike the English Channel, is almost tideless? Shakespeare probably knew Dover and the Kent and Sussex coast, because that was part of the usual itinerary of his company on tour; he was thinking of English seas, not the seas of Greece, when he wrote the famous lines in *Timon of Athens*:

> Come not to me again: but say to Athens,
> Timon hath made his everlasting mansion
> Upon the beached verge of the salt flood;
> Who once a day with his embossed froth
> The turbulent surge shall cover . . .

A natural mistake for an actor-dramatist familiar only with his native island, but a mistake that would have been impossible to a travelled nobleman like Derby or Rutland or Oxford. Nor could Bacon, who wrote a book on horology, have possibly made the mistake of putting clocks into the Rome of *Julius Caesar* and the ancient Ephesus of *The Comedy of Errors*.

'Shakespeare drew more essential history from North's Plutarch than most men could from the whole of the British Museum.' These words of Mr. T. S. Eliot are profoundly true, of course, but the emphasis rests on the word 'essential'. Shakespeare was the very opposite of a learned man: he was a great literary artist, interested above all in human nature, including his own. He could grasp the essentials of history because of his profound knowledge of the human soul, comparable to that of Blake or Bunyan or Dickens. He could draw the fundamentals of history from Plutarch and Holinshed, but the mere information—totally unimportant, of course, in literary art—he took equally from history and legend. If you read Shakespeare like an encyclopaedia, you gain a good deal of accurate knowledge, copied by the author from his sources, together with a good deal of inaccurate or legendary knowledge, copied by the author from the same sources. I can well believe those writers who point out that in some cases Shakespeare has been proved right, after all, and the critics of his inaccuracy wrong; I do not dispute this for a moment, but I do not believe we can praise Shakespeare for being right in these cases any more than we should blame him for being wrong in others. Being a literary artist, not a scholar, he was interested in the fundamentals of human nature, and his putting cannons into *Macbeth*, pistols into *Henry the Fourth*, Childe Roland into *King Lear*, Cato and Galen into *Coriolanus*, Aristotle into *Troilus and Cressida*, and other mistakes of the sort, are merely the incidental weaknesses of his supreme strength. A scholar would not have made any of these mistakes, any more than a travelled nobleman like Derby would have confused the Mediterranean with the English Channel, but would either have been capable of writing *Macbeth* or *King Lear*?

III

I have given selections from the publishing list of Richard Field, drawn largely from Mrs. Stopes and Dr. Wright. But it was Vautrollier *and* Field, of course; and it was presumably the senior partner's Huguenot extraction that accounts for the preponderance of books and pamphlets about France and the French language. How well did Shakespeare himself know French? Scholars have always disagreed: 'he was as much a stranger to French as to Latin' (Gerard Langbaine, c. 1688); '*il savait le français à fond*' (Mathias Morhardt, 1938). I should think it likely that the truth lies somewhere between these two conflicting statements. We know, at any rate, that he put a French scene into *Henry the Fifth* and that there are various French phrases and allusions in other plays, notably of course in *Love's Labour's Lost*. But we also know of the existence of the pamphlets published by Field, some of them in French and English, others in French only; we know, too, that Field, like the present writer, married a lady of French origin, and that Shakespeare himself lodged for some years with Christopher Mountjoy, a Huguenot wigmaker and hairdresser, and was an intimate friend of the family. If Shakespeare knew insufficient French to write that scene in *Henry the Fifth*, he had only to enlist the help of Mountjoy or Mrs. Field. It is not a scene which requires a very profound knowledge of the French language either to write or to understand; otherwise, how could it have been intelligible to the audiences at the Globe?

There are various minor points in the Derby case still to be discussed. What, for instance, of the knowledge of music shown so obviously in the plays? We know that Derby, like his father-in-law Oxford, was a talented amateur in music; but what knowledge of music did Shakespeare have?

He must have had a great deal, otherwise he could not have been an actor. An actor in Elizabethan times had to be a trained dancer, a trained musician, a trained swordsman, and a trained acrobat. A combination of modern acting, modern ballet, and modern circus would approximate to the one Elizabethan profession. 'A wrestling match in *As You Like It*, a fencing match in *Hamlet*, Sir Andrew Aguecheek's illustration of dancing feats in *Twelfth Night*, all would be genuine skilled exhibitions by trained experts'

(C. J. Sisson, 'The Theatres and Companies', *Companion to Shakespeare Studies*, p. 35).

'. . . it was no special casting problem [writes Miss Chute] to find an actor who could play a musical instrument. When Shakespeare's fellow actors like Pope and Bryan appeared at the Danish Court of Elsinore, part of their business was to "attend with their fiddles and instruments". After more than a decade as a successful actor Edward Alleyn was still being styled "musician", and Kempe was listed as an "instrumentalist". When Augustine Phillips died he willed his various musical instruments to his apprentices as a natural part of their equipment as actors, and they were certainly expected to know how to use them' (*Shakespeare of London*, pp. 140–1; compare Jusserand, *Shakespeare en France sous l'ancien régime*, p. 49 sq., and Cohn, *Shakespeare in Germany*, p. 23 sq.).

Another point raised by the Derby theory is Shakespeare's supposed knowledge of the Chester plays. I believe Lefranc has made a mistake here, a mistake natural perhaps to a foreigner. Why the Chester plays in particular? an Englishman would ask. Such popular performances had gone on for centuries, not only in Chester but in Coventry and elsewhere. The attribution to an aristocratic author of knowledge much more familiar to the mass of the nation is rather paradoxical. Shakespeare and his audiences had been brought up on traditional plays of the sort good-humouredly satirized in *A Midsummer Night's Dream*; they had them in their blood. It is not necessary to stress Lefranc's un-English mistake, because there exists the book by his fellow-countryman Aristide Marie, *À la recherche de Shakespeare*, which shows how much the dramatist owed to his own native county of Warwickshire, its popular traditions and folklore.

The rest of the Derby position can be summed up in Lefranc's assertion that in the plays Derby was embodying circumstances of his own life. This would be more convincing were we able to take either Shakespeare or Derby in isolation. But we cannot do this. If Shakespeare's plays are autobiographical, why not Webster's also? From a knowledge of *The White Devil* and *The Duchess of Malfi*, one would naturally conclude that the author was an Italian nobleman; actually he was the son of a London tailor. And what of Derby? You cannot treat him in isolation, either. He is not the only aristocrat whose personal experiences are said to have been embodied in *Hamlet*, the *Sonnets*, etc. Raleigh, Oxford, Rutland, Essex, Bacon, Devonshire—all these and many more are supposed to have embodied their life-stories in the plays and poems; and the lives of these aristocrats were very different. The autobiographical part of the Derby case is the weakest link in a very weak chain.

CHAPTER V

THE CASE AGAINST RUTLAND

You know my methods, Watson.
CONAN DOYLE: *The Complete Sherlock Holmes Short Stories*.
I thank thee, Jew, for teaching me that word.
SHAKESPEARE: *The Merchant of Venice*.

I

I believe it is of the highest significance that the latest writer to advocate the authorship of Roger Manners, Earl of Rutland, should have engaged the services of Mr. Sherlock Holmes of Baker Street, the most famous sleuth in all detective fiction. Mr. Sykes is not the only unorthodox theorist to compare the question of the Shakespeare authorship to criminal detection. Roderick Eagle, a Baconian, refers to 'this fascinating study—as exciting as anything in a detective story'; Slater, a Group Theorist, thought 'the exploration of the Shakespeare Mystery is one of the most fascinating of detective stories'. Galsworthy declared Looney's '*Shakespeare*' *Identified* to be 'the best detective story' he had ever read.

Mr. Sykes's book, *Alias William Shakespeare?*, is itself written like a detective story. Like all other detective-story writers, he adopts a method precisely opposite to the advice given by the King of Hearts in *Alice in Wonderland*: instead of starting at the beginning and going on to the end, he starts at the end and goes steadily backward to the beginning. He has already found his author of Shakespeare, just as Conan Doyle and his successors know the identity of their criminals before they start. It is Mr. Sykes's aim to try to fool the reader into thinking that Sherlock Holmes has discovered the author of Shakespeare's works by a process of logical deduction, just as Doyle and his successors, already aware of the solution of their mysteries, try to fool the reader—in this case with the reader's consent—into imagining that Holmes or one of his rivals has tracked down the murderer by the same method. Mr. Sykes has already picked his man, but the reader first comes across the identity as late as Chapter 16 in an 18-chaptered book. The earlier chapters are a skilful attempt to persuade the reader that a study of the plays alone has driven Mr. Sykes—in the dressing-gown of Sherlock Holmes—to the inescapable conclusion that only Rutland could have written them! Thus, the author of Shakespeare's plays is claimed to have visited Verona, because Mr. Sykes already knows that Rutland visited Verona; but the author's personal ignorance of Rome is equally emphasized, because Mr. Sykes knows that Rutland probably never visited Rome (though Peter Alvor claims that he did). And so on, all through the book. Do I, then, accuse Mr. Sykes of dishonesty? Not at all: I accuse him of writing a detective story.

I enjoy detective stories as much as most people, and like Mr. Sykes I am particularly fond of those of Doyle's featuring Sherlock Holmes. Regarded as a detective story, bearing not the slightest relation to real life, Mr. Sykes's book is highly enjoyable. But there are two reasons why we cannot accept it as a serious contribution to the question—or the alleged question—of the Shakespeare authorship.*

In the first place, Mr. Sykes, as we have observed, has not played fair with his readers. This would not matter at all if his readers realized he was writing a detective story. The readers of detective stories say to their authors: go on, make a fool of us! Try to fool us into thinking that Mr. Brown or Mr. White committed the murder of Mrs. Green, when all along you know it was Dr. Black! The reader, in other words, is fooled with his own consent, even in those cases where he does spot the real murderer—for the author's motive is the same: to try to fool the reader into choosing the wrong person.

But this method will not do at all in matters of cultural history and literary criticism. Mr. Sykes had already chosen his author before he started to write; he should have told us so, and proceeded to give his reasons. A dull, straightforward method? Perhaps; but the contrary method, the method of the detective story—the right method, the only possible method, for that kind of writing—is the wrong method for his subject.

In the second place, what is a detective story? It is a more sophisticated version of the fairy story of our childhood. Its rela-

---

* To me, as to the vast majority of Shakespeare's readers, there is no question as to the authorship. But I agree with M. Connes that one can talk logically of there being a question while people exist who sincerely think there is some doubt about it.

tion to real life is either tenuous or non-existent, and this particularly applies to those which feature an amateur detective like Holmes who knows so much more than the professional police and is invariably right where they are invariably wrong. And I need scarcely point out that these stories are the most popular.

Has there ever been, in real life, an amateur detective who solved crimes which baffled the professional police? No: the amateur detective who does the professional's work for him is as much a product of fantasy as the noble Elizabethans who are alleged to have written Shakespeare's plays. In real life, crimes are solved by the professional police, as professional plays for the public theatres in the time of Shakespeare were written by professional dramatists like Shakespeare himself, Jonson, or Webster. Though partly founded upon some traits of the Edinburgh surgeon, Dr. Joseph Bell, Sherlock Holmes as the baffler of the police is a product of Doyle's imagination, as much an impossibility as the talking animals of our childhood stories. Cows cannot really converse, any more than an amateur sleuth can do better than the professionals, but in certain moods and at certain times we like to believe so, we like to believe in the impossibility because the reality appears so commonplace.

The various noble authors put forward as the real Shakespeare have much in common with Sherlock Holmes and other heroes of romantic fiction—not as they really were, of course, but as they are imagined by their devotees. (The Rutland of reality bears the same relation to the Rutland of Mr. Sykes and Prof. Porohovshikov as Dr. Bell to Sherlock Holmes.) It will be remembered that Holmes is addicted to drugs and is furthermore a heavy smoker; yet at a moment's notice he can twist iron bars or outbox the toughest criminals of the East End of London. We are bound to be reminded of Francis Bacon as seen by Baconians, the Earl of Rutland as seen by Rutlandians, and other figures of the romantic imagination. Bacon could denounce the public theatre and yet write its chief works, could be at the same time Lord Chancellor of England and a busy professional dramatist, could write in *The Conference of Pleasure* the most amateur of all amateur masques and in *Lear* and *Antony* the supreme masterpieces of the professional stage; Raleigh could be one of the most noted explorers of his era, a man whose life was simply packed with various activity, and at the same time write over thirty plays of a professional competence hardly matched in the literary history of Europe; Oxford could combine a career at Court with musical powers superior to Byrd's and with the composition of eight or nine plays written after his death; while Rutland could creep unwillingly to school and be at the same time the author of *Venus and Adonis*, *The Rape of Lucrece*, and *Henry the Sixth*, Parts One, Two and Three . . . It is all very agreeable, but there comes a time when we close these fairy stories and awake from our day-dreams.

II

There was no professional police force, as we understand the term, in the time of Shakespeare, but the secret police under Walsingham and Cecil—their leader was a man called Topcliffe [1]— were highly skilled in tracking down political or politico-religious offenders. It seems to me that Mr. Sykes under-rates their efficiency in the pages he devotes to the authorship of *Richard the Second*.

A special performance of this play was commissioned by the fellow-conspirators of Essex in 1601, in the hope that the spectacle of a king being deposed by his subjects might embolden the London citizens to follow Essex against the Queen. After the failure of the rising, the conspirators, who included Southampton and Rutland, were brought to trial, and naturally a great deal was made by the prosecution, which included Bacon, of this special performance of *Richard the Second*. Mr. Sykes truly says that if Bacon had written the play this would surely have been known to his former friend and patron Essex, and all Essex would have had to do, when the matter came up at the trial, would be to point out that the play in question had been written by the eminent counsel for the prosecution (*Alias William Shakespeare?*, p. 142). And Bacon would have followed Essex to the Tower and perhaps to the block.

But Mr. Sykes fails to realize that the same argument applies even more strongly to Rutland. If Rutland had written *Richard the Second* the fact would surely have been known to his friend and fellow-conspirator Essex. Rutland had turned Queen's Evidence and had made a statement which—Mr. Sykes himself says—was of considerable assistance to the prosecution. In the eyes of Essex, then, Rutland was a turn-coat, and if he had written

Richard the Second there was nothing to prevent Essex from pointing this out. The result would have been that Rutland as well as Essex would have been executed.

Why did nothing happen to Shakespeare himself? Rutlandians and Baconians alike believe that this was because the secret police of the Privy Council had found out that Shakespeare was just a cover for a noble author. They underestimate the methods used by Topcliffe and his men. Sir John Hayward was kept in the Tower for months because it was wrongly suspected that his *Life and Reign of King Henry the Fourth* (1599) had been written by a noble author with a treasonable purpose. (The book was dedicated to Essex and included an account of the deposition of Richard II: many Baconians confuse this history book with Shakespeare's play.) Shakespeare would have been treated with the same degree of severity, and *if* he had been a cover for Rutland or Bacon or Oxford or some other noble, he would have been forced to confess the identity of the real author. But there is no evidence that he was ever taken to prison at all, let alone 'put to the question'.

Topcliffe and his men were very efficient, and they must have been satisfied beyond any doubt that the ostensible author of the play, the colleague of the players who performed it, was in fact the real author. They were persons trained to be suspicious of everything, and the result of their investigations, which must have been extremely thorough, was that Shakespeare was—Shakespeare. These secret police I believe to have been the very first persons— years before Dr. Wilmot—to suspect that Shakespeare might have been the cover for a noble author; they investigated the matter with their usual thoroughness—'you know our methods, Sir John Hayward'—and came to the conclusion that Shakespeare had really written the play.

Which is why I put 1601 as the date of the origin of the Shakespeare authorship question. If Shakespeare, in Topcliffe's professional opinion, wrote *Richard the Second*, then he must be presumed to have written the other plays also. The original manuscript was probably still in existence, to be compared with Shakespeare's handwriting, and if Topcliffe had suspected—as he would have done if there had been any suspicious circumstances at all— that Shakespeare had merely copied out a manuscript by Rutland or Bacon or another, then the actor would certainly have been tortured to reveal the name of the dramatist. And it is extremely unlikely that Shakespeare would have remained silent. The crime was the capital one of treason, and if Rutland could turn Queen's Evidence with a clear conscience, why not Shakespeare?

How could such trained investigators possibly have been mistaken? They must have found evidence of Shakespeare's authorship so utterly convincing that there was no need even to take the author to the Tower and torture him. The evidence which they found convincing must also have convinced the Queen, one of the shrewdest politicians in English history and at that moment the most suspicious person in England. The innocence of Shakespeare was not that of a figurehead for a noble author, as Mr. Sykes supposes, because if he *had* been a figurehead, the secret police, suspecting just that thing, would have got the name of his noble author out of him in less time than it takes Mr. Sykes to murmur 'Manners'. Shakespeare's innocence was that of a professional dramatist who had written the play as one of a series of historical subjects, with no thought of a contemporary application. It was an *old* play in 1601, as Phillips pointed out to the conspirators when they asked him to revive it. The original performances about 1597 had taken place without government censure, though this was probably due to the deposition scene having been cut out.

III

The other play which Mr. Sykes emphasizes in his case for Rutland's authorship is, of course, *Hamlet*. Shakespeare probably never visited Denmark, but Rutland did, and Mr. Sykes thinks it obvious that the author of *Hamlet* must have done so.

But this is by no means obvious. Most scholars agree that there was an older play of *Hamlet*, possibly by Kyd, which is now lost. No one knows how much of the detail of Shakespeare's play might have been taken from it. And in what precisely does this detail consist?

Mr. Sykes mentions one in particular: the famous scene (III, 4) where Hamlet points, symbolically or literally, to the portraits of his father, and his uncle:

> Look here, upon this picture, and on this,
> The counterfeit presentment of two brothers . . .

Mr. Sykes explains that in the hall of the castle at Elsinore there actually existed portraits of the kings of Denmark, and he thinks this evidence of a personal visit.

But Shakespeare's scene takes place in 'the Queen's closet'. 'Probably Shakespeare'—meaning Rutland to Mr. Sykes—'deliberately transferred it there.' And this is the man who accuses the Baconians of wanting to eat their cake and have it! The accusation is true, of course, of most of the unorthodox, and we cannot except Mr. Sykes. His first argument is that Shakespeare's knowledge of the portraits proves that he visited Denmark; when he realizes that he made a mistake over their location, he shifts his ground and claims it was a deliberate mistake, for dramatic convenience!

The truth of the matter is probably much simpler. Either Shakespeare took over this detail and this mistake from the older *Hamlet*, or else he had heard about the portraits from somebody else but had not troubled to enquire their exact location. Who, then, could have been his informant?

Evidently one of the actors of the Earl of Leicester's Company who visited the Danish Court in 1585 and again in 1586. Several members of this Company, including Kempe, Pope, and Bryan, later became colleagues and intimate friends of Shakespeare's in the Chamberlain's Company. Only if Shakespeare can be proved to have been stone deaf could he fail to have heard about these portraits, many times. He was probably sick and tired of hearing about them. The mistake in their location is much more likely to have been made by the bored listener to a colleague's reminiscence —'Have I ever told you, Will, about our visit to Elsinore?'— than by a man who had actually visited the Danish Court himself.

Mr. Sykes (following Demblon) says that the names of the characters 'Rosencrantz and gentle Guildenstern' were taken from the names of some fellow-students of Rutland's at Padua, whom he may have met again at Elsinore. M. Morhardt, a supporter of Derby, says that the names of the characters 'Guildenstern and gentle Rosencrantz' were taken from those of some students at Wittenberg University, whom Stanley probably met in his travels through Denmark and Germany. Mr. Roderick Eagle, a Baconian, says that the names of these characters were taken from a portrait of the astronomer Tycho Brahe which Bacon had probably seen. Much more likely than any of these wild conjectures is that

Shakespeare took the names from the older play of *Hamlet*, together with the names of most of the other characters. But this is too reasonable an explanation to find favour with the unorthodox.

Mr. Sykes devotes an entire chapter to Italy, which country he says truly Shakespeare cannot be proved to have visited. Rutland was certainly there, but can you treat this fact in isolation? Many of the Tudor nobility visited Italy: did they therefore all write *The Merchant of Venice*? And did Rutland write *The Duchess of Malfi*, *The White Devil*, *Women Beware Women*, *The Revenger's Tragedy*, and all the other Elizabethan plays set in Italy or other foreign countries? If not, I should very much like to know the reasons Mr. Sykes or Prof. Porohovshikov could advance against his authorship.

Mr. Sykes points out truly that the theme of brother against brother is extremely common in the plays of Shakespeare. Nothing is known of any ill-feeling in Shakespeare's personal relations with his brothers; he seems to have got on well with them all, and one brother, Edmund, followed him into the acting profession. Whereas Rutland was on very bad terms with his younger brother, who may actually have murdered him to gain the earldom.[2]

The argument would be sounder, like so many unorthodox arguments, could we treat Shakespeare in isolation. But we cannot do this. 'The brother complex', as Mr. Sykes calls it, was one of the stock themes of Elizabethan drama. It is, furthermore, one of the stock themes of historical romance, as well as a fact common in actual history. Three of Mr. Sykes's six instances—*Lear*, *Hamlet*, *King John*—were founded on history or historical romance. It is always dangerous to assume a personal parallel in an author's writings, particularly of course in a dramatist: 'Sophocles wrote the gloomiest of tragedies,' Prof. Thomson reminds us, 'yet the cheerful serenity of his temper was almost proverbial' (*Shakespeare and the Classics*, p. 224). Bastards come into the plays of Shakespeare, as they do into many other plays of the period, for instance Tourneur's *Revenger's Tragedy*. But there is no need to assume from this that the entire body of Elizabethan dramatists were born the wrong side of the blanket. And did all the nobles who are supposed to have written Shakespeare go mad in unison about the year 1606, so that they could use their personal experience of insanity to write *King Lear*?

IV

Resuming the dressing-gown of Sherlock Holmes, Mr. Sykes tells us that the author of Shakespeare's plays died young. Rutland died young, too: at the age of 36. But Shakespeare of Stratford lived to 52, 'a ripe age by contemporary standards'.

What makes Mr. Sykes think that the author of Shakespeare's plays died young? He is going by the verses which J.M. wrote for the First Folio:

> We wondered, Shakespeare, that thou wentst so soon
> From the world's stage to the grave's tiring-room . . .

But these lines do not bear Mr. Sykes's interpretation; they refer, not to the age of the poet, but to the number of years that had elapsed between Shakespeare's retirement and his death: about five to six years, so far as is known. There is an obvious play upon the words 'stage' and 'tiring-room' by which J.M. refers to the profession from which Shakespeare retired.

Now who was this J.M.? Mr. Sykes quotes Dowden to the effect that he was probably James Mabbe, Fellow of Magdalen College, Oxford, who afterwards became Prebendary of Wells. He was a friend of Jonson and Florio, and adds Mr. Sykes, 'must have been at least on the edge of the circle which knew or guessed the secret of Shakespeare's identity.' The question then remains: was it part of the function of a distinguished clergyman to tell a deliberate lie?

For this is what Mabbe was doing—on Mr. Sykes's interpretation. The Folio was not published till 1623, eleven years after Rutland's death, but Mr. Sykes thinks it was still necessary for the Earl's authorship to be kept a secret—in a volume dedicated to two other Earls and introduced by the chief poet of the time, the former bricklayer of whose 'tribe' young aristocrats, amateurs of letters, were only too anxious to be sealed;[3] though this involved not only Jonson telling lies when he spoke of the Swan of Avon, and Digges telling lies when he spoke of the Stratford monument, but the Rev. James Mabbe telling lies, too, when he referred to Rutland's early death in the same context as the poems of Jonson and Digges. Is it likely that a distinguished cleric would deliberately sin against one of the Commandments by lending his initials to a lie?

Mr. Sykes is once again trying to have it both ways—as we do ourselves when we read of Sherlock Holmes being so excitingly addicted to cocaine and being able at the same time to bend iron bars or knock down a bruiser. Surely either the contributors to the Folio's prefatory verses must have been entirely ignorant of the authorship, or they must have known all about it. If they were entirely ignorant, then Mabbe's verses cannot refer to Rutland's early death; if they knew all about it, then the chief poet of the age and a distinguished clergyman were lending themselves to a deliberate fooling of the public. And the public *were* fooled, for neither Milton nor Dryden, nor any of the seventeenth-century poets or critics, doubted that the actor from Stratford was the author. Dryden mixed in Court circles, the very circles who were inclined to disparage Shakespeare's plays for their want of breeding and refinement, but neither he nor they realized that this ungentlemanly fellow Shakespeare was really the Earl of Rutland!

The public were fooled, furthermore, for no purpose. Both the Queen and Rutland were long dead: how could the avowal of the authorship have affected the Rutland family as late as 1623? James I was nearing the end of his life, and Charles was to succeed only two years later. And it is known that Charles so shared the admiration of his father for the plays of Shakespeare that—according to the accusation of the Puritans, which he may have taken as a compliment—he read his own copy of the Folio more than the Bible.

Was Shakespeare's age when he died 'a ripe age by contemporary standards'? This is a small point, but interesting as an example of Mr. Sykes's inaccuracy. His own book contradicts him. Among the contemporaries or near-contemporaries of Shakespeare he mentions are Titian (who lived to 99); Queen Elizabeth (69); Bacon (65); Ben Jonson (64); Burghley (78); Dekker (67); Heywood (88); Chapman (75); Sir John Hayward (73); Florio (72); Joseph Hall (82); Lady Pembroke (66); Raleigh (64, executed); Catherine de' Medici (70); King Philip II (71); Coke (82); and Derby (84).

Compare Dr. Bénézet, the Oxfordian, and Mr. Hoffman, who supports Marlowe: 'It was unusual in those days for a man to live past 60 years of age . . . A man of 40 in the court of Elizabeth, as in the modern steel mills, was ready for the scrap heap' (*Shakspere, Shakespeare and de Vere*, p. 21); 'When a man approached his thirtieth year in Elizabethan England he had passed over the threshold of middle age. The life expectancy of the average man during those times was (to be liberal) 40. Both Marlowe and Shakespeare were well in their middle-aged prime during the year of 1593' (*The Man who was Shakespeare*, pp. 23–4).

Mr. Sykes has probably been misled by two facts: first, that a striking number of Elizabethan dramatists *did* die early: Greene, Peele, Kyd, Lyly, Fletcher, Beaumont, among them. (This was partly the reason why Shakespeare had so few lasting rivals.) Secondly, it was a common assumption at the time that a man whom we should call middle-aged had one foot in the grave; I believe Montaigne speaks of himself as old at 40, like Shakespeare in the *Sonnets*:

> When forty winters shall besiege thy brow,
> And dig deep trenches in thy beauty's field . . .

Nevertheless, Montaigne lived to 59 and his compatriots Brantome to 75, Amyot to 80 and Pasquier to 84. Lee in his *Life of Shakespeare* quotes Daniel at the age of 29, Barnfield at 20, and Drayton at 31, all describing themselves as old (2nd. ed., p. 86 *note*). Daniel lived to 57, Barnfield to 53, Drayton to 68. The illusion was perhaps part of the cult of melancholy at the period: to be really sad, you needed a few grey hairs, either in fact or in fancy. I believe Forbes-Robertson played Hamlet when he was over 60; he would not have attempted Romeo at the same age.

In making the common unorthodox point that the author of Shakespeare's plays must have been educated at Cambridge, because of Lear's remark, 'to scant my sizes', Mr. Sykes writes:

'The Oxford Dictionary states that the use of the word [in the sense of cutting a poor student's rations] is peculiar to Cambridge and the two American universities, Harvard and Yale. Since several centuries had to elapse before the two latter were founded, the obvious inference is that Shakespeare learnt it at Cambridge.'

But Harvard was founded by John Harvard, son of a London butcher, in 1636, only twenty years after Shakespeare's death, and Yale in 1701. 'The obvious inference' is not drawn by Mr. Sykes because of this very mistake in dating. 'Scant my sizes' was evidently an Elizabethan or Jacobean expression, which survived in universities but died out elsewhere.

N

On a more important point, Mr. Sykes is similarly reasoning from false evidence. Like Mark Twain and the Baconians, he cannot understand why no mention of Shakespeare's manuscripts was made in his will, nor why some of the plays were printed anonymously. The answer to both questions is plain and has been pointed out many times. Shakespeare's plays were written for the company he belonged to, and they were the owners of the manuscripts. The reason why Shakespeare did not mention them in his will was because they were not at Stratford to mention: they were in their proper place, in the library at the Globe Theatre. What happened to them afterwards nobody knows, but this is not peculiar to Shakespeare. Hardly any manuscripts of Elizabethan plays survive: some of Jonson and Massinger, none of Marlowe, none of Beaumont, none of Fletcher, none of Kyd, none of Webster, none of Tourneur. . . .

Nor is there any mystery why plays were sometimes printed anonymously. Mr. Sykes is precisely wrong, most exactly in error, when he writes:

'. . . Then come the quarto editions of *Titus Andronicus* (1594) and *Romeo and Juliet* (1597), both of which are anonymous. But why? the intelligent reader will ask. Surely the actor who had just started a career as a playwright *and had succeeded in getting two plays printed* [my italics] would have wanted all the publicity he could get, and would have taken care that his name appeared on the title-page. Or was there some cogent reason why he preferred to remain anonymous?' (pp. 11–12; compare Kent, p. 6).

It is not an 'intelligent reader' who will ask these questions, but an extremely ignorant one. The truth of the matter is precisely opposite to what Mr. Sykes has said. Only when a play was losing its popularity did the theatre company allow it to be printed, but they could not prevent publishers from printing 'pirated' versions which they had procured by various means. In neither case did the author himself have anything to do with the matter, unless he happened to be also one of the partners in the company. Shakespeare's position as partner in the Globe Theatre from 1599 enabled him to have a say—if only a tenth say—in the question as to which plays by himself and others were now sufficiently stale for there to be no danger of losing custom by having them published. When he became better known, no play of his was printed anonymously; on the contrary, publishers unblushingly printed plays by other people under his name.

The related question, so often asked by unorthodox theorists, has an equally simple answer. Why did Shakespeare make no move to collect his plays together and publish them in a permanent form during his lifetime? Because during his lifetime such a thing was unheard of. Hundreds of plays were performed on the stage, and a good many found their way into print, authorized or unauthorized, but not a single professional dramatist collected his plays together—as would be natural today. The first to do so was Ben Jonson, a few months after Shakespeare's death, and he was good-humouredly derided for giving his plays the dignified title of 'works'. No other of Shakespeare's dramatic rivals followed Jonson's example. The first collected Beaumont and Fletcher appeared in 1647, after their death; most of the others had to wait till the nineteenth century.

NOTES

1. G. B. Harrison, *Shakespeare's Fellows*, p. 71 *note*. Marlowe 'railed at Mr. Topcliffe', according to Richard Cholmeley's evidence in 1593.

2. William Stanley was similarly rumoured to have murdered his brother Ferdinando to gain the Earldom of Derby. We may agree with the exclamation of the unorthodox, who throw up their hands in wonder before such Elizabethan nobles: 'How this transports us from the provincial upbringing of Shakespeare at Stratford!' It does, indeed.

3. 'Every courtier who could scan a line aspired to be one of "Ben's Sons"' (Harrison, p. 181).

CHAPTER VI

THE CASE AGAINST OXFORD AND OTHERS

The time has been,
That when the brains were out, the man would die,
And there an end: but now they rise again . . .
And push us from our stools.

SHAKESPEARE: *Macbeth.*

I

On 8 November 1955 Mr. Christmas Humphreys cross-examined a panel of Oxfordians on the difficulties of their case. I read the account in the *Shakespeare Fellowship News-Letter* for Spring, 1956, hoping to be informed how the Oxfordians get around the embarrassing fact that Edward de Vere died in 1604, before some of Shakespeare's greatest plays were written. But Mr. Humphreys did not ask this question, and so no answer was forthcoming.

I am afraid that I cannot allow the matter to rest there. All the other arguments against the case for Oxford's authorship—and they are as many as against other aristocratic amateurs of letters—are unimportant beside the fact that he was so inconsiderate as to die before *Macbeth*, *King Lear*, *Antony and Cleopatra*, *Coriolanus*, *Timon of Athens*, *Cymbeline*, *The Winter's Tale*, and *The Tempest* were written. To get an answer to the problem we must first of all turn to Looney's '*Shakespeare*' *Identified*, the pioneer work on the Oxfordian claim.

This book has been regarded with something approaching to veneration by subsequent believers. William McFee, in his introduction to the American reprint, tells us that the book 'resembles in its general tenor *The Origin of Species*. In my own opinion . . . "*Shakespeare*" *Identified* is destined to occupy in modern Shakespeare controversy the place Darwin's great work occupies in evolutionary theory' (p. xix). Slater, after summarizing Looney's arguments, exclaims: 'If I could, I would now present the case against this theory, but I cannot. To the best of my knowledge no reply to the Oxfordians has been published. Nor can I make out any substantial adverse case myself' (*Seven Shakespeares*, p. 205).

I think a possible reason for Slater's helplessness was the fact that he was himself a believer in a Group Theory with Oxford at the head, as a possible reason for Mr. Humphreys failing to put the obvious and embarrassing question is the fact that he himself is President of the Shakespeare Fellowship, a body primarily concerned to push the claims of Edward de Vere.

To compare Looney's book with *The Origin of Species* is an insult to Darwin. For example, Looney takes over from Donnelly all the old Baconian legends about the illiteracy of Shakespeare's parents (p. 16 sq.). The equivalent in Darwin would have been the stressing in the *Origin of Species* of the scientific reliability of the Book of Genesis (see above, p. 150 sq.).

Nor would Darwin, I believe, have taken social prejudices to be facts of cultural history, as when Looney writes:

'He [Shakespeare] lodged at one time in Bishopsgate and later on in Southwark. We know this, not because *lords and ladies in their coaches drove up to the door of the famous man* [my italics] . . . but because he was a defaultant taxpayer' (p. 40).

This revealing passage indicates what Looney considered to be evidence of literary accomplishment: that lords and ladies in their coaches should roll up to the author's door! If this is so, the majority of great English writers have not been great at all: they lacked the necessary qualification.

Looney, then, is not the 'cool, scientific' observer of Mr. McFee's imagination. (Mr. Allen speaks of his 'remorseless logic'.) He confessed he was no literary critic, either, but he does in fact make one venture into literary criticism. And this is extremely interesting, as he not only makes it for the express purpose of answering the question as to the authorship of Shakespeare's post-Oxford works, but in answering this question he dismisses the whole of the Oxfordian case. To those who still believe that there is no answer to Looney, I would say: read your Looney again and notice how his argument answers itself.

II

The literary criticism in Looney is virtually restricted to his Appendix I, on *The Tempest*. He has previously entitled his Chapter XIII, 'Manhood of Edward de Vere: Final or Shakespearean

Period (1590–1604)', and he is so conscious of the need to compress the plays into a period of about fifteen years that he affects to wonder how Shakespeare could have compressed them into a period of about twenty or twenty-three years! He speaks ironically of 'a series of stupendous creative efforts . . . the rapid succession of which betokened a genius of almost superhuman fecundity' (p. 315). This is really a most extraordinary argument for the authorship of a man who, on Looney's own showing, had even less time to perform the work.

At the beginning of his long appendix on *The Tempest*, Looney admits that some difficulties have arisen in connection with his case, but 'the surprising thing has been that they have proved so few and unformidable. Up to the present, the greatest obstacle is that presented by one play, *The Tempest*.' Why this play in particular? we must ask; considering that Oxford, the alleged author, died not only before this play was written, but before all the others we have mentioned. Luckily, Looney in answering the objections raised over *The Tempest* also answers the objections raised over these other plays—and in so doing dismisses the Oxfordian case.

His conclusion will be astonishing to the unprepared reader, but one must admit that it follows logically from his arguments:

'We are prepared to maintain, then, on the strength of the various points indicated, that *The Tempest* is no play of "Shakespeare's" . . . The discovery brings additional support to the supposition that the author of the genuine work was indeed Edward de Vere' (p. 452).

It proves, as a matter of fact, the exact opposite.

Now what made Looney believe that *The Tempest* was un-Shakespearean? He had previously spoken of the verse of the later plays in general—from about *Antony and Cleopatra* onward—as '"rag-time" verse', 'so-called "blank-verse" hardly distinguishable to the ear from honest prose' (p. 349 sq.). This is the argument developed at length in regard to *The Tempest*. He speaks of what he imagines to be its 'un-Shakespearean' style, such as the use of 'and' and 'but' and 'that' at the end of lines; he speaks of its 'attempt at blank verse'. 'Throughout the play there is a general thinness, so far as first-class literary matter and the figurative language which distinguishes the best poetry are concerned.' He is particularly upset by the 'defect', as he sees it, of the running-over of one line into the next, as in 'have Put', 'had Burnt', 'must Take', 'and The', 'and A', etc. (p. 448 sq.).

Prof. Porohovshikov, the Rutlandian, agrees with Looney that *The Tempest* is of poor literary quality. He speaks of its 'glaring defects' and 'bad scansion' and believes that Shakespeare (meaning Rutland) wrote only two passages in the play: the first scene and Stephano's song in II, 2: 'The master, the swabber, the boatswain and I.' 'Apart from this, there is little in the dialogue which we could confidently ascribe to Shakespeare' (*Shakespeare Unmasked*, p. 225 sq.). Rutland, unlike Oxford, was still alive at the time when Shakespeare wrote this play.

I do not agree with Looney, but I cannot fault him in the internal consistency of his literary arguments. I believe it is precisely in that internal consistency that there lies the time-bomb which explodes the Oxfordian case.

Looney has spoken of un-Shakespearean defects. What we want to know is: by what standard is he judging? And he tells us. He is judging *The Tempest* by the standard of *Hamlet*:

'Taking *Hamlet* as our standard for measuring Shakespeare's style of versification, we do not find a single example of this defect in the great masterpiece. . . . Never once does this form of intimate connection between the end of one line and the beginning of the next appear in *Hamlet*. How it is possible to hold, in the face of a comparison of this kind, that the versification of both plays came from the same pen, is most difficult to understand' (p. 448).

Now this is perfectly sound literary criticism: the alleged 'defect' is *not* a feature of *Hamlet*, save in a few examples; it is not a feature of any play written about the same time as *Hamlet*, still less is it a feature of any play written before; but it is an increasingly common feature of the later plays, from about *Antony and Cleopatra* onward. Looney's criticism, I believe, is perfectly sound, both to those who agree with him that the point raised is a 'defect' and to those of us who think it an improvement.

The blank-verse style of Shakespeare *did* change in the way Looney has pointed out. It changed from the rigid style of the earliest plays, where each line halts at the end like a soldier on sentry-go, very gradually to a more conversational style. It is by this change from rigid blank-verse to what is virtually 'free verse' —or to Looney 'rag-time verse'—that literary critics are enabled to date most of Shakespeare's plays with some general degree of accuracy. No one disputes that, by this stylistic evidence, *Romeo* is early or fairly early, *Hamlet* middle or middle-approaching-late, and *The Tempest* very late. Looney is precisely wrong when he speaks of *The Tempest* as 'a play apart': it bears the strongest relation, both in style and theme, to *The Winter's Tale* and *Cymbeline*. All three of these plays were written during the same period, all have the conversational style at its highest pitch of literary art—those 'defects of style' which Looney reprobated by the standard of *Hamlet*.

Can we treat *Hamlet* as the standard of Shakespeare's style? Evidently not, unless we believe with Looney that Shakespeare died soon after he had written it and that most of the later plays were finished by inferior playwrights from Oxford's uncompleted manuscripts:

'The people who were "finishing off" these later plays [*Antony*, *Coriolanus*, etc.] took straightforward prose, either from the works of others, or from rough notes collected by "Shakespeare" in preparing his dramas, and chopped it up, along with a little dressing, to make it look in print something like blank verse . . .

'The general stamp, then, of this later work is greatness, suggestive of unfailing powers; and defects suggestive of unfinished workmanship and the intervention of inferior pens: a combination which we claim can only be explained by the death of the dramatist' (p. 349 sq.).

Shakespeare's career extended from about 1590 to about 1612, and *Hamlet*, written about 1600, comes therefore about half-way through. It comes at the end of the middle period or at the very beginning of the late; so far from it being the 'culmination' of the 'great series of Shakespearean dramas', as Looney suggested, it would be truer to say it was the beginning of them. The great tragedies, the apex of Shakespeare's achievement, can be said to *begin* with *Hamlet*, they cannot be said to end with it: *Hamlet* was followed by *Macbeth*, *Lear*, and *Antony*, to mention the chief. In *The Age of Shakespeare* (Vol. 2 of the Pelican *Guide to English Literature*), Shakespeare's plays are considered in four chapters: (1) 'The Young Dramatist'; (2) 'The Middle Plays', including *Hamlet*; (3) '*King Lear* and the Great Tragedies'; and (4) 'The Last Plays', including *The Tempest*.

What is important is the point Looney himself stressed: that the conversational style of *The Tempest* (and, he could have added with almost equal truth, of *Antony and Cleopatra*) is not generally found in *Hamlet*. It was, in fact, *a later development*, a perfectly logical development, for *Hamlet* itself is 'conversational' or 'free' compared with *Romeo*. And this later development, which Looney deplored and which most literary critics today admire as the supreme culmination of Shakespeare's dramatic art, took place after Oxford's death. Looney, in other words, has disproved the Oxfordian case.

There are two possible ways out of the dilemma. One, as we have seen, was suggested by Looney himself; the other has been suggested by his followers. Looney suggested that perhaps the unfinished manuscripts and notes of such plays as *Antony* and *Coriolanus* were found at Oxford's death and completed for the stage by inferior playwrights; later Oxfordians have suggested that the whole question of the dating of Shakespeare's plays is now an open one and that the entire series, even including *The Tempest*, can be easily fitted into the lifetime of Oxford.

But neither of these suggestions can be substantiated. Let us take Looney's first. The question is again one of literary dramatic style, the question that Looney himself raised in dismissing *The Tempest* as spurious. The development of Shakespeare's style, I make no apology for repeating, was towards conversation, towards a free use of blank verse that inevitably reminds us today of the 'free verse' of modern poets like Eliot. Looney should have realized that the style of *Antony and Cleopatra*, for example, is all of a piece throughout. To suggest that this masterpiece of art is the result of inferior playwrights completing for the stage an unfinished *Hamlet*-like manuscript of Oxford's is preposterous. *Antony* is not another *Hamlet* spoiled by inferior pens; it is the product of a later development in Shakespeare's art and—though a great admirer of *both* plays, I should myself add—the product of a much deeper insight into human nature.

One cannot therefore suggest that these later plays, most of which are among Shakespeare's greatest achievements, were crowded, even in an unfinished state, into a short period immediately preceding Oxford's death. (Would *anyone* have suggested this had Oxford lived ten years longer?) For the development of Shakespeare's style was a very slow development. Gradually, very gradually, the rigid forms of blank verse were turned into a style reminiscent of natural conversation, and I need hardly remind the reader that such a development must have come easier to a professional dramatist who was also a professional actor than to anybody else. It was partly Shakespeare's professional knowledge of *speaking* verse that led him—very gradually—to substitute for the declamation of *King Henry the Sixth* those 'defects' which Looney spotted in *The Tempest*—and which are, of course, simply the conversational style common to all Shakespeare's later plays.

It was a development which extended in all over about twenty or twenty-three years. At no point in this gradual process could the development have been suddenly speeded up, not even to comply with the inconvenient fact that Oxford died in 1604. *Hamlet* was written around the turn of the century; seven years of gradual development brought Shakespeare to *Antony*; four or five years more brought him to *The Tempest*. As Looney himself has unconsciously proved, the plays mentioned belong to three different periods, three stages in Shakespeare's development: *Hamlet* to the middle period, *Antony* to the period of the great tragedies (of which *Hamlet*, if you like, was the forerunner), and *The Tempest* to the final period. To claim *Hamlet* as belonging to the final period is as plainly wrong as to suggest that ten or twelve years of development could have been telescoped into five or six.

On Looney's showing, if I have read him correctly, Oxford wrote the first draft of *Hamlet* about 1600, then wrote but left unfinished *Macbeth, Lear, Antony, Coriolanus, Timon, Cymbeline* and *The Winter's Tale*—all between 1600 and 1604, together with *Twelfth Night, All's Well, Measure for Measure* and *Othello*—and then went back to *Hamlet* and produced the revised 2nd Quarto of 1604 just before he died. This suggestion completely contradicts the evidence of style which Looney himself pointed out. We are asked to believe that after writing such plays as *Antony* and *The Winter's Tale* in a style similar to that of the 'spurious' *Tempest*, Oxford went back to *Hamlet*—and his middle style! To say nothing of the fact that if *The Tempest* is spurious by reason of its conversational style, then *Antony, Coriolanus, The Winter's Tale*, etc. must be spurious, too.

A literary artist can no more go back to a style he has outworn than can an artist in paint or music. And he cannot crowd ten or twelve years' stupendous development into half that time. Neither suggestion will find any support except among those already committed to the Oxfordian case, and it will find such support among them, not on literary grounds, but simply and solely because they have to explain away the uncomfortable fact that Oxford died in 1604. If it was suddenly proved that the date of Oxford's death was a mistake, that he really died in 1612, we should hear nothing further of these suggestions.

III

The other argument, made by more recent Oxfordians, seems on the surface to have much more to commend it. It does not involve any drastic curtailment of Shakespeare's stylistic development, or any putting of a late play like *Antony* before a middle play like *Hamlet*, since it recommends a bodily removal of the entire development to an earlier period: the same plays, even *The Tempest*, with the same slow development of style from early to middle, from middle to late, from late to final, but simply transferred in a body to about twelve years earlier. It is an attractive theory; can it therefore be accepted?

I believe it would stand a greater chance of acceptance by non-Oxfordians were it not for one fact, a fact which I have often had to point out in these pages: Shakespeare cannot be treated in isolation; he was not the only dramatist of his time. The development I have mentioned, from sentry-like blank verse to a more natural style reminiscent of actual conversation, was not the work of Shakespeare alone, though he played the chief part in it (or the chief part after Marlowe's death). If we remove Shakespeare's work bodily to a period twelve years earlier, then we have to do the same for Marlowe and the rest. It is a wholesale removal or nothing. Let us look at this difficulty in more detail.

I have said 'twelve years earlier', though there is not full agreement among Oxfordians as to the extent of the shifting desired. I am going by the theory in *Edward de Vere, the Real Shakespeare* (1947) by William Kent and Another, which is merely *one* of the theories that have been advanced.

The theory is put forward by Mr. Kent's collaborator on p. 26 of their joint pamphlet. He takes over the suggestion of Dr. A. S. Cairncross in *The Problem of Hamlet* (1936), to the effect that 'the

Complete *Hamlet* Quarto (1604) was written for the Queen's Men by Shakespeare late in 1588 or early in 1589':

'This demolishes the artificially constructed chronology which had to fit in everything between 1597 and 1616 to suit the life of the Stratford man—and accordingly did so. Dr. Cairncross proves that *Hamlet* was written at least twelve years earlier than the orthodox date, and was certainly not one of the earliest plays; Sir Edmund Chambers puts twenty-one of them before it!'

This, then, is the theory put forward by one set of Oxfordians, with the help of Dr. Cairncross: the 1604 *Hamlet*, the end of Shakespeare's middle period, was really written about 1588, instead of about 1600–1 as most scholars believe, and the earliest of Shakespeare's plays belong accordingly to about 1580. This would also fit in with Miss Gwynneth Bowen's suggestion, in *Shakespeare's Farewell* (1951), that *The Tempest* is not spurious, after all, but written by Oxford in 1604, just before his death. As Mr. Kent's colleague can enlist Dr. Cairncross on his side, so Miss Bowen, in a scholarly well-reasoned pamphlet, can quote the opinion of a distinguished nineteenth-century German critic: 'Karl Elze places *The Tempest* between the tragedy of *Darius*, by the Earl of Sterling (published in Edinburgh, 1603, and London, 1604) and Ben Jonson's *Volpone* (1605)' (p. 8).

The case seems reasonable enough—on the surface. But we should realize that the opinions of Karl Elze and Dr. Cairncross have found little support among scholars and literary critics. And the reason why they have found little support has nothing whatever to do with the dates of Shakespeare's birth and death. It is a far more serious argument than any 'artificially constructed chronology' which the Oxfordians have to face.

They have to face the fact that you cannot treat Shakespeare's plays in isolation. The Oxfordian date for *Hamlet* is now 1588, Oxford–Shakespeare's first plays having been written around 1580. The accepted date of the first part of Marlowe's *Tamburlaine* is about 1587; the accepted date for *The Spanish Tragedy* about 1588–9. This means that when Oxford–Shakespeare had completed his middle period, and had progressed far beyond the sentry-go style of his first plays, Marlowe and Kyd were still on sentry-go. The accepted chronology, which dates *Tamburlaine, The*

Spanish Tragedy, *Titus Andronicus*, and *Henry the Sixth* within a few years of one another, is surely more reasonable.

Dramatists do not exist in isolation: they influence each other. If Shakespeare had already advanced to his middle period by about 1585–6 why on earth should Kyd and Marlowe persist in writing in a style outworn? Marlowe, with his great genius, would have followed Shakespeare with a difference, of course; what he could not possibly have done was to have written *Tamburlaine* in the style that his rival had long discarded.

The alternative to this horn of the Oxfordian dilemma is the even more serious horn of shifting Marlowe back twelve years earlier as well. This would mean that he wrote the first part of *Tamburlaine* about 1575, when he was a child of eleven—and that is too great a precocity even for Rutlandians like Mr. Sykes to swallow. The Oxfordians would have to assume, too, that Marlowe wrote nothing during the last twelve years of his life, unless they go the whole hog and 'prove' that his death took place in 1581, not 1593.

There are other disadvantages. Francis Meres published in 1598 his celebrated *Palladis Tamia*, in which he mentioned twelve of Shakespeare's plays, practically a complete list of all that had been written up to that date. But if we carry the whole series back twelve years! That would mean that Meres had the bad literary taste to mention among Shakespeare's tragedies *Titus Andronicus*, but not *Lear*, *Antony*, *Hamlet* or *Macbeth*; and among the comedies *The Two Gentlemen of Verona*, but not *Twelfth Night* or *Measure for Measure*. Unless the Oxfordians again go the whole hog and date Meres's book 1586, and if they do this there is no logical reason why they should not hold that the de Vere family came over with the Conqueror, not in 1066, as had previously been supposed, but in 1054.

I do not believe this tampering with history can do anybody any good in the long run. What is the suggestion, after all, but an ingenious attempt to bolster up a theory which is, in any case, without foundation? For if Oxford could be proved to have lived till 1612, that would not make him the author of Shakespeare's plays. The fact of his early death is the most obvious point against the theory, and in itself it is, I believe, decisive—as it is decisive against the theories supporting Essex, Devonshire, Queen Elizabeth, and the elder Florio (not to mention Cardinal Wolsey). But there are many other points against the Oxfordian theory, most of which we have already covered in earlier chapters. Oxford was a nobleman, an enthusiastic amateur and generous patron of the arts, and therefore no more able to compose the professional plays of Shakespeare than the professional music of Byrd. He is alleged to have written his life-story in the plays and *Sonnets*; the same plays and *Sonnets* are alleged by other theorists to contain the autobiographies—all very different—of Raleigh, Essex, Derby, Bacon, Rutland, and numerous others. The logical inference is not that one of these theories is correct, but that none of them is correct. He is supposed in Sonnet 125 to be referring to his duty as Lord High Chamberlain of bearing the canopy over the Queen's head; the supporters of Raleigh, Derby, Sidney, and Anne Whateley give other explanations—all very different—of the same passage. The logical inference, again, is not that one of these theories is correct, but that none of them is correct.

I cannot close this chapter without expressing my concern at the way Dr. Bénézet has misquoted Emerson. It is bad enough having Emerson always quoted by Baconians as a Baconian, but this error rests upon their taking down a quotation out of its context without troubling to find out what Emerson really wrote. I have already quoted his actual words (p. 68 above) and since the passage is short I will quote them again here, with the addition of the very next sentence—which proves that he was not a Baconian. 'The Egyptian verdict of the Shakespeare Societies comes to mind, that he was a jovial actor and manager. I cannot marry this fact to his verse. Other admirable men have led lives in some sort of keeping with their thought; but this man, in wide contrast. Had he been less, had he reached only the common measure of great authors, of Bacon, Milton, Tasso, Cervantes, we might leave the fact in the twilight of human fate' (*Representative Men*, World's Classics ed., p. 309). On p. 294 Emerson refers to Shakespeare leaving Stratford for London; the whole essay, in fact, is entirely orthodox. Emerson was simply under the mistaken impression that Shakespeare should have lived the life of a lay-preacher or philosopher like himself instead of the actor's life he actually led.

The Baconians can be forgiven for their error, which does not involve any actual misquotation, but it is more difficult to condone the treatment of Emerson by Dr. Bénézet, President of the American branch of the Shakespeare Fellowship. After making a list of all the hoary old legends about Shakespeare's untaught parents, illiterate daughter, bookless house, etc., Dr. Bénézet writes: 'Says Emerson: "I cannot marry these facts to this verse" ' (*Shakspere, Shakespeare and de Vere*, p. 3). The passage from Emerson that Dr. Bénézet was thinking of has just been quoted: it does not bear much relation to the Oxfordian's revised version. Dr. Bénézet, in fact, has made Emerson responsible for the 'facts' which he himself has drawn from Donnelly and others. Emerson makes no mention of Shakespeare's allegedly untaught parents, illiterate daughter or bookless house.

CHAPTER VII

SOME MINOR THEORIES CONSIDERED

Nothing like leather, quoth the cobbler.
ANON: *Old saw.*

I

That Shakespeare was a lawyer has long been clear to many of those who are themselves in the legal profession. That he was a sailor has been similarly obvious to those who have been down to the sea in ships and whose calling has taken them into deep waters. The dramatist's intimate acquaintance with military life has long been evident—to professional soldiers. While his knowledge of medicine and pathology has become more and more apparent through the years—to doctors and psychologists. Whole books have been devoted to Shakespeare's familiarity with printing, zoology, botany, classical scholarship, Biblical studies, and practically every other subject under the sun; and the authors of these books have been, almost invariably, those professionally engaged in the subject under discussion.

To this *embarras de richesses* the Baconians have their answer ready in the alleged familiarity of Francis Bacon with 'all knowledge'. Since this is a purely romantic idea, being based, as we have seen, upon a remark of Bacon's lifted out of its context, it is not important for the rest of us. More important to realize is what the poet and critic T. S. Eliot once wrote when considering some recently-published books on Shakespeare:

'. . . I believe that I have as high an estimate of the greatness of Shakespeare as poet and dramatist as anyone living; I certainly believe that there is nothing greater. And I would say that my only qualification for venturing to talk about him is, that I am *not* under the delusion that Shakespeare in the least resembles myself, either as I am or as I should like to imagine myself. It seems to me that one of the chief reasons for questioning Mr. Strachey's Shakespeare, and Mr. Murry's, and Mr. Lewis's, is the remarkable resemblance which they bear to Mr. Strachey, and Mr. Murry, and

208

Mr. Lewis respectively. I have not a very clear idea of what Shakespeare was like. But I do not conceive him as very like either Mr. Strachey, or Mr. Murry, or Mr. Wyndham Lewis, or myself' ('Shakespeare and the Stoicism of Seneca', 1927, *Selected Essays*, 1934 ed., p. 128).

This is wise advice to remember whenever we are tempted to succumb to the natural weakness of thinking Shakespeare, or any other great dramatist or novelist, either like ourselves personally or else a member of our own particular profession. It is no accident that so many lawyers have belonged to the Francis Bacon Society: they like to think Shakespeare one of themselves. It is no accident, either, that the general ranks of the unorthodox have held so many aristocrats, or those who would like to be aristocrats.

Luckily, as we have seen, there is no unanimity among lawyers as to the extent of Shakespeare's legal knowledge, and the idea that he could possibly have been Bacon has filled some of them with mingled amusement and disgust. There is similar encouraging reading in the latest book devoted to Shakespeare's alleged intimacy with the classics: *Shakespeare and the Classics* (1952) by J. A. K. Thomson. Prof. Thomson comes to conclusions similar to those of Ben Jonson and the seventeenth century in general: that Shakespeare had little Latin and less Greek.

A German Baconian, Dr. Konrad Meier, once suggested that Jonson's famous line in the First Folio: 'And though thou hadst small Latin and less Greek', should be read in the sense of 'Even if . . .' This has since been accepted by most modern Baconians. But Jonson's opinion does not stand alone; it was the accepted opinion of the age. In a verse-letter to Jonson, written about 1615, Beaumont wrote:

> Here I would let slip
> (If I had any in me) scholarship,
> And from all Learning keep these lines as clear
> As Shakespeare's best are . . .

In his 'commendary verses' to the 1640 edition of Shakespeare's *Poems*, his Stratford friend Leonard Digges wrote:

> . . . Nature only helped him, for look thorough
> This whole book, thou shalt find he doth not borrow
> One phrase from Greeks, nor Latins imitate.

o

This opinion of Shakespeare's contemporaries was also that of their seventeenth-century successors: Shakespeare's 'Nature' was always contrasted with Jonson's 'Art'—the latter word having a classical, not a dramatic, significance. For instance, H. Ramsay wrote in *Jonsonius Virbius* (1637):

> That Latin he reduced and could command
> That which your Shakspere scarce could understand.

Richard Flecknoe in his *Essays on the English Stage* (c. 1660) wrote that 'Shakespeare excelled in a natural vein . . . Johnson in gravity and ponderousness of style . . . Comparing him with Shakespeare, you shall see the difference betwixt Nature and Art.'

Let us refresh our memory with the contrary opinion of the unorthodox. Dr. Titherley speaks of 'Shakespeare's saturation with the classics', of his being 'deeply versed in ancient classical lore' and says that 'his erudition was unbounded, the Plays and Poems teeming with classical allusion'; Holmes wrote of Shakespeare as 'a classical scholar'; Ellis of his 'stupendous knowledge of the classics'; Morgan of his 'massive draught upon antiquity'; Durning-Lawrence of his 'prodigious amount of knowledge of classical lore'; Mr. Johnson speaks of the plays being 'literally stuffed with classical allusions'; and so on.

It seems a shame after this to turn to Prof. Thomson and observe what chilly water he pours upon such enthusiastic illusions. The unorthodox are never weary of throwing up their hands in wonder before those not very distinguished poems *Venus and Adonis* and *The Rape of Lucrece*; they refer to them as 'teeming with classical allusion,' 'the fruit of much classical learning', etc. Of the former, Mr. Johnson writes: 'Polished and scholarly indeed is this extraordinary poem, imbued with the highest culture of the age in which it was written'; and a Barrister writes that 'the work exhibits a degree of classical learning unequalled in the English tongue'; Stotsenburg thought it 'unquestionably written by a scholar. . . . It is indisputable that no one but a learned man could have written the *Venus and Adonis*'; while Greenwood speaks of it as 'imbued with the spirit of the highest culture of the age in which it was written. A courtly, scholarly poem, saturated with Ovid.' Let us see what a modern classical scholar has to say:

'There are in the general body of *Venus and Adonis* a number, but, considering the subject and the conventional way of treating such a subject, a surprisingly small number, of allusions to classical tales and persons. All these allusions are of a perfunctory character and such as could be plucked in Elizabethan times from every hedgerow . . .

'Of *The Rape of Lucrece* the general character is the same . . . There are casual references to Narcissus, to Orpheus before Pluto, to Philomel—the commonplaces of Renaissance poetry, and all, as it happens, to be found in the *Metamorphoses*, whence comes nine-tenths of Shakespeare's classical mythology. Of classical *learning* there is no trace. . . .

'Ovid's own poetry is loaded in every rift with mythological allusion, and his Renaissance imitators, both in Latin and in their mother tongues, had followed him in this. But anyone who reads the *Poems* of Shakespeare with an eye solely to their matter will be astonished to find how meagre and perfunctory is the element of classical allusion. We, who think little of such allusions and rarely find them in contemporary verse . . . do not notice this character-istic of *Venus and Adonis* and *Lucrece*. But it was noticed in Shakespeare's own day' (*Shakespeare and the Classics*, pp. 42–3, 181–2).

Precisely: the cultural background was different. And what the Baconians and others, living in a different cultural environment, have taken to be Shakespeare's 'profound classical learning' seemed to his contemporaries, such as Jonson and Digges, very perfunctory indeed, at most the mere 'odds and ends of classical scholarship'—to quote Prof. Thomson on *Love's Labour's Lost*. In this play, he says, 'while there is a great deal of classical quotation and allusion, it is all of the kind that could be picked up by any intelligent person in Shakespeare's age' (pp. 76–7). Prof. Thomson examines this play in some detail (pp. 66–76) and concludes that the only thing we can be certain of is that Shakespeare had read Lily's *Grammar* and part at least of Erasmus's *Colloquia Familiaria*. According to Mrs. Stopes and Miss Chute, both these were ex-tensively used in the lower forms of Elizabethan grammar schools. Have, then, unorthodox writers simply underrated the classical culture of Elizabethan England?

I believe the correct answer to this question is: yes and no. They have underrated the extent to which classical allusions were household words in the sixteenth century, but at the same time

they have grossly overestimated the classical scholarship of the
Court and upper classes.

To take the latter point first. Dr. Titherley repeats the old
legend that 'Queen Elizabeth was an accomplished scholar,
familiar with Greek and Latin', to which and similar legends Prof.
Thomson makes this reply: 'If one finds it written that Queen
Elizabeth or Lady Jane Grey knew Greek, it is impossible to take
that very seriously. Some Greek they certainly knew, but it cannot have been much, for their very preceptors did not know
much' (p. 18).

On the other hand, the unorthodox have much underrated the
extent of the popular classical knowledge of the time. It was not in
the least a scholarly knowledge, any more than the average man's
acquaintance with scientific matters today is truly scientific. But
as the man in the street nowadays knows the names of such things
as radar and atomic energy, without being able to give a scientific
description of them, so the average member of the Globe audience
knew enough about the classics to recognize references to mythological figures. He had seen them portrayed often enough in the
streets outside:

'. . . some knowledge of Greece and Rome was impressed upon the
most illiterate Elizabethan. There was an almost continuous succession of masques, shows, revels, processions, royal progresses
and the like, in each of which there was sure to be one or more
characters drawn from ancient history or mythology. . . . Who-
ever in reading Shakespeare finds allusions to Jove with his
thunderbolt . . . or Venus with her doves should not conclude
from this that the poet was remembering what he had read in
books. It is rather more likely that he was remembering what he
had seen in London streets' (Thomson, pp. 37–8; compare Robertson, *Baconian Heresy*, p. 180 sq., on the classical allusions in
homilies and popular plays).

The unorthodox always speak of 'knowing Latin', as if it were a
question of knowing that 2 plus 2 equals 4. The true question—
how *much* Latin?—is avoided. Any Elizabethan who had been to
school at all must have known *some* Latin, for little else was taught.
Today, for a man to know any Latin is to be one in a thousand;
in Elizabethan times, we find that 'Sturley, a Stratford alderman,

wrote in Latin to his fellow-townsman Quiney, and the latter at the age of eleven wrote a Latin letter to his father' (Connes, p. 275). The fact that young Quiney could write in Latin is an indication that he was being educated at the local Grammar School, where little else but Latin was taught. The very instructions of the master (quoted in *Love's Labour's Lost*) were in the ancient tongue. If Richard Quiney, whose son later married Shakespeare's daughter, was educated at the Grammar School, why not Shakespeare himself? Both were the sons of aldermen, and the two families had been friends since the days of Shakespeare's grandfather at Snitterfield.

Much is made by the unorthodox of the fact that in *Love's Labour's Lost* Holofernes quotes the first line of the *Eclogues* of Mantuanus. This is evidently one of those 'classical' allusions which so impress them with the profundity of Shakespeare's erudition. They should look a little deeper. In the first place, 'Mantuanus' is not a classical author at all: it was the clerical name of Johannes Baptista Spagnuoli, a Carmelite monk who died in 1516. In the second place, his *Eclogues* was a favourite grammar-school text in Elizabethan times, being considered suitable for third-form reading. (Mrs. Stopes, p. 233; Thomson, pp. 19, 33–4; Baldwin, *Shakspere's 'Small Latine and Lesse Greeke'*, II: p. 543.) Thomson agrees with Robertson (*The Baconian Heresy*, pp. 178–375) that we should be wary before accepting the opinion of Churton Collins, the Victorian scholar, that Shakespeare was necessarily quoting the classics at first-hand in all such passages. Applying the tests of 'thought' and 'wording', similar to Robertson's, Thomson concludes that it is surprising how few of the suggested allusions and imitations 'survive the ordeal' (p. 31).

As long ago as 1767, Richard Farmer proved by parallel quotations that in most cases where Shakespeare was apparently following classical authors, he was really following their translators. We must ask those who imagine him to have been a profound classical scholar why he should have followed translators at all. Oxfordians make much of the fact that de Vere's uncle was Arthur Golding, translator of the *Metamorphoses* (1567), but a scholar would not have needed Golding to read Ovid any more than Holland to read Pliny, North to read Plutarch—North himself knew no Greek, but took his Plutarch from a French translation—or Bernard to read Terence.* The *Metamorphoses* was a fourth-form text in the grammar-schools of the period, so it is likely that Shakespeare knew a little Ovid in the original. He could have borrowed a very nice edition of the original from his publisher Field. The fact that he mostly followed Golding is proof, however, that he was not sufficient of a scholar to trust to his own learning.

Latin was the international language of the sixteenth century, the means by which statesmen, churchmen, theologians, scholars, and philosophers addressed each other across the frontiers of Europe. The use by Shakespeare of whatever translations lay to his hand surely proves that his works could not have been written either by a university man or by a churchman or by one trained for government. This rules out Bacon, Derby, Rutland, and Oxford, of those theories already considered, as well as Raleigh, Marlowe, Devonshire, Burton, Anne Whateley, Essex, Cecil, Southampton, Stirling, Shirley, not to mention the Jesuits, among the minor theories. It leaves us in fact with just such a man as we know Shakespeare to have been, living in just such a time as we know the Elizabethan age to have been.

II

I have discussed the question of Shakespeare's alleged classical scholarship in this final chapter of our Criticism section for two reasons: first, because it was the only important question which remained outstanding; secondly, because there is one exception to the general unorthodox rule that sees the 'real' Shakespeare as an aristocrat and that is the theory which sees him as a university scholar. Such a scholar was Burton, and even more interesting is the theory which gives Shakespeare to Christopher Marlowe. Born into much the same circumstances as Shakespeare himself, Marlowe was not a 'better' in any social sense, but he was educated

---

* Montaigne thought the plays of Terence, a Carthaginian slave, were really written by his patrons Laelius and Scipio the younger. This is an interesting forerunner of the anti-Shakespearean heresies, and many of the unorthodox have taken the epigram of John Davies of Hereford to 'our English Terence, Mr. Will Shake-speare' to be a covert reference to Shakespeare being a cover for some noble patron (see, e.g., Johnson, *Francis Bacon of St. Albans*, pp. 33-4). Classical scholars today, however, do not agree with Montaigne that Terence was incapable of writing his own plays; the utmost they will allow is that he may have been helped by his patrons. See Gilbert Norwood's *Art of Terence* and the *Oxford Classical Dictionary*.

at Cambridge and must have known a great deal more about the classics than his rival.

We have seen in an earlier chapter how greatly Mr. Hoffman has underestimated the publishing and the popular reading of the Elizabethan age (see above, p. 173 sq.); now we have seen how greatly he has overestimated the classical knowledge revealed in Shakespeare. Between these two errors in estimation sails the frail bark of his theory: that Marlowe, because of his university training, must have written the works.

I will say this for his theory: for the first time we have a hypothetical Shakespeare who was *capable* of writing the plays. This is quite a new thing for unorthodoxy. Bacon was a philosopher, at the furthest extreme in literature from dramatic art; Raleigh was a minor poet; Oxford and others were very minor poets; Rutland's literary works, like those of Anne Whateley and Robert Cecil, are non-existent. . . . It is decidedly refreshing to have an author put forward who was a professional dramatist. With all the other theories, we seem to be travelling in the opposite direction to Shakespeare; with the Marlowe theory, we seem to be coming back again.

And so in truth we are. For the educational assumption of Mr. Hoffman is as illusory as the aristocratic assumption of earlier theorists. Neither has any basis in reality. Shakespeare's plays no more reveal profound classical knowledge than they reveal intimacy with Court life or foreign countries. Prof. Thomson adds that they do not reveal, either, any *feeling* for the Latin language, a point of supreme importance in literature and literary history. 'There is in him no feeling for Latin as Latin; he is not thrilled by Latin poetic style, as Jonson was . . . or Milton.'

So what remains of Mr. Hoffman's theory? If we cancel out Marlowe's educational superiority—and on the evidence of Prof. Thomson it seems to me that we are bound to cancel it out—in what way is he supposed to be a more suitable author? He was born the same year as Shakespeare, into much the same social environment, and he came up to London and became a professional dramatist and actor. How does this differ from Shakespeare? The only point of difference that I can see is that Marlowe unfortunately was killed and Shakespeare went on living. And I see nothing suspicious in the fact that Marlowe's death coincided with the closing of the theatres because of the plague and the consequent writing of

Venus and Adonis and *Lucrece* by a man of the theatre who was temporarily unemployed. It is simply not the case that Marlowe's death coincided with the beginning of Shakespeare's career; he was already an actor and a dramatist.

Mr. Hoffman's book makes much more interesting reading than the majority of unorthodox literature. But the fact must be faced that, apart from the one point of aristocracy—admittedly a big exception—he is a perfectly 'orthodox' unorthodox writer. He agrees, for instance, with the Baconians and the rest that Shakespeare's plays reveal a personal knowledge of foreign countries, which he supposes Marlowe–Shakespeare to have acquired when he fled abroad after his faked death. But most of Marlowe's own plays are set in foreign countries, too: if Shakespeare had to make a personal visit to Venice in order to write *The Merchant*, why did not Marlowe need to visit Asia in order to write *Tamburlaine*? The degree of 'local colour' in any Elizabethan play is a matter upon which no two critics agree; it is amusing to read the difference of opinion among unorthodox writers, each of whom is trying to fit Shakespeare's plays into the travels of his particular candidate.

I wonder when Marlowe visited Scotland in order to be able to write *Macbeth*? Peter Alvor answers this question in regard to Southampton, and the candidacy of the Earl of Stirling must be reckoned to have its chief weight in his intimate knowledge of his native country. But the advocates of Raleigh, while stressing Sir Walter's acquaintance with the sea and the Indies that led him to be able to write *The Tempest*, simply say that he wrote *Macbeth* in the Tower of London in order to please the King! It must be regarded as a logical corollary that if Raleigh could imagine Scotland from the Tower of London, then Shakespeare could imagine it from Cripplegate.

The truth is, of course, that we cannot judge the extent of a dramatist's personal travels from the settings of his plays. The majority of the minor theories agree with the Baconians, the Group Theorists, the Derbyites, the Rutlandians and the Oxfordians in assuming that we can do precisely this. The Earl of Stirling wrote plays, certainly; but they were at the opposite extreme from Shakespeare's, being 'closet dramas' like those of Lady Pembroke's Wilton coterie of poets. The only other 'proof' that Stirling wrote Shakespeare is in his knowledge of the country of *Macbeth*, but then he had to write *The Tempest* from his own reading and imagination just as Raleigh had to write *Macbeth* from the Tower of London. . . .

And so we could go on. For each candidate's 'strong' point is balanced by a score of weak ones, and the logical conclusion is that all these minor theories are equally spurious—as spurious as Bacon–Shakespeare, Group–Shakespeare, Derby–Shakespeare, Rutland–Shakespeare and Oxford–Shakespeare. Which is saying a good deal.

I do not find the centre of Elizabethan–Jacobean literature either in the Court at Whitehall or in Gorhambury, Belvoir Castle, Wilton or any other of the country houses of the aristocracy, old or new. In so far as it had a centre at all, I find it either in the Globe Theatre, Southwark, or in Silver Street, Cripplegate. It was at the Globe Theatre that the supreme masterpieces of English literature were first performed, and it was at his lodgings with the Mountjoy family in Cripplegate that Shakespeare probably wrote most of them. Wilton produced Sidney's *Arcadia* and Daniel's *Cleopatra*, works by no means to be despised; but Cripplegate produced *King Lear* and *Antony and Cleopatra*. It is permissible to take one's choice.

In the neighbouring parish of Aldersgate lived Shakespeare's colleagues John Heminges and Henry Condell—described by Pemberton as 'two journeymen actors, whose names are unknown to literature' (*Shakspere and Sir Walter Ralegh*, p. 16). Unknown to literature! England and the world owe a tremendous debt to these men: 'more is their due than more than all can pay'. By the 1620's, they were the last survivors of the original Chamberlain's Company, and if they had not had the foresight and the wisdom to start collecting Shakespeare's plays together, it is extremely likely that many of them would have been lost.

It is easy to forgive the jibes of the unorthodox at Shakespeare himself; they affect his stature not at all. It is more difficult to condone the unorthodox sneers at Heminges and Condell, and at Ben Jonson. All three collaborated in that embarrassment to unorthodoxy, the First Folio. The unorthodox have tried to cover their embarrassment by suggesting a number of unpleasant things about these three distinguished people, to whom we owe so much. Heminges and Condell have usually been dismissed as ignorant dolts, sometimes for no better reason than that the one ended his days as a grocer, the other as a publican; and Jonson has been credited with deliberate falsehood and the willingness to write anything for money. It is hard to forgive these insults to the men to whom we owe the preservation of the greatest masterpieces of English literature—written, as they pointed out, by the actor William Shakespeare of Stratford-on-Avon.

CONCLUSION

The theories of the alchemists paved the way for chemistry; and there are few
fields of inquiry in which a true explanation of facts has not been reached through
a trial of extravagantly false hypotheses.

W. H. MALLOCK: *New Facts Relating to the*
Bacon–Shakespeare Question.

O monstrous! but one half-pennyworth of bread to this intolerable deal of sack!

SHAKESPEARE: *The First Part of King*
Henry the Fourth.

I

The first part of this book summarized the case against Shakespeare's authorship, and the corresponding case for various alternative authors or groups of authors, as put forward by unorthodox
theorists. The second part consisted of a criticism of these alternative theories, from the point of view of literary criticism and
cultural history, and a corresponding backing of the traditional
authorship. A true conclusion should perhaps sum up the evidence
from an entirely neutral angle.

The difficulty is to find a neutral angle—or any authority who is
truly impartial. Some have claimed to be so, but their claims are
unfounded. Lord Penzance's *Judicial Summing-Up on the Bacon–
Shakespeare Controversy* is correctly described by Robertson as 'a
grossly *ex parte* statement . . . entitled to neither lay nor professional respect'—an opinion proved by the number of occasions
on which Baconians cite Penzance as one of their advocates. Stotsenburg's *Impartial Study of the Shakespeare Title* is only impartial as regards various anti-Shakespearean theories; it is very
biased against Shakespeare himself, as we should expect from its
dedication to Mrs. Pott for her 'exposure' of 'the Shaksper fraud'.
Stotsenburg remarks on p. 513 that 'with Shaksper entirely
eliminated, the path of discovery is open to every disinterested
searcher'.

Gilbert Standen's more recent *Shakespeare Authorship: A Summary of Evidence* is written from the point of view of a Group
Theorist who believes Oxford to be the leading figure. Neither
this nor Slater's *Seven Shakespeares* nor the various works of

Greenwood can truly claim to be unbiased towards the traditional authorship. It would be surprising if they were.

Nor do we find any neutrals in the traditional camp, however conscientious they may be in endeavouring to summarize fairly the anti-traditional case. M. Connes's *Shakespeare Mystery* is probably the most unbiased work on the traditional side: in its summary of the main theories, it has a use even for those who dissent from its conclusions. But neither M. Connes nor myself can claim to be neutral. It would be surprising if we were.

Have we, then, to give up entirely our search for a neutral investigator? Since Shakespeare's death, yes; but we must not forget that the first suspicion that he might have been the mask for an aristocratic author probably arose in his lifetime, when the Privy Council were enquiring into that special performance of *Richard the Second* commissioned by the Essex conspirators. Topcliffe and his men did not care one way or the other who wrote *Richard the Second*: they were simply in pursuit of the truth. Their complete neutrality is as obvious as the advantages they had over the Baconians and other later theorists. They were on the spot, they were trained investigators, and they were searching for a noble author at the express command of the Queen. I do not believe they could possibly have been mistaken, or possibly have been bribed. The reason why Shakespeare did not share the imprisonment of Sir John Hayward was, presumably, because the investigators found convincing proof that the supposed author of *Richard the Second* was in fact the real author. If there had been any doubt about it, Shakespeare would have been imprisoned until he revealed the identity of the nobleman they assumed to be behind him.

I want to stress the importance of this investigation of 1601. It is not only the sole neutral enquiry we have any record of, but all later enquiries seem frivolous by comparison. I do not mean that these later enquirers—Baconian and other—have not been sincere; I mean that nothing vital was at stake. The original investigation was personal and to the point, and the charge was the capital one of treason. Shakespeare was alive, to be tortured if necessary by the same men who, four years afterwards, tortured Guy Fawkes; there was a suspected noble author, who, if he had existed, must have been trembling for his head. Under these circumstances, the investigation was bound to have been thorough and the proof of Shakespeare's authorship—and consequently of the non-existence of any noble author behind him—absolutely convincing. It seems to me that here political history comes to the aid of cultural history to support the traditional case.

II

Has all the labour of the Baconians and other unorthodox theorists gone for nothing, then, or can we agree with W. H. Mallock that it is not necessary to accept any of their theories in order to claim that they have performed a notable service towards the truth?

The parallel with the alchemists drawn by Mallock is tempting to accept, but nevertheless I believe it ought to be firmly rejected. For what, after all, is the 'true explanation of facts' towards which all these theories have been leading? It is the authorship of the plays and poems attributed to William Shakespeare of Stratford-on-Avon. How can these theories be held to have advanced us towards a truer understanding of that authorship?

At best I feel that they have brought us nearer to the truth in a purely negative fashion. Their insistence on the aristocratic nature of Shakespeare's work has led to a testing by literary criticism and cultural history of the 'familiarity with Court and noble life' that has been discovered therein. And by this test the aristocratic assumption has been disproved.

Their insistence that the plays and poems must have been written by a classical scholar has also been tested and found wanting. So have their parallel insistences that the works were written by a traveller returned from France, Italy, Germany, Denmark, America and the West Indies, or by an intellectual giant possessed of the specialized knowledge open to professional lawyers, professional doctors of medicine, professional soldiers, and so forth. What remains, then, after all these assumptions have been cleared away, but the recognition that the traditional authorship is correct, that Heminges, Condell, Ben Jonson, Leonard Digges, and J.M. were neither credulous fools nor deliberate liars but simply telling the truth in a perfectly straightforward manner? The fact that James Boswell the younger, in the late eighteenth century, started a tradition that there was something fishy about the First Folio does not mean there was something fishy about the First Folio; it means that James Boswell the younger with his followers, orthodox and unorthodox, were mistaken. Which is a much more likely state of affairs.

M. Connes came to the conclusion that there was an atom of truth in all the main unorthodox theories: he did not believe that either Bacon, Derby, Rutland or Oxford wrote the works, but thought it possible that Shakespeare was acquainted with all four of these courtiers. I see nothing either in the plays themselves or in the cultural history of the period to warrant such a possibility. The only courtier who can be proved to have had any connection with Shakespeare is the Earl of Southampton, and the Earl's biographer failed to find any evidence that the connection was either intimate or lasting. Until we find other evidence, it is safest to assume what is, in any case, most probable: that Shakespeare mixed, not with courtly amateurs of letters, but with his fellow-professionals in drama, acting, music and publishing. In that high cultural company, rather than in the high social and political company of the Court, is where we should naturally expect to find a man of Shakespeare's genius.

That high Elizabethan society could sometimes be highly cultured, too, is a fact, but it is also a fact that only in the short period of the closing of the theatres in the plague years 1593–4 do we find Shakespeare in the role of a courtly poet. When the theatres reopened, and the companies reformed, he went back to working for the public stage and remained there until his retirement. He had a slight taste of the courtly view of literature through his brief acquaintance with Southampton, but those who make much of this do not explain why, if he liked it, he should have turned away from it immediately he was able to do so. The inference is surely obvious: talented as were the best of the courtly men of letters, they were only amateurs, bound furthermore by half-understood 'rules' of literature they had picked up in their reading or brought from abroad. It was as unlikely that a professional dramatist of Shakespeare's calibre—and of all English dramatists he is the most professional—should have remained in that narrow atmosphere as that a professional artist like Raphael should have allowed the Papal Court to show him how to paint. As patrons and protectors of dramatic companies, the Elizabethan and Jacobean aristocracy must have had Shakespeare's profound gratitude, but he knew better than they did what the freedom of the popular stage meant to the achievement of his art.

His art, his dramatic poetry . . . It is astonishing how little attention is paid to this by those desirous of showing that the plays were written by a nobleman or a group of noblemen. All the emphasis lies on the mere information displayed therein, as if any noble, by virtue of his birth, could be a great dramatic poet! As a matter of fact, there was no great poet, though many distinguished minor ones, among the Elizabethan aristocracy; the nearest to an aristocrat among the great poets of the period was, of course, Spenser. But in the generation immediately succeeding Shakespeare's, the nobility *did* produce a great poet—the Rev. George Herbert (1593–1633), younger brother of Lord Herbert of Cherbury. Herbert seems to me one of the greatest poets of the seventeenth century. Could he, then, if he had been born a little earlier, have written Shakespeare? Compared with those of Bacon and Oxford, not to mention Derby and Rutland and the rest, his claims are tremendous: he really was a great poet. But not even Herbert could have written Shakespeare. In order to do so, he would have had to resign his rectory at Bemerton and become a professional man of the theatre. His poems can be truly compared with the *Sonnets*—I would not care to say which is the greater—but the plays required the poetic genius of the *Sonnets* intimately bound up with a professional knowledge of dramatic art. The combination is naturally rare, but then Shakespeares are only common in a book like this.

SELECTED BIBLIOGRAPHY

Mainly restricted to works and authors mentioned in this book, with some characteristic additions under various headings up to the end of the year 1957.

I: ORIGINS OF THE AUTHORSHIP QUESTION.
    (1) Literary.
    (2) Pictorial.
    (3) Some Modern Authorities.

II: THEORIES OF THE NINETEENTH AND TWENTIETH CENTURIES.
    (1) Anti-Shakespeare in General.
    (2) Group and Dual Theories.
    (3) Francis Bacon.
    (4) Anthony Bacon.
    (5) William Butts.
    (6) Wolsey.
    (7) Raleigh.
    (8) Essex.
    (9) Cecil.
    (10) Burton.
    (11) Southampton.
    (12) Shirley.
    (13) Derby.
    (14) Rutland.
    (15) Barnard.
    (16) Devonshire.
    (17) Stirling.
    (18) Oxford.
    (19) Florio.
    (20) Marlowe.
    (21) Queen Elizabeth.
    (22) Anne Whateley.
    (23) Dyer.
    (24) Other Theories; Satires; Burlesques.
    (25) Discussions; *Résumés*; Bibliographies.

III: SOME PARALLEL THEORIES.

    (1) Terence.
    (2) Molière.
    (3) Emily Brontë.
    (4) Music.

IV: PRO-SHAKESPEARE REJOINDERS.

    (1) Anti-Baconian.
    (2) Anti-Unorthodox in General.

V: SOME RELATED QUESTIONS.

    (1) Biographical.
    (2) Cultural.
    (3) Law.
    (4) Travel.

I: ORIGINS OF THE AUTHORSHIP QUESTION

(1) LITERARY

ANON. (? Capt. Goulding) *An Essay against too much Reading*. London, 1728.

ANON. (? Herbert Lawrence) *The Life and Adventures of Common Sense: An Historical Allegory*. London, 1769.
Vie et aventures de Sens Commun: histoire allégorique, traduite de l'anglais. Avignon & Yverdon, Switzerland, 1777.

ANON. (?? Herbert Lawrence or James Wilmot) *The Learned Pig*. London, 1786.

COWELL, James Corton. 'Some Reflections on the Life of William Shakespeare: a Study read before the Ipswich Philosophical Society.' Unpublished MS dated 7 Feb. 1805, owing its original conception to the author's conversations with the Rev. James Wilmot in 1785.

RICCOBONI, Louis. *Réflexions historiques et critiques sur les différents Théâtres de l'Europe*. Paris, 1738.

TOWNLEY, Rev. James. *High Life below Stairs: a Farce in Two Acts*. London, 1759.

WILMOT, Rev. James. See under *Cowell* above.

(2) PICTORIAL

BACON, Francis. *Sermones Fideles, Ethici, Politici, Oeconomici*. Holland, 1641. Pictorial title-page.
Historia Regni Henrici Septimi. Holland, 1642. Pictorial title-page.
De Augmentis Scientiarum. Holland, 1645, 1662, 1694. Pictorial title-pages.

'GUSTAVUS SELENUS' (? Duke of Brunswick) *Cryptomenytices et Cryptographiae*. Lüneburg, 1624. Pictorial title-page.

MONTAIGNE, Michel de. *Essays*, tr. Florio. 3rd ed., London, 1632. Pictorial title-page.

(3) SOME MODERN AUTHORITIES

LEFRANC, Abel. '*La question Shakespearienne au XVIIIe siècle*.' App. A, *A la Découverte de Shakespeare*, Vol. I. (See below under *Derby*.)

MALLOCK, W. H. 'New Facts Relating to the Bacon–Shakespeare Question.' *Pall Mall Magazine*, XXIX, 117–18; London, Jan.–Feb. 1903.

NICOLL, Allardyce. 'The First Baconian.' *Times Literary Supplement*, London, 25 Feb. 1932.

SYDENHAM OF COMBE, Lord. *The First Baconian*. London, n.d.

II: THEORIES OF THE NINETEENTH AND TWENTIETH CENTURIES.

(1) ANTI-SHAKESPEARE IN GENERAL.

BRIGHT, John. Report of speech denying Shakespeare's authorship of *Othello*. *Rochdale Observer*, 27 March 1889.

DISRAELI, Benjamin. *Venetia*. London, 1837. Chap. VI.

EDWARDS, W. H. *Shaksper not Shakespeare*. Cincinnati, 1900.

FREUD, Sigmund. *Outline of Psychoanalysis*. London, 1940.

GREENWOOD, Sir George. *The Shakespeare Problem Restated*. London, 1908; condensed by Elsie Greenwood, with foreword by Lord Ponsonby, 1937.

Is there a Shakespeare Problem? London, 1916.

Shakespeare's Law and Latin. London, 1916.

Shakespeare's Law. London, 1920.

Ben Jonson and Shakespeare. London, 1921.

Introduction to *Baconian Essays*, ed. Smithson, q.v.

JAMES, Henry. Letter to Violet Hunt, 26 Aug. 1903. *Letters of Henry James*, 1920. Vol. I, p. 432.

MOORE, George. *The Making of an Immortal: A Comedy*. London, 1927.

*'Comment se fait un immortel, ou le Poète malgré lui'; tr. Louis Gillet with a preface, *Revue des Deux Mondes*, Paris, 15 Jan. 1930.

O'CONNOR, William D. *Mr. Donnelly's Reviewers*. Chicago, 1889.

PICHOT, Amédée. *'Shakespeare a-t-il existé?' Revue Britannique*, Paris, Sept. 1856.

TWAIN, Mark. *Is Shakespeare Dead?* New York & London, 1909; Leipzig, 1911.

(2) GROUP AND DUAL THEORIES

ALVOR, Peter. *Das Neue Shakespeare-Evangelium*. Munich, 1906; 2nd ed., Hanover, 1907.

Der heutige Stand der Shakespeare-Frage. Leipzig, 1907.

Die Lösung der Shakespeare-Frage. Leipzig, 1909.

ANON. (initialled J. G. B.) *Who wrote Shakespeare's Plays?* London, 1887.

BACON, Delia. 'Shakespeare and his Plays: An Inquiry.' *Putnam's Magazine*, New York, Jan. 1856.

The Philosophy of Shakespeare's Plays Unfolded. With a Preface by Nathaniel Hawthorne. London, 1857.

BROOKS, Alden. *Will Shakspere: Factotum and Agent*. New York, 1937.

Will Shakspere and the Dyer's Hand. New York, 1943.

CASTLE, Edward James. *Shakespeare, Jonson, Bacon and Greene: A Study.* London, 1897.

CUNNINGHAM, Dr. W. M. *The Tragedy of Sir Francis Bacon, Prince of England.* Los Angeles, 1940.

DENNING, W. H. 'Who Wrote the Shakespeare Sonnets?' *English Review,* XL; London, June 1925.

Dressing Old Words New. London, 1933.

DE PEYSTER, J. Watts, General. *Was THE Shakespeare after all a Myth?* New York & London, 1888.

DOUGLAS, Montagu W. *Lord Oxford and the Shakespeare Group.* See below under *Oxford.*

EVANS, A. J. *Shakespeare's Magic Circle.* London, 1956.

'Who was Shakespeare?' *The Humanist,* London, July 1957.

FORREST, H. T. S. *The Five Authors of Shakespeare's Sonnets.* London, 1923.

HART, Joseph C. *The Romance of Yachting.* New York, 1848.

HUTCHESON, W. J. Fraser. *Shakespeare's Other Anne.* Glasgow, 1950.

JAMIESON, Robert. 'Who Wrote Shakespeare?' *Chambers's Journal,* Edinburgh, 7 Aug. 1852.

JOHNSON, Harold. *Did the Jesuits write 'Shakespeare'?* Chicago, 1916.

MARSCHALL, Wilhelm. *Aus Shakespeares Briefwechsel.* Heidelberg, 1926.

Die neun Dichter des 'Hamlet'. Heidelberg, 1929.

MORGAN, Appleton. *The Shakespeare Myth: William Shakespeare and Circumstantial Evidence.* Cincinnati, 1881.

Der Shakespeare-Mythus; tr. Karl Müller-Mylius. Leipzig, 1885.

Shakespeare in Fact and in Criticism. New York, 1888.

MUSKAT, C. G. *Die Lösung der Shakespeare-Frage.* Leipzig, 1925.

O'CONNOR, William D. *Harrington: A Story of True Love.* Boston, 1860.

Hamlet's Note-Book. Boston, 1886.

POROHOVSHIKOV, Pierre S. *Shakespeare Unmasked.* See below under *Rutland.*

REICHEL, Eugen. *Shakespeare-Litteratur.* Stuttgart, 1887.

'Das Porträt des Herrn W. H.' *Die Gegenwart,* Berlin, 1902.

ROBERTSON, J. M. *An Introduction to the Study of the Shakespeare Canon.* London & New York, 1924.

The Genuine in Shakespeare: A Conspectus. London & New York, 1930.

ROSS, William. *The Story of Anne Whateley and William Shaxper as revealed by 'the Sonnets to Mr. W. H.' and other Elizabethan Poetry.* Glasgow, 1939.

SLATER, Gilbert. *Seven Shakespeares.* London, 1931.

STANDEN, Gilbert. *Shakespeare Authorship: A Summary of Evidence.* London, 1930.

STOTSENBURG, John H., Judge. *An Impartial Study of the Shakespeare Title.* Louisville, Kentucky, 1904.

WHITE, T. W. *Our English Homer.* London, 1892.

YEATMAN, J. P. *The Gentle Shakspere.* London, 1896.

ZEIGLER, Wilbur Gleason. *It was Marlowe: A Story of the Secret of Three Centuries.* Chicago, 1895.

(3) FRANCIS BACON

ANON. *'Shaksperes Geheimnis und Bacons Promus'.* Deutsche Allgemeine Zeitung, Berlin, 1 March 1883.

ANON. *The Bacon-Shakespeare Controversy;* by a Barrister. London 1927.

ARENSBERG, W. C. See below under *William Butts.*

BACON, Delia. See above under *Group and Dual Theories.*

BACON SOCIETY, THE FRANCIS. *Baconiana: A Journal devoted to the study of the works of Francis Bacon, his character, genius and influence on his own and succeeding times.* Originally called *The Journal of the Bacon Society.* London, 1886–in progress.

American Baconiana. New York, 1923–31.

Deutsche Baconiana. Leipzig, 1930–2.

BAXTER, J. P. *The Greatest of Literary Problems: The Authorship of Shakespeare's Works.* Boston, 1917.

BEAUMONT, William Comyns. *The Private Life of the Virgin Queen.* London, 1947.

BLACK, Hugh. 'Bacon's Claim and Shakespeare's "Aye",' *North American Review,* Toronto, Oct. 1887.

BONAC-MELVRAU, F. *Défense de Will.* Paris, 1951.

BOOTH, W. S. *Some Acrostic Signatures of Francis Bacon.* Cambridge, Mass., 1909.

Subtle Shining Secrecies. Boston, 1925.

BORMANN, Edwin. *Das Shakespeare Geheimnis.* Leipzig, 1894.

Neue Shakespeare-Enthüllungen. Leipzig, 2 vols., 1895.

Bacon-Shakespeare: 'Venus and Adonis'. Leipzig, 1899.

Die Kunst des Pseudonyms. Leipzig, 1901.

BÜCHNER, Alexandre. 'Shakespeare ou Bacon?' *Revue Britannique,* Paris, May 1885.

BURR, William H. *Bacon and Shaksper.* Washington, 1885.

CARTIER, Henri, Général. *Un Problème de Cryptographie et d'Histoire.* Paris, 1938.

CORNWALL, A. B. *Francis, the First Uncrowned King of England.* Birmingham, 1936.

CREWE, E. *Who Wrote Shakespeare?* Cape Town, 1927.
CUNINGHAM, Granville C. *Bacon's Secret Disclosed in Contemporary Books.* London, 1911.
DAWBARN, C. Y. C. *Uncrowned: The Story of Queen Elizabeth and Bacon.* London, 1913.
DENHAM-PARSONS, John. *Non-Partisan Shakespeare Decipherings.* London, 1927.
Report on the Poet Shakespeare's Identity: submitted to the Trustees of the British Museum. Chiswick, Middlesex, 1930.
DODD, Alfred. *Shakespeare: Creator of Freemasonry.* London, 1937.
Who was Shake-speare? London, 1947.
(ed.) *The Personal Poems of Francis Bacon.* Liverpool, 1931.
DONNELLY, Ignatius. *The Great Cryptogram: Francis Bacon's Cipher in the so-called Shakespeare Plays.* New York, 2 vols., 1888.
'Did Francis Bacon write the Shakespeare Plays?' Motion (lost) at the Union, Cambridge, during visit to England, 1888.
The Cipher in the Plays and on the Tombstone. New York, 1899.
Ben Jonson's Cipher. Minneapolis, 1900.
DURNING-LAWRENCE, Sir Edwin, Bart. *Bacon is Shake-speare.* London, 1910.
The Shakespeare Myth. London, 1912.
EAGLE, Roderick L. *Shakespeare: New Views for Old.* London, 1930; enlarged ed., n.d.
ELLIS, Walter. *The Shakespeare Myth.* London, n.d.
FRANCO, Johan. *Bacon-Shakespeare Identities revealed by their Handwritings.* London, 1947.
FURNESS, W. H. Letter of support to Nathaniel Holmes, New York, 29 Oct. 1866.
GALLUP, Mrs. E. W. *The Biliteral Cypher of Francis Bacon.* Detroit, 2 vols., 1899.
HOLMES, Nathaniel, Judge. *The Authorship of Shakespeare.* New York, 2 vols., 1866.
HOOS, F. *A Shakespeare-drámák-szerzöségi kérdése.* Ersekujvar, Hungary, 1914.
ILIJĆ, V. *Šekspir ili Bekon.* Sobodija, Serbia, 1883.
JOHNSON, Edward D. *The First Folio of Shakespeare.* Birmingham, 1932.
The Shaksper Illusion. Birmingham, 1944; 2nd enlarged ed., London, 1951.
The Mystery of the First Folio of the Shakespeare Plays Birmingham, 1945; 2nd ed., London, n.d.
Will Shakspere of Stratford. London, 1954.
Francis Bacon of St. Albans. London, 1955.

MASNOVO, O. *Come Shakespeare potè leggere Euripide: piccolo contributo alla questione baconiana.* Parma, 1909.

MATHY, Ludwig. *Der wahre William Shakespeare: Prinz Francis Tudor.* Frankfurt-on-Main, 1929.

MEIER, Konrad. Article in German on the First Folio; tr., *Baconiana*, Oct. 1907.

MELSOME, W. S. *The Bacon-Shakespeare Anatomy.* ed. Roderick Eagle. London, 1945.

MILLAR, J. S. L. *The Man in the Shakespeare Mask.* London, 1946.

MUDIE, Alfred. *The Self-Named William Shakespeare.* London, 1925.

MÜLLER-MYLIUS, Karl. *Der Shakespeare-und-Bacon-Streit.* Leipzig, 1884.

O'NEILL, Rev. George. *Could Bacon have written the Plays?* Dublin, 1909.

OWEN, Orville. *Francis Bacon's Cipher Story.* Detroit & New York, 5 vols., 1893–5; London, 1 vol., 1894.

PENZANCE, Lord. *A Judicial Summing-Up on the Bacon-Shakespeare Controversy.* London, 1902.

PLATT, Isaac Hull. *Are the Shakespeare Plays signed by Francis Bacon?* Philadelphia, 1897.

Debate with Appleton Morgan. *New Shakespeareana*, Westfield, New Jersey, April–July 1903.

POPOVIĆ, B. *Šekspir ili Bekon.* Glasnik, Serbia, 1907.

POTT, Mrs. Henry. *Did Francis Bacon write 'Shakespeare'? Part One: 32 Reasons for believing that he did.* New York, 1884; *Part Two: The Lives of Bacon and Shakspere Compared.* New York, 1885.

Francis Bacon and his Secret Society. New York, 1891.

(ed.) Bacon's *Promus of Forms and Elegancies.* New York, 1883.

ROE, J. E. *The Mortal Moon: Bacon and his Masks.* New York, 1891.

Sir Francis Bacon's Own Story. New York, 1918.

SHEPPARD, Thomas. *Bacon is Alive!* Hull, Yorkshire, 1911.

SLOCOMBE, R. S. 'Was Lord Bacon the Author of Shakespeare's Plays?' *Notes and Queries*, 27 Dec. 1857.

SMITH, William Henry. *Bacon and Shakespeare: An Inquiry touching Players, Playhouses and Play-Writers in the Days of Elizabeth.* London, 1856.

SMITHSON, E. W. 'Ben Jonson's Pious Fraud.' *Nineteenth Century & After*, London, Nov. 1913.

Baconian Essays. With Introduction and Two Essays by Sir George Greenwood. London, 1922.

SPECKMAN, H. A. W. *Francis Bacon is Shakespeare.* Arnhem, 1916.

STRZELECKI, Adolf. *Szekspir i Bakon.* Krakov, 1898.

THEOBALD, Bertram G. *Shake-speare's Sonnets Unmasked.* London, 1929.

THEOBALD, R. M. *Shakespeare Studies in Baconian Light.* London, 1904.

(ed.) *Dethroning Shakspere: A Selection of Letters to the 'Daily Telegraph'.* With notes and comments. London, 1888.

THOMPSON, William. *The Political Purpose of the Renascence Drama: The Key of the Argument.* Melbourne, 1878.

Our Renascence Drama, or History Made Visible. Melbourne, 1880.

William Shakespeare in Romance and Reality. Melbourne, 1881.

Bacon and Shakespeare. Melbourne, 1881.

The Political Allegories in the Renascence Drama of Francis Bacon. Melbourne, 1882.

VITZTHUM VON ECKSTÄDT, Carl Friedrich, Graf. *Shakespeare und Shakspere: zur Genesis der Shakespeare-Dramen.* Stuttgart, 1888.

WEBB, Eric. 'Some Aspects of the Baconian Theory.' Lecture to the Humanist Fellowship, Manchester, 15 Dec. 1956.

WEBB, T. E., Judge. *The Shakespeare Mystery.* New York, 1902.

WEBER-EBENHOFF, Alfred von. *Bacon–Shakespeare–Cervantes.* Vienna & Leipzig, 1917.

WIGSTON, W. F. C. *Bacon and the Rosicrucians.* London, 1889.

WINDLE, Mrs. C. F. A. *On the Discovery of the Cipher of Francis Bacon.* San Francisco, 1881–2.

WOODWARD, Parker. *Sir Francis Bacon: Poet-Philosopher-Statesman-Lawyer-Wit.* London, 1920.

(4) ANTHONY BACON

ALVOR, Peter. *Die Lösung der Shakespeare-Frage.* (See above under *Group and Dual Theories.*)

DENNING, W. H. See above under *Group and Dual Theories.*

POTT, Mrs. Henry. *Francis Bacon and his Secret Society.* (See above under *Francis Bacon.*)

(5) WILLIAM BUTTS

ARENSBERG, W. C. *The Secret Grave of Francis Bacon at Lichfield.* San Francisco, 1923.

The Shakespearean Mystery. Pittsburgh, 1928.

Francis Bacon, William Butts and the Pagets of Beaudesert. Pittsburgh, 1929.

The Magic Ring of Francis Bacon. Pittsburgh, 1930.

(6) WOLSEY

ANON. (initialled J. G. B.) *Who wrote Shakespeare's Plays?* (See above under *Group and Dual Theories.*)

(7) RALEIGH

BACON, Delia. See above under *Group and Dual Theories.*

CALDWELL, G. S. *Is Sir Walter Ralegh the Author of Shakespeare's Plays?* Melbourne, 1877.

O'CONNOR, William D. *Hamlet's Note-Book.* (See above under *Group and Dual Theories.*)

PALK, Robert. Letter on Raleigh and Shakespeare. *Times Literary Supplement,* London, 20 April 1916.

PEMBERTON, Henry, Jr. 'Topical Allusions in the *Sonnets.*' *New Shakespeareana,* Westfield, New Jersey, May 1909.

Shakspere and Sir Walter Ralegh. ed. S. L. Pemberton & C. Smyth. Philadelphia & London, 1914.

(8) ESSEX

DAVIS, Latham. *Shakespeare: England's Ulysses.* Seaford, Delaware, 1905.

REICHEL, Eugen. '*Das Porträt des Herrn W. H.*' (See above under *Group and Dual Theories.*)

(9) CECIL

MAXWELL, J. M. *The Man behind the Mask: Robert Cecil, first Earl of Salisbury, the only True Author of William Shakespeare's Plays.* Indianapolis, 1916.

(10) BURTON

'MULTUM IN PARVO' (M. L. Hore). *Who wrote Shakespeare?* Denver, Colorado, 1885.

Theory mentioned in *Shakespeare-Jahrbuch: XXII,* Leipzig, 1887.

(11) SOUTHAMPTON

NICOL, J. C. *The Real Shakespeare.* London, 1905.

(12) SHIRLEY

HARRIS, C. Shirley. 'Sir Anthony Sherley the author of Shakespeare's Plays.' *Notes and Queries,* London, 13 March 1897.

SURTEES, Scott F. *William Shakespere of Stratford-on-Avon.* Dinsdale-on-Tees, 1888.

(13) DERBY

ANON. (initialled D.T.U.) 'Another Concealed Poet of the Elizabethan Age.' *Baconiana,* London, July 1897.

BOULENGER, Jacques. *L'Affaire Shakespeare.* Paris, 1919.

DEPOIN, J. *L'énigme Shakespearienne: les deux William, Shakespeare et Stanley.* Paris, 1919.

EVANS, A. J. See under *Group and Dual Theories*.

FRAZER, Robert. *The Silent Shakespeare*. Philadelphia, 1915.

GREENSTREET, James. 'A Hitherto Unknown Noble Author of Elizabethan Comedies.' *The Genealogist*, July 1891.
'Further Notices of William Stanley.' *Ibid.*, Jan. 1892.
'Testimonies against the Accepted Authorship of Shakespeare's Plays.' *Ibid.*, May 1892.

LAMBIN, Prof. G. Articles in *Les Langues Modernes*. Paris, 1955.
'Shakespeare in Milan.' *Shakespeare Fellowship News-Letter*, Autumn 1957.

LEFRANC, Abel. *Sous le masque de William Shakespeare: William Stanley, VIe Comte de Derby*. Paris, 2 vols., 1919.
La réalité dans le 'Songe d'une Nuit d'été.' Geneva, 1920.
'Du nouveau sur Shakespeare: le Secret du "Songe d'une Nuit d'été".' *L'Opinion*, Paris, 16–23 Oct. 1920. tr., *London Illustrated News*, 30 Oct. 1920.
'Du nouveau sur Shakespeare: à propos des "Joyeuses Commères de Windsor".' *L'Opinion*, Paris, 5–12 July 1921.
'*L'Origine d'Ariel.*' *Cinquantenaire de l'Ecole pratique des Hautes Etudes*, ed. Champion. Paris, 1921.
Le Secret de William Stanley: Etude sur la question Shakespearienne. Brussels, 1923.
Hélène de Tournon: Celle qui mourut d'amour et l'Ophèlie d' 'Hamlet.' Paris, 1926.
'*Hamlet.*' *Revue bleue*, Paris, 7 May 1932.
A la découverte de Shakespeare. Paris, Vol. I, 1945; II, 1950.

LUCAS, R. Macdonald. 'Did Lord Derby write Shakespeare?' *National Review*, London, Jan. 1922.
Shakespeare's Vital Secret. London, 1938.

MORHARDT, Mathias. *A la recontre de William Shakespeare*. Paris, 1938.

TITHERLEY, A. W. *Shakespeare's Identity: William Stanley, Sixth Earl of Derby*. Winchester, 1952.
(ed.) *Shakespeare's Sonnets, as from the pen of William Stanley, Sixth Earl of Derby*. Liverpool, 1939.

(14) RUTLAND

ALVOR, Peter. *Das neue Shakespeare-Evangelium*. (See above under *Group and Dual Theories*.)

BLEIBTREU, Carl. *Der wahre Shakespeare*. Play in 5 acts; 3rd ed., with Introduction, Munich, 1907.
Shakespeares Geheimnis. Berne, 1923.

BOSTELMANN, Lewis F. *An Outline of the Life of Roger Manners, Fifth Earl of Rutland.* New York, 1911.
Roger of Rutland: a Drama in 4 Acts. New York, n.d.
DEMBLON, Célestin. *Lord Rutland est Shakespeare.* Paris, 1912.
L'Auteur d' 'Hamlet' et son monde. Paris, 1914.
DESSART, A. *Lord Rutland est-il Shakespeare?* Liège, 1913.
PACI, S. 'El misterio Shakespeare.' *Nosotros,* Buenos Aires, Dec. 1928.
POROHOVSHIKOV, Pierre S. *Shakespeare Unmasked.* New York, 1940; London, 1955.
SCHNEIDER, Carl. *Neues Zeugnis für Rutland-Shakespeare.* Berlin, 1922.
SYKES, Claud W. *Alias William Shakespeare?* With a Preface by Sir Arthur Bryant. London, 1947.

(15) BARNARD

BARNARD, Finch. *Shakespeare and the Barnard Family.* London, 1914.
More Light on Shakespeare. London, 1914.
Science and the Soul. London, 1918.

(16) DEVONSHIRE

ALVOR, Peter. *Neue Shakespeare Biographie.* Würzburg, 1930.

(17) STIRLING

Theory mentioned in: ALVOR, Peter. *Die Shakespeare-Frage und das Ben Jonson-Problem.* Würzburg, 1930.

(18) OXFORD

ALLEN, Percy. *The Case for Edward de Vere, Seventeenth Earl of Oxford, as 'Shakespeare.'* London, 1930.
AMPHLETT, Hilda. *Who was Shakespeare?* Introduction by Christmas Humphreys. London, 1955.
BARRELL, Charles Wisner. *Elizabethan Mystery Man.* New York, 1940. Articles on the *Sonnets* and Oxford's son. *Shakespeare Fellowship News-Letter,* New York, 1942–3, and *Tomorrow Magazine,* New York, Feb.–March 1946.
BÉNÉZET, Louis P. *Shakspere, Shakespeare and de Vere.* Manchester, New Hampshire, 1937.
BOWEN, Gwynneth. *Shakespeare's Farewell.* Buxton, Derbyshire, 1951.
CLARK, Mrs. Eva Turner. *Axiophilus; or Oxford alias Shakespeare.* New York, 1926.
Hidden Allusions in Shakespeare's Plays. New York, 1931. (Published in London under title *Shakespeare's Plays in the Order of their Writing.*)

The Satirical Comedy 'Love's Labour's Lost'. New York, 1933.

The Man who was Shakespeare. New York, 1937.

DOUGLAS, Montagu W., Lt.-Col. *Lord Oxford and the Shakespeare Group*. Oxford, 1952.

EGGAR, Katharine E. *The Unlifted Shadow*. London, 1954.

HOLLAND, H. H., Rear-Admiral. *Shakespeare through Oxford Glasses*. London, 1923.

HUMPHREYS, Christmas. Cross-examination of a panel of Oxfordians. Shakespeare Fellowship meeting, London, 14 Jan. 1956.

KENNEDY-SKIPTON, H. K., and MALVIN, W. G. Lectures on the Oxfordian theory. Dublin Shakespeare Society, winter 1956–7.

KENT, William, and ANOTHER. *Edward de Vere, the Real Shakespeare*. London, 1947.

LOONEY, J. Thomas. *'Shakespeare' Identified in Edward de Vere, the Seventeenth Earl of Oxford*. London, 1920; reprinted New York, 1949, with Introduction by William McFee, and Afterwords and Notes by Charles Wisner Barrell.

' "Shakespeare": Lord Oxford or Lord Derby?' *National Review*, London, Feb. 1922.

'The Earl of Oxford as "Shakespeare": New Evidence.' *The Golden Hind*, Oct. 1922.

(ed.) *The Poems of Edward de Vere*. London, 1921.

OGBURN, Dorothy and Charlton. *This Star of England*. New York, 1952.

The Renaissance Man of England. New York, 1955.

PIER, Arthur Stanwood. Lecture on the Oxfordian case. Massachusetts Historical Society, Boston, 13 Dec. 1956.

PHILLIPS, G. W. *Shake Spears Sonnets*. Horley, Surrey, 1954.

RENDALL, Gerald H., Canon. *Shakespeare's Sonnets and Edward de Vere*. London, 1930.

SHAKESPEARE FELLOWSHIP. *News-Letter*, London, 1922—In progress.

Quarterly (formerly *News-Letter*), New York, 1939—In progress.

SLATER, Gilbert. STANDEN, Gilbert. See above under *Group and Dual Theories*.

WAINEWRIGHT, Ruth M. D., with BOWEN, Gwynneth, and ADAMSON, T. L., *versus* EVANS, A. J. Debate: Oxford *versus* Derby. Shakespeare Fellowship, London, 16 Jan. 1957.

WARD, B. M., Capt. *The Seventeenth Earl of Oxford*. London, 1928.

'Shakespeare and the Anglo–Spanish War.' *Revue Anglo–Américaine*, Paris, April, Dec. 1929, April 1930.

WARD, B. R., Col. *The Mystery of Mr. W. H.* London, 1923.

'Shakespeare and Elizabethan War Propaganda.' *Royal Engineers Journal*, Dec. 1928.

(19) FLORIO

PALADINO, Santi. *Shakespeare sarebbe il pseudonimo di un Poeta Italiano.* Reggio, 1929.

REGER, Erik. 'Der Italiener Shakespeare.' *Deutsche Allgemeine Zeitung,* Berlin, nos. 453–6, 1927.

VILLA, Carlo. New book announced in *Daily Telegraph,* 12 Oct. 1956.

(20) MARLOWE

HOFFMAN, Calvin. *The Man who was Shakespeare.* New York & London, 1955.

WRAIGHT, Mrs. Dolly. Lecture on Marlowe's authorship of the *Sonnets.* Old Vic Theatre, London, 11 Nov. 1956.

ZEIGLER, Wilbur Gleason. See above under *Group and Dual Theories.*

(21) QUEEN ELIZABETH

APPLEBY, John. See below under *Other Theories; Satires; Burlesques.*

SWEET, George Elliott. *Shake-speare the Mystery.* Stanford, California, 1956.

(22) ANNE WHATELEY

See HUTCHESON and ROSS above under *Group and Dual Theories.*

(23) DYER

See BROOKS above under *Group and Dual Theories.*

(24) OTHER THEORIES; SATIRES; BURLESQUES

ALLEN, H. L. 'Was Shakespeare an Irishman?' *Academy,* London, 26 Feb. 1898.

ANON. *Raleigh wrote Shakespeare; or the Grate Crab-Tree-Grave.* Glasgow, 1888.

ANON. 'Did Adam Smith write Burns?' *Chicago Tribune,* 17 March 1902.

ANON. (initialled W. H. T.) 'Who wrote *Paradise Lost?*' *Macmillan's Magazine,* London, March 1902.

APPLEBY, John. *The Stuffed Swan.* London, 1956.

DE FONSEKA, J. P. 'The Plays of Mrs. Shakespeare.' *G. K.'s Weekly,* London, 3 March 1938.

EWEN, C. l'Estrange. *Shakespeare, Automatist or Nothing.* Paignton, Devon, 1946.

FEELY, J. M. *The Shakespearean Cypher.* Rochester, New York, 1931.

FORBIS, J. F. *The Shakespeare Enigma and an Elizabethan Mania.* New York, 1924.

KNOX, Ronald A. 'The Authorship of *In Memoriam.*' *Essays in Satire.* London, 1928.

NEWCOMEN, George. 'A New Shakespeare Cryptogram: Was the Author of Shakespeare's Plays an Irishman?' *Academy*, London, 25 Dec. 1897.

SHATFORD, Sarah. (ed.) *My Proof of Immortality;* by *Sir* William Shakespeare. New York, 1924.

STEPHEN, Sir Leslie. 'Did Shakespeare write Bacon?' *Men, Books and Mountains*, London, 1956.

(25) DISCUSSIONS; RÉSUMÉS; BIBLIOGRAPHIES

AIZEN, N. 'Shakespeare or Bacon.' *Journal of Literature*, St. Petersburg, 12 Nov. 1894.

CHERNIGOVETZ, O. *William Shakespeare.* St. Petersburg, 1889.

CHIARINI, Giuseppe. *Studii Shakespeariani.* Leghorn, 1897.

COCHIN, M. 'La vie de Shakspeare et le paradoxe Baconien.' *Revue des Deux Mondes*, Paris, Nov. 1885.

CONNES, Georges. *The Shakespeare Mystery.* (See below under *Pro-Shakespeare Rejoinders.*)

GALLAND, J. S. *Digesta anti-Shakespeariana.* Microfilm, North-Western University, Illinois, 1949. (The most complete bibliography.)

McGACHAN, M. 'Shakespeare or Bacon.' *Novosty*, No. 256, St. Petersburg, 1887.

MEESHEL, M. 'Shakespeare or Bacon.' *The Illustrated World*, No. 4, St. Petersburg, 1898.

MEZ, John R. *Edward de Vere—or 'Shakespeare.'* London, 1952.

NOURISSON, V. '*Shakspere et Shakespeare.*' *Nouvelle Revue*, Alexandria, Nov. 1903.

PERRY, Marsden. *A Preliminary List of Books, Pamphlets and Newspapers relating to the Bacon–Shakespeare Controversy.* Providence, Rhode Island, 1897.

RAPP, C. Max. *William Shakespeare oder Francis Bacon.* Ulm, 1887.

RAYNAL, Louis de. *Une controverse littéraire: Shakespeare et Bacon.* Paris, 1888.

ROZ, Firmin. '*Le troisième centenaire de Shakespeare et la question Shakespearienne.*' *Revue des Deux Mondes*, Paris, April 15 1916.

SCHUCK, Henrik. '*Den nya teorien om forfätterskapet till Shaksperes arbeten.*' *Ny Svensk Tidskrift*, Stockholm, 1883.

III: SOME PARALLEL THEORIES

(1) TERENCE

MONTAIGNE, Michel de. *Essays*, tr. Florio: I, 39. (Believed Terence's
plays were written by his patrons, Laelius and Scipio the Younger:
'For to prove the labour to be theirs, the exquisite eloquence and
excellent invention thereof, doth sufficiently declare it.')
Against this theory: NORWOOD, Gilbert. *The Art of Terence*. London,
1923. *Oxford Classical Dictionary*, 1949. (Some *assistance* from
Terence's patrons not denied.)

(2) MOLIÈRE

FRASER, Elizabeth. *La Mort de Solon: pièce attribuée à Pierre Corneille*.
Paris, 1949. Introduction. (Prolegomenon to extensive theory that
Corneille wrote all Molière's works.)

(3) EMILY BRONTË

LAW, Alice. *Patrick Branwell Brontë*. London, 1924.
Emily Jane Brontë and the Authorship of 'Wuthering Heights'.
Altham, 1926. (Believes Branwell was the author.)
Against this theory: WILLIS, Irene Cooper. *The Authorship of
'Wuthering Heights'*. London, 1936.
MALHAM-DEMBLEBY, J. *The Confessions of Charlotte Brontë*. Bradford,
1954. (Believes Emily's works were written by Charlotte.)

(4) MUSIC

CUDWORTH, Charles L. 'Ye Olde Spuriosity Shoppe.' *Notes*, Washington, Dec. 1954 & Sept. 1955. (A complete listing of all musical
authorship theories.)

IV: PRO-SHAKESPEARE REJOINDERS

(1) ANTI-BACONIAN

ANON. (initialled B. J. A.) 'The Humbug of Bacon.' *New York
Herald*, 5 Oct. 1874.
ANON. Review of Mrs. Windle's Baconian Cipher. *San Francisco
Chronicle*, 20 Aug. 1882.
ANON. (initialled G. B. A.). 'Mask Torn Off.' *Detroit Free Press*,
17 June 1888.
BAILDON, H. Bellyse. Introduction to *Titus Andronicus*. Arden ed.
London, 1904.
BÖGHOLM, Niels. *Bacon og Shakespeare: en sproglig sammenligning*.
Copenhagen, 1906.

BRANDES, Georg. *William Shakespeare.* Copenhagen, 3 vols., 1896; tr., London, 2 vols., 1898.

CAMPBELL, John, Lord. *Life of Bacon.* London, 1865.

CHURCHILL, R. C. 'The Baconian Heresy: A Post-Mortem.' *Nineteenth Century & After,* London, Nov. 1946.

COLLINS, John Churton. *Studies in Shakespeare.* London, 1885.

CRAWFORD, Charles. 'The Bacon-Shakespeare Question.' *Collectanea,* 2nd series. Stratford-on-Avon, 1907.

CROLL, D. *De Bacon-Shakespeare Mythe.* Rotterdam, 1914.

DEVECMON, William C. See below under *Some Related Questions: Law.*

DOWDEN, Edward. Review of Judge Webb's *The Shakespeare Mystery,* q.v. *National Review,* London, July 1902.

EICHLER, Albert. *Anti-Baconianus: Shakespeare-Bacon?* Vienna & Leipzig, 1919.

FISCHER, Kuno. *Shakespeare und die Bacon Mythe.* Heidelberg, 1895.

FOARD, J. T. 'The Bacon–Shakespeare Craze.' *Papers of Manchester Literary Club,* 1895.

GERVINUS, G. G. *Shakespeare Commentaries.* Heidelberg, 1849–52; tr. London, 1862; new ed. with Introduction by F. J. Furnivall, 1875.

GREG, Sir Walter. *Facts and Fancies in Baconian Theory.* London, 1903.

HARENDRAKUMARA, Mukhopadhyaya. *The Authorship of the Shakespearean Plays: An Answer to the Baconians.* Calcutta, 1915.

IRVING, Sir Henry. 'Shakespeare and Bacon.' Lecture at Princeton University, New Jersey, 19 March 1902.

KEETON, George W. See below under *Some Related Questions: Law.*

KING, Thomas. *Bacon versus Shakespeare: A Plea for the Defendant.* Montreal, 1875.

KNOX, Ronald A. See above under *Other Theories; Satires; Burlesques.*

LEE, Sir Sidney. Letter to the *Times,* London, 30 March 1898.

MALLOCK, W. H. 'New Facts relating to the Bacon–Shakespeare Question.' (See above under *Origins of the Authorship Question.*) Article on Mrs. Gallup's Baconian Cipher. *Nineteenth Century & After,* London, July 1902.

MENDENHALL, Thomas Corwin. 'A Mechanical Solution of a Literary Problem.' *Popular Science Monthly,* New York, Dec. 1901.

MORSE, Herbert. *Back to Shakespeare.* London, 1915.

NICHOLSON, Rev. R. B. *No Cipher in Shakespeare: A Refutation of the Hon. Ignatius Donnelly's 'Great Cryptogram'.* London, 1888.

RÉMUSAT, Charles de. *Bacon, sa vie, son temps, sa philosophie et son influence.* Paris, 1857.

Q

ROBERTSON, J. M. *Montaigne and Shakespeare; and other essays on cognate questions.* London & New York, 1909.
The Baconian Heresy: A Confutation. London & New York, 1913.
The Problem of the Shakespeare Sonnets. London & New York, 1926.
ROLLINS, H. E. (ed.) *Shakespeare's Sonnets.* Variorum ed., 2 vols., Philadelphia, 1944.
SCHIPPER, Jakob. *Zur Kritik des Shakespeare–Bacon–Frage.* Vienna, 1889.
STEEL, Charles F. *Is there any Resemblance between Shakespeare and Bacon?* New York, 1888.
STEPHEN, Sir Leslie. See above under *Other Theories; Satires; Burlesques.*
STOPES, Mrs. Charlotte Carmichael. *The Bacon–Shakspere Question Answered.* 2nd enlarged ed., London 1889.
THURSTON, Fr. Herbert. Article on Mrs. Gallup's Baconian Cipher. *The Month,* London, Aug. 1902.
TOWNSEND, G. H. *William Shakespeare not an Impostor; by an English Critic.* London, 1857.
WHITE, Richard Grant. 'The Bacon–Shakespeare Craze.' *Studies in Shakespeare.* London, 1885. Essay first published in the *Atlantic Monthly,* Boston, April 1883.
WILLIS, William, Judge. *The Baconian Mint: Its Claims Examined.* London, 1903.
WRIGHT, E. M. *Rustic Speech and Folk-Lore.* Oxford, 1913.

(2) ANTI-UNORTHODOX IN GENERAL

BEECHING, H. C., Canon. *William Shakespeare, Player, Playmaker and Poet: A Reply to Mr. George Greenwood.* London, 1908.
BRYANT, Sir Arthur. Preface to Sykes, q.v. above under *Rutland.*
CHAMBRUN, Comtesse de. Discussion with Boulenger on Derby theory. *Revue de Paris,* during 1919.
Shakespeare: Actor-Poet. New York, 1927.
Shakespeare: A Portrait Restored. London, 1957.
CHUTE, Marchette. *Shakespeare of London.* (See below under *Some Related Questions: Biographical.*)
CONNES, Georges. Article in *Revue Anglo-Américaine,* Paris, Aug. 1924.
Le Mystère Shakespearien. Paris, 1926. Originally lectures at University of Dijon, 1925. Abridged tr., London, 1927.
'De nouveau sur de Vere.' *Revue Anglo-Américaine,* Feb. 1929.
FRIEDMAN, Col. William F. & Mrs. Elizebeth S. *The Shakespearean Ciphers Examined.* Cambridge, 1957.
GRILLO, Ernesto. See below under *Some Related Questions: Travel.*

HARRISON, G. B. Review of Oxfordian book. *London Mercury*, Oct. 1929.

JOSEPH, Bertram. 'Who Was Shakespeare?' *The Humanist*, London, May 1957.

LANG, Andrew. *Shakespeare, Bacon and the Great Unknown.* London, 1912.

LEE, Sir Sidney. Article on Rutland theory. *Illustrated London News*, 25 Jan. 1919.

MARGRIE, William. *Shakespeare Vindicated: An Exposure of Oxford and Bacon Nonsense.* London, 1946.

MARIE, Aristide. *A la recherche de Shakespeare.* Paris, 1924.

MONTGOMERY, C. M. *Shakespearean Afterglow.* Melbourne, 1944.

ROBERTSON, J. M. 'Another "Ghost" for Shakespeare.' *Observer*, London, 2 March 1919. (Review of Derby theory.)

SAMPSON, George. *The Concise Cambridge History of English Literature.* Cambridge, 1941. p. 256 sq.

SMITH, Logan Pearsall. *On Reading Shakespeare.* London, 1933. Chap. I.

THOMPSON, Godfrey. 'Who didn't write Shakespeare?' *Humberside*, Hull, Yorkshire, Autumn 1956.

V: SOME RELATED QUESTIONS

(1) BIOGRAPHICAL

BAKELESS, John. *The Tragicall History of Christopher Marlowe.* Cambridge, Mass., 2 vols., 1942.

BROWN, Ivor. *Shakespeare.* London, 1949.

CARTER, Rev. T. *Shakespeare: Puritan and Recusant.* London, 1897.

CHAMBERS, Sir Edmund. *William Shakespeare: A Study of Facts and Problems.* Oxford, 2 vols., 1930.

CHAMBRUN, Comtesse de. *John Florio.* Paris, 1921.

CHUTE, Marchette. *Shakespeare of London.* New York, 1950; London, 1951.

Ben Jonson of Westminster. New York, 1953; London, 1954.

DAVIES, Hugh Sykes. "The Consul and the Gifted Woman." Dramatised talk on Hawthorne's friendship with Delia Bacon. B.B.C. Home Service, 9 July 1957.

DE GROOT, John Henry. *The Shakespeares and 'the Old Faith'.* New York, 1946.

HALLIWELL-PHILLIPPS, J. O. *Outline of the Life of Shakespeare.* Brighton, Sussex, 1887.

HARRISON, G. B. *Introducing Shakespeare.* Penguin Books, Harmondsworth, Middlesex, and Baltimore, revised ed., 1954.

HAWTHORNE, Nathaniel. 'Recollections of a Gifted Woman' (Delia Bacon). *Our Old Home.* Boston, 1863.

HOTSON, Leslie. *The Death of Christopher Marlowe.* London, 1925. *'I, William Shakespeare . . .'* London, 1937.

LEE, Sir Sidney. *A Life of Shakespeare.* London, 1898.

SERRES, Olivia Wilmot. *The Life of the Author of the Letters of Junius: the Rev. James Wilmot, D.D.* London, 1813.

SPEDDING, James. *Letters and Life of Francis Bacon.* London, 7 vols., 1861–74.

(ed.) *A Conference of Pleasure: from MS. belonging to Duke of Northumberland.* London, 1870.

STOPES, Mrs. Charlotte Carmichael. Article on Shakespeare's Monument at Stratford. *Monthly Review*, London, April 1904.

Shakespeare's Warwickshire Contemporaries. Stratford-on-Avon, 1907.

Article on John Shakespeare, emblem-maker. *Athenæum*, London, 16 May 1908.

The Life of Henry, Third Earl of Southampton. Cambridge, 1922.

WALLACE, C. W. 'New Shakespeare Discoveries.' *Harper's Magazine*, New York, March 1910.

(2) CULTURAL

BALDWIN, T. W. *William Shaks⸱ re's 'Small Latine and Lesse Greeke'.* Urbana, Illinois, 2 vols., 1944.

BLOM, Eric. *Music in England.* Penguin Books, Harmondsworth & Baltimore, revised ed., 1947.

CHAMBERS, Sir Edmund. *The Elizabethan Stage.* Oxford, 4 vols., 1927.

COHN, Albert. *Shakespeare in Germany.* London, 1865.

ELIOT, T. S. *Selected Essays.* London, 1934.

FARMER, Richard. *An Essay on the Learning of Shakespeare.* Cambridge, 1767.

FORD, Boris (ed.) *The Age of Shakespeare. Pelican Guide to English Literature*, Vol. 2. Harmondsworth & Baltimore, 1955.

GRANVILLE-BARKER, Harley, and HARRISON, G. B. (eds.) *A Companion to Shakespeare Studies.* Cambridge, 1934.

HALLIWELL-PHILLIPPS, J. O. *The Visits of Shakespeare's Company of Actors to the Provincial Cities and Towns of England.* Brighton, Sussex, 1886.

HARRISON, G. B. *Shakespeare's Fellows.* London, 1923.

HOTSON, Leslie. *The First Night of 'Twelfth Night'.* London, 1954. *'Falstaff's Death and Greenfield's.' Times Literary Supplement*, London, 6 April 1956.

JUSSERAND, Jean Jules. *Shakespeare en France sous l'ancien régime.* Paris, 1898.

KNIGHTS, L. C. 'Bacon and the Seventeenth-Century Dissociation of Sensibility.' *Explorations,* London, 1946.

LEE, Sir Sidney, and ONIONS, C. T. (eds.) *Shakespeare's England.* Oxford, 2 vols., 1916.

MELLERS, Wilfrid. *Music and Society.* London, 1946.
'Words and Music in Elizabethan England.' *The Age of Shakespeare. Pelican Guide to English Literature,* Vol. 2. ed. Ford, q.v.

POLLARD, A. W. *The History of the Title-Page.* London, 1903.

PORTA, Baptista. *De Furtivis Literarum Notis.* Naples, 1568; Strasburg, 1606.

SCHENK, Wilhelm. 'The *Cortegiano* and the Civilization of the Renaissance.' *Scrutiny,* Cambridge, June 1949.

TENISON, Thomas, Archbishop. *Baconiana.* London, 1679.

THOMSON, J. A. K. *Shakespeare and the Classics.* London, 1952.

TREVELYAN, G. M. *English Social History.* New York, 1942; London, 1944.

VIGENÈRE, Blaise de. *Traité des chiffres; ou Secrètes manières d'escrire.* Paris, 1586.

WILKINS, John, Bishop. *Mercury; or The Secret and Swift Messenger.* London, 1641.

WORDSWORTH, John, Bishop. *On Shakespeare's Knowledge and Use of the Bible.* London, 1864.

WRIGHT, Louis B. *Middle-Class Culture in Elizabethan England.* Chapel Hill, North Carolina, 1935.

(3) LAW

CAMPBELL, John, Lord. *Shakespeare's Legal Acquirements Considered.* London, 1859.

CASTLE, Edward James. See above under *Group and Dual Theories.*

COLLINS, John Churton. 'Was Shakespeare a Lawyer?' *Studies in Shakespeare.* London, 1885.

DAVIS, Cushman, Senator. *The Law in Shakespeare.* St. Paul, Minnesota, 1884.

DEVECMON, William C. *In re Shakespeare's 'Legal Acquirements'.* New York, 1899.

GREENWOOD, Sir George. See above under *Anti-Shakespeare.*

KEETON, George W. *Shakespeare and his Legal Problems.* With a Foreword by Lord Darling. London, 1930.

MORSE, Herbert. See above under *Pro-Shakespeare Rejoinders.*

PENZANCE, Lord. See above under *Francis Bacon.*

ROBERTSON, J. M. 'The Argument from Legal Allusions in Shakespeare: Lord Campbell's Case'; 'The Argument from Legal Phraseology: Mr. Grant White's Case'; 'The Argument from Legal Phraseology: Mr. Rushton, Senator Davis, Mr. Castle'; 'Litigation and Legalism in Elizabethan England.' *The Baconian Heresy*, Chaps. IV–VI, q.v. above under *Pro-Shakespeare Rejoinders*.

RUSHTON, W. L. *Shakespeare a Lawyer*. Liverpool, 1858.
Shakespeare's Testamentary Language. London, 1869.
Shakespeare Illustrated by the Lex Scripta. London, 1870.
Shakespeare's Legal Maxims. London, 1907.

WHITE, Richard Grant. *Studies in Shakespeare*. London & New York, 1885.

(4) TRAVEL

ANON. Article on Shakespeare's knowledge of the sea. *Chambers's Journal*, Edinburgh, 20 March 1852.

ANON. 'Shakespeare a Seaman.' *St. James's Magazine*, London, July 1862.

CLEMENTS, Rex. 'Shakespeare as Mariner.' *Shakespeare Fellowship News-Letter*, London, Autumn 1956.

ELZE, Karl. 'Italienische Skizzen zu Shakespeare.' *Shakespeare-Jahrbuch* VIII, Leipzig, 1873.
'The Supposed Travels of Shakespeare.' *Essays on Shakespeare*, tr. Dora Schmitz. London, 1874.

ELZE, Theodore. 'Bellario und die Studenten in Padua.' *Shakespeare-Jahrbuch* XIII, Leipzig, 1878.

GRILLO, Ernesto. *Shakespeare and Italy*. Glasgow, 1949.

REBORA, Piero. *L'Italia nella Dramma inglese*. Milan, 1925.

SARRAZIN, G. 'Shakespeare in Mantua.' *Shakespeare-Jahrbuch* XXIX–XXX, Leipzig, 1894–5.
'Der Rauberwald in der Lombardie.' *Ibid.*, XXXIX, 1903.
'Shakespeare in Mailand.' *Ibid.*, XLVI, 1910.

STEFFANSON, Yan. 'Shakespeare in Elsinore.' *Contemporary Review*, London, Jan.–June 1896.

SULLIVAN, Sir Edward. 'Shakespeare and the Waterways of North Italy.' *Nineteenth Century & After*, London, Aug. 1908.
'Shakespeare and Italy.' *Ibid.*, Jan.–Feb. 1918.

WHALL, W. B. *Shakespeare's Sea Terms Explained*. London, 1910.

ZUPUTZA, Julius. 'Ueber die Fabel in Shakespeare's "Two Gentlemen"' *Shakespeare-Jahrbuch* XXIII, Leipzig, 1888.

INDEX